SHARKY!

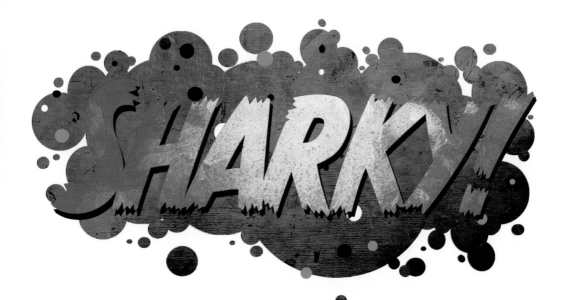

It's only comics...

Dedications:

Alex: Ray Harryhausen, Go Nagai,
John Buscema, Rich Corben
and Frank Frazetta.
Also for Selina and Tiger, who
shared my studio and kept me
company when I was working
on this.

Dave: June & Geoff, Mike &
Yvonne and especially two
amazing characters that made
their first comic appearance here;
Crazy Amy & Loopy Lizzy.

Dave & Alex: To Jack and Rosalind
Kirby, without whom the inspiration
wouldn't have been there.

9001081062

SHARKY!

Written by:
Dave Elliott

Art by:
Alex Horley

Colors by: Bad @$$
Colors on Intro:
Sunny Gho
Letters by: John Green
Cover by: Alex Horley
Additional art:
"Blazing Glory"
Written and inks by: Dave Elliott
Pencils by: Paris Cullins
Colors by Lovern Kindzierski
Letters by: Bambos

"Secret Origin"
sketchbook art:
Alex Horley, Jerry Parris,
Simon Bisley and Dave Elliott

Special thanks: Merv
Garretson, Mike Lopez, Dave
Johnson, Mike Richardson, John
Green, Jerry Paris, Paris Cullins,
Michael T. Gilbert, Evan Dorkin,
Bob Burden, Keith Giffen, Joe
Quesada, Jimmy Palmiotti,
Erik Larsen, Jerry Ordway, Dave
Bogart, Garry Leach and Simon
Bisley.

TITAN MAGAZINES

Senior Comics Editor
Steve White
Titan Comics Editorial
Andrew James, Mark
McKenzie-Ray, Jon
Chapple
Production Supervisors
Kelly Fenlon, Jackie
Flook
Interim Production
Controller
Mo Adams
Production Controller
Bob Kelly
Art Director Oz Browne
Studio Manager Selina
Juneja
Circulation Manager
Steve Tothill
Marketing Manager
Ricky Claydon
Advertising Manager
Michelle Fairlamb
Publishing Manager
Darryl Tothill
Publishing Director
Chris Teather
Operations Director
Leigh Baulch
Executive Director
Vivian Cheung
Publisher Nick Landau

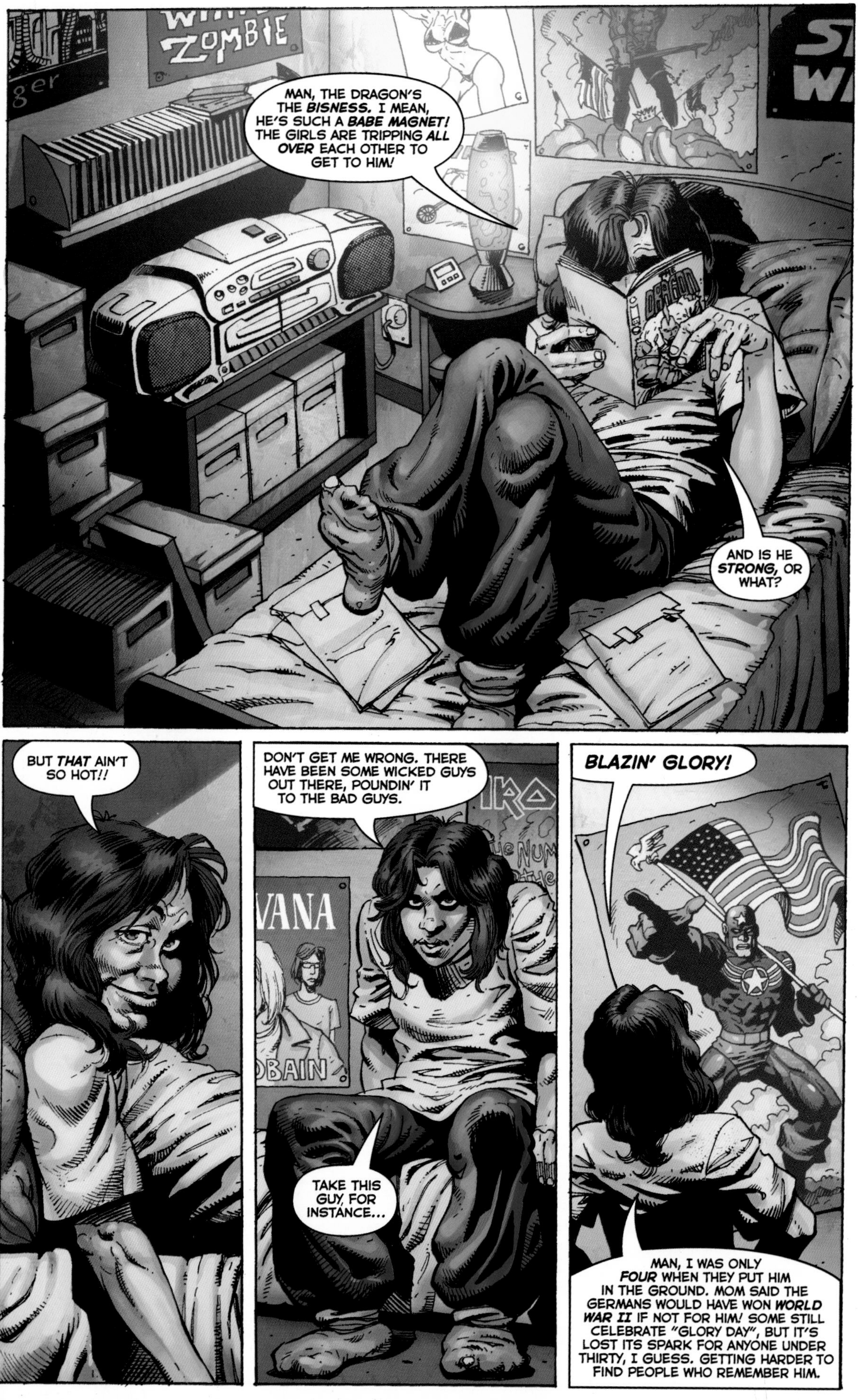
MAN, THE DRAGON'S THE *BISNESS.* I MEAN, HE'S SUCH A *BABE MAGNET!* THE GIRLS ARE TRIPPING *ALL OVER* EACH OTHER TO GET TO HIM!
AND IS HE *STRONG,* OR WHAT?
BUT *THAT* AIN'T SO HOT!!
DON'T GET ME WRONG. THERE HAVE BEEN SOME WICKED GUYS OUT THERE, POUNDIN' IT TO THE BAD GUYS.
TAKE THIS GUY, FOR INSTANCE...
BLAZIN' GLORY!
MAN, I WAS ONLY *FOUR* WHEN THEY PUT HIM IN THE GROUND. MOM SAID THE GERMANS WOULD HAVE WON *WORLD WAR II* IF NOT FOR HIM! SOME STILL CELEBRATE "GLORY DAY", BUT IT'S LOST ITS SPARK FOR ANYONE UNDER THIRTY, I GUESS. GETTING HARDER TO FIND PEOPLE WHO REMEMBER HIM.

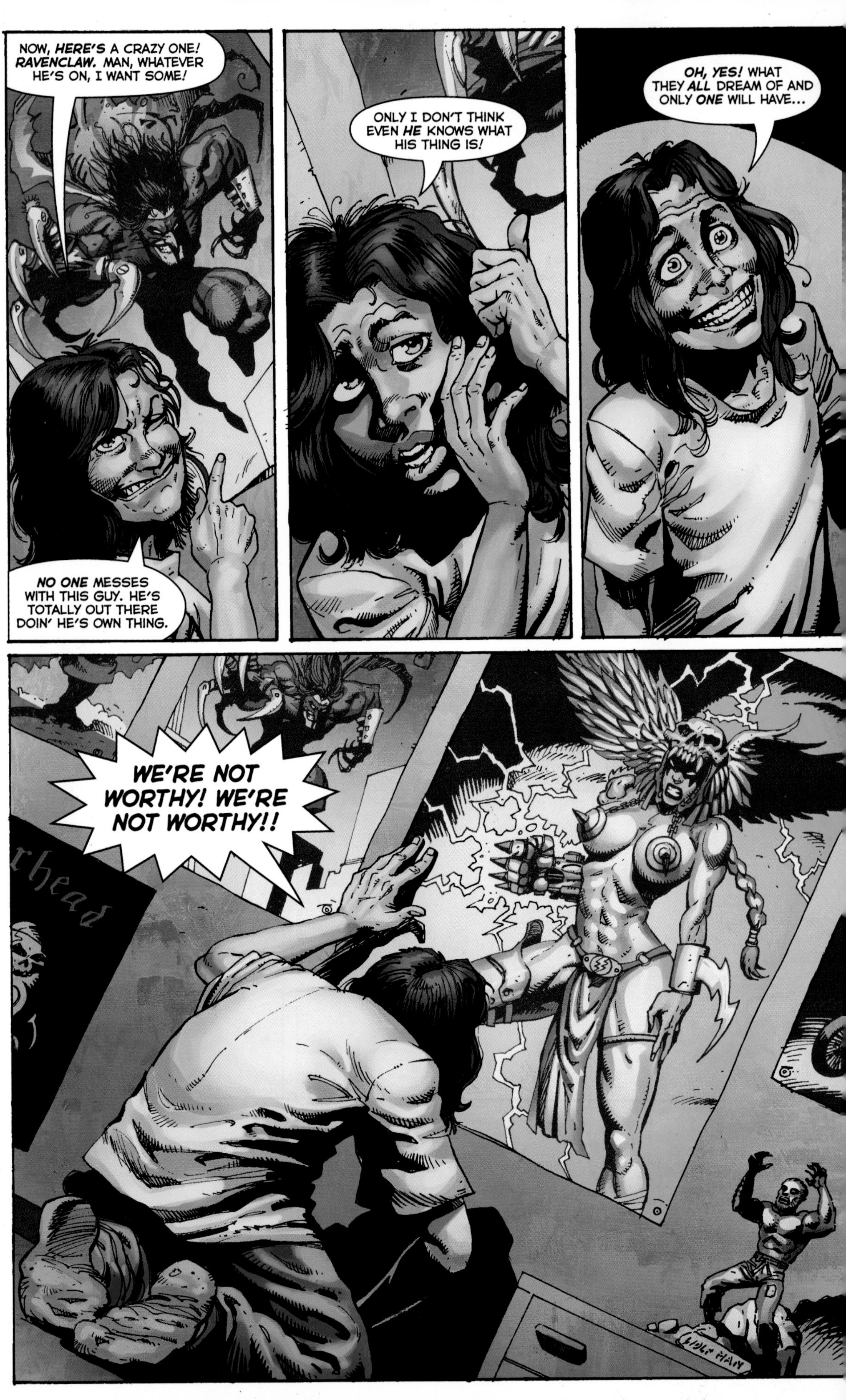
NOW, HERE'S A CRAZY ONE! RAVENCLAW. MAN, WHATEVER HE'S ON, I WANT SOME!
NO ONE MESSES WITH THIS GUY. HE'S TOTALLY OUT THERE DOIN' HE'S OWN THING.
ONLY I DON'T THINK EVEN HE KNOWS WHAT HIS THING IS!
OH, YES! WHAT THEY ALL DREAM OF AND ONLY ONE WILL HAVE...
WE'RE NOT WORTHY! WE'RE NOT WORTHY!!

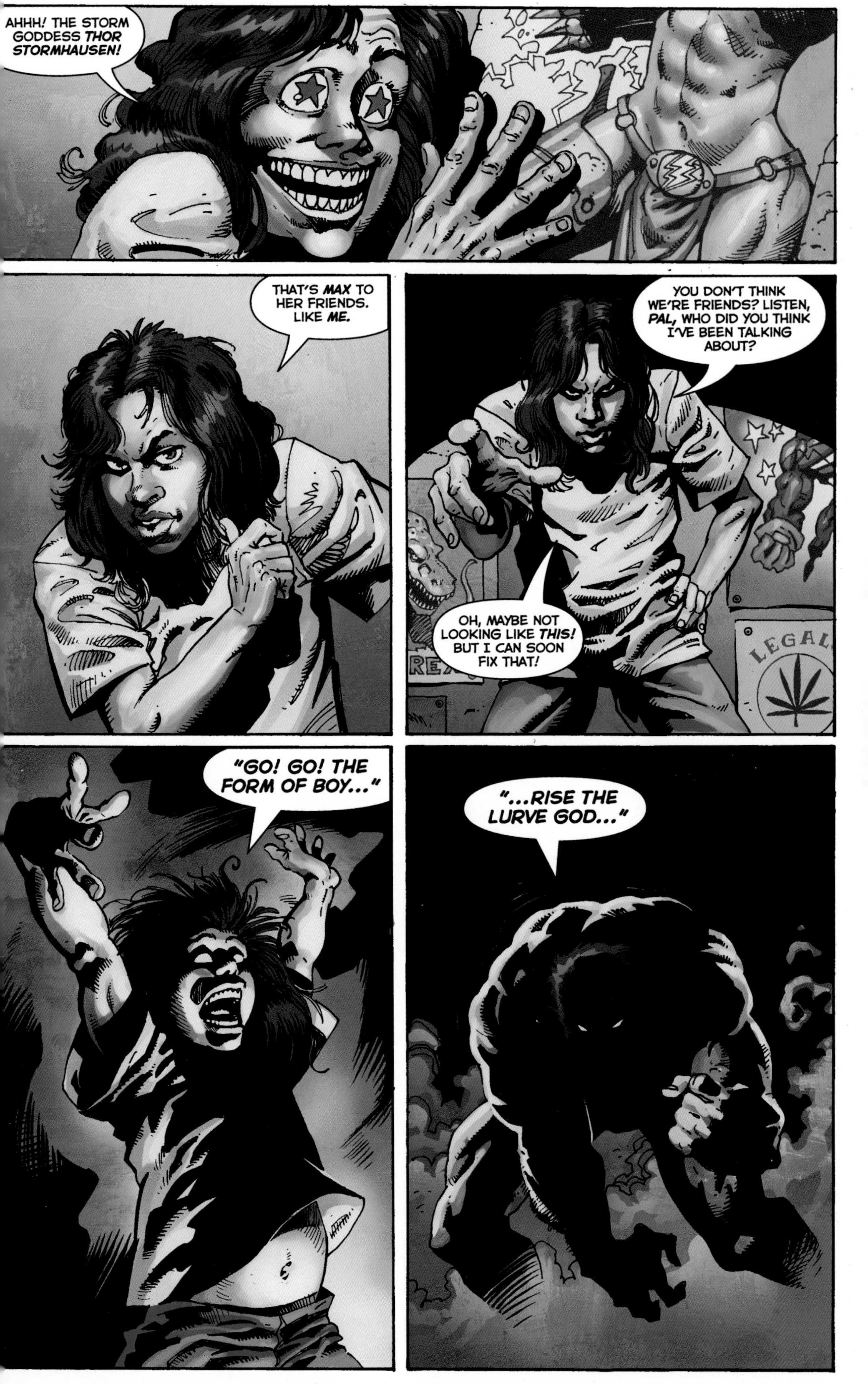
AHHH! THE STORM GODDESS THOR STORMHAUSEN!
THAT'S MAX TO HER FRIENDS. LIKE ME.
YOU DON'T THINK WE'RE FRIENDS? LISTEN, PAL, WHO DID YOU THINK I'VE BEEN TALKING ABOUT?
OH, MAYBE NOT LOOKING LIKE THIS! BUT I CAN SOON FIX THAT!
LEGAL
"GO! GO! THE FORM OF BOY..."
"...RISE THE LURVE GOD..."

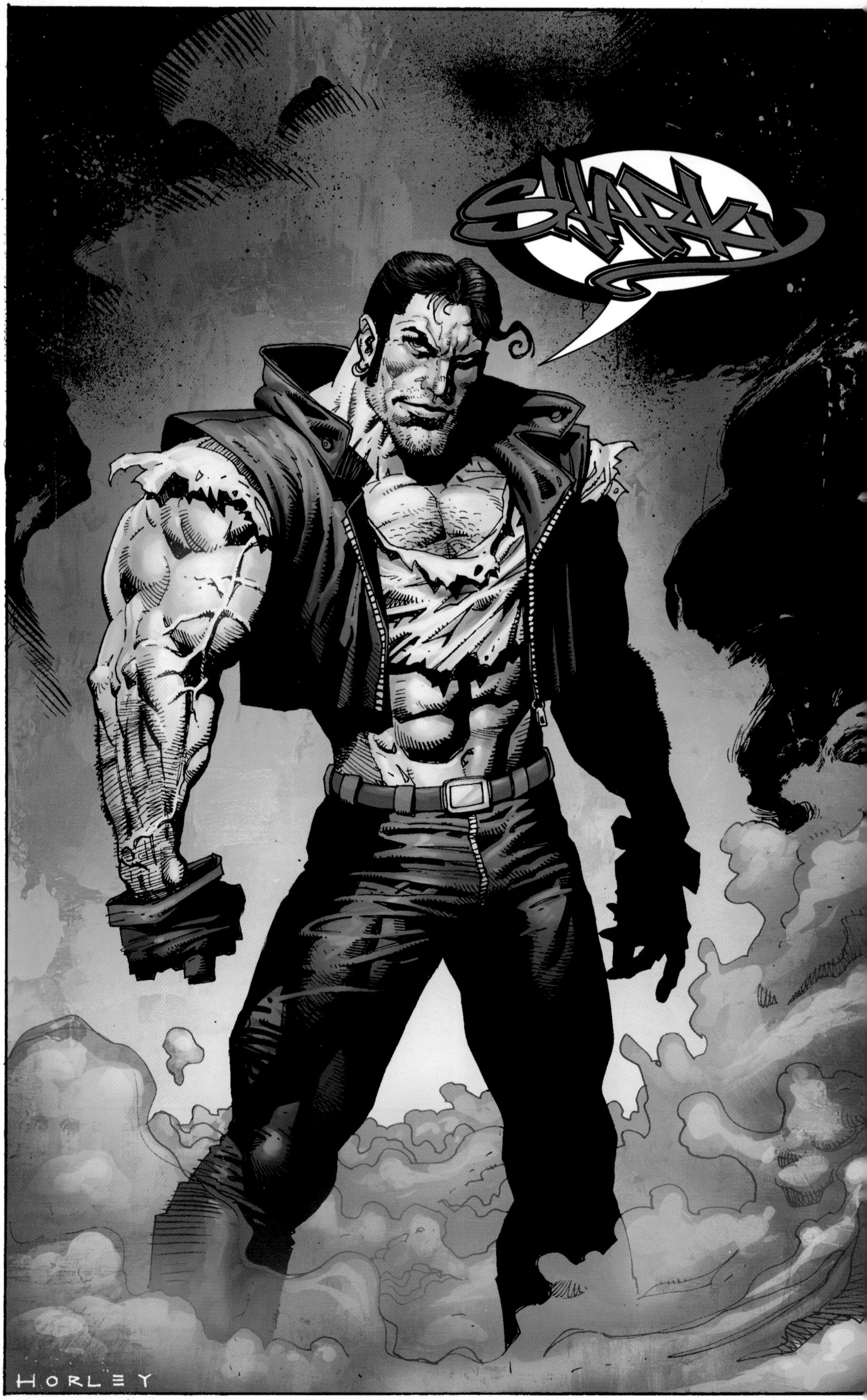
SHARKY
HORLEY

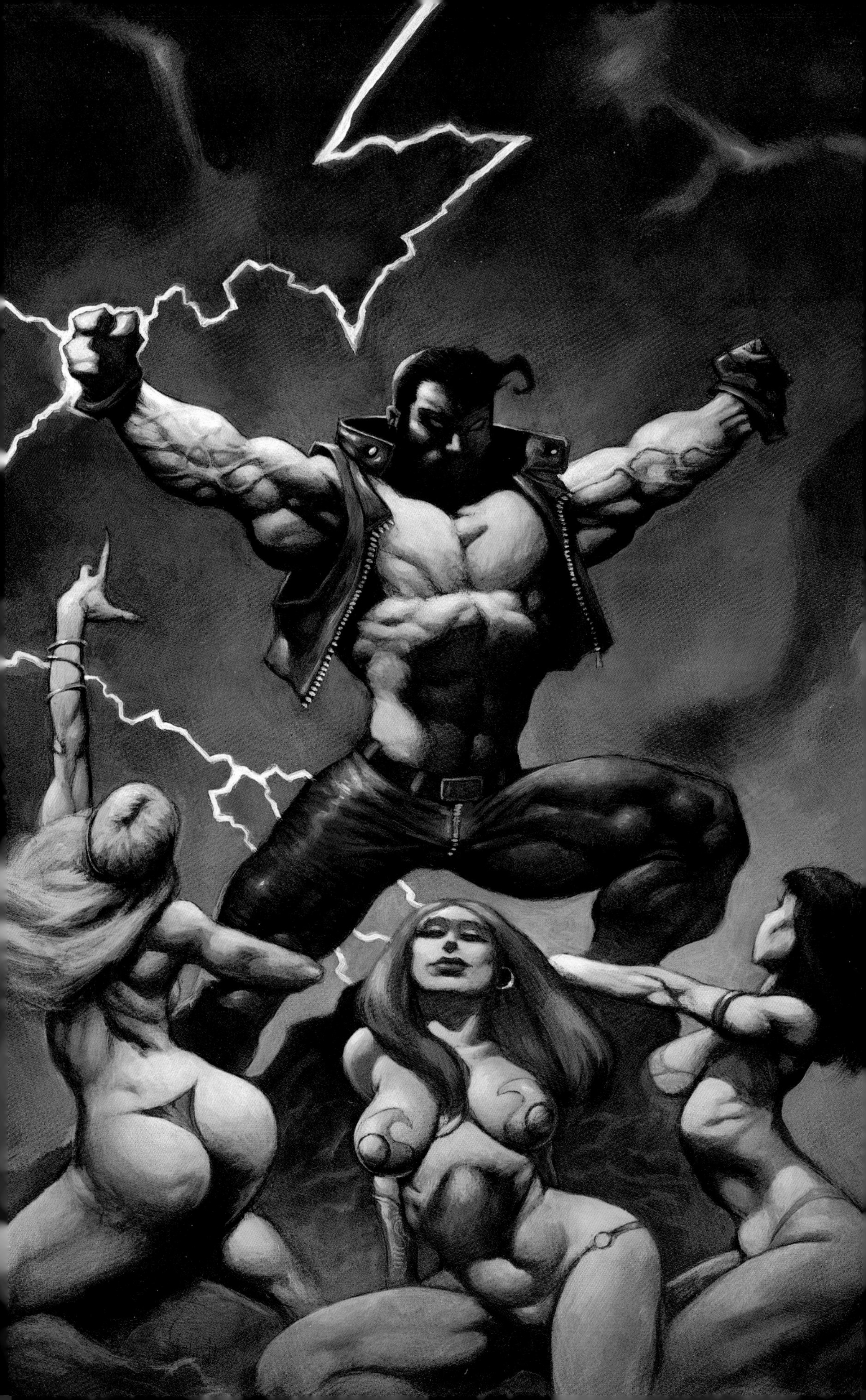

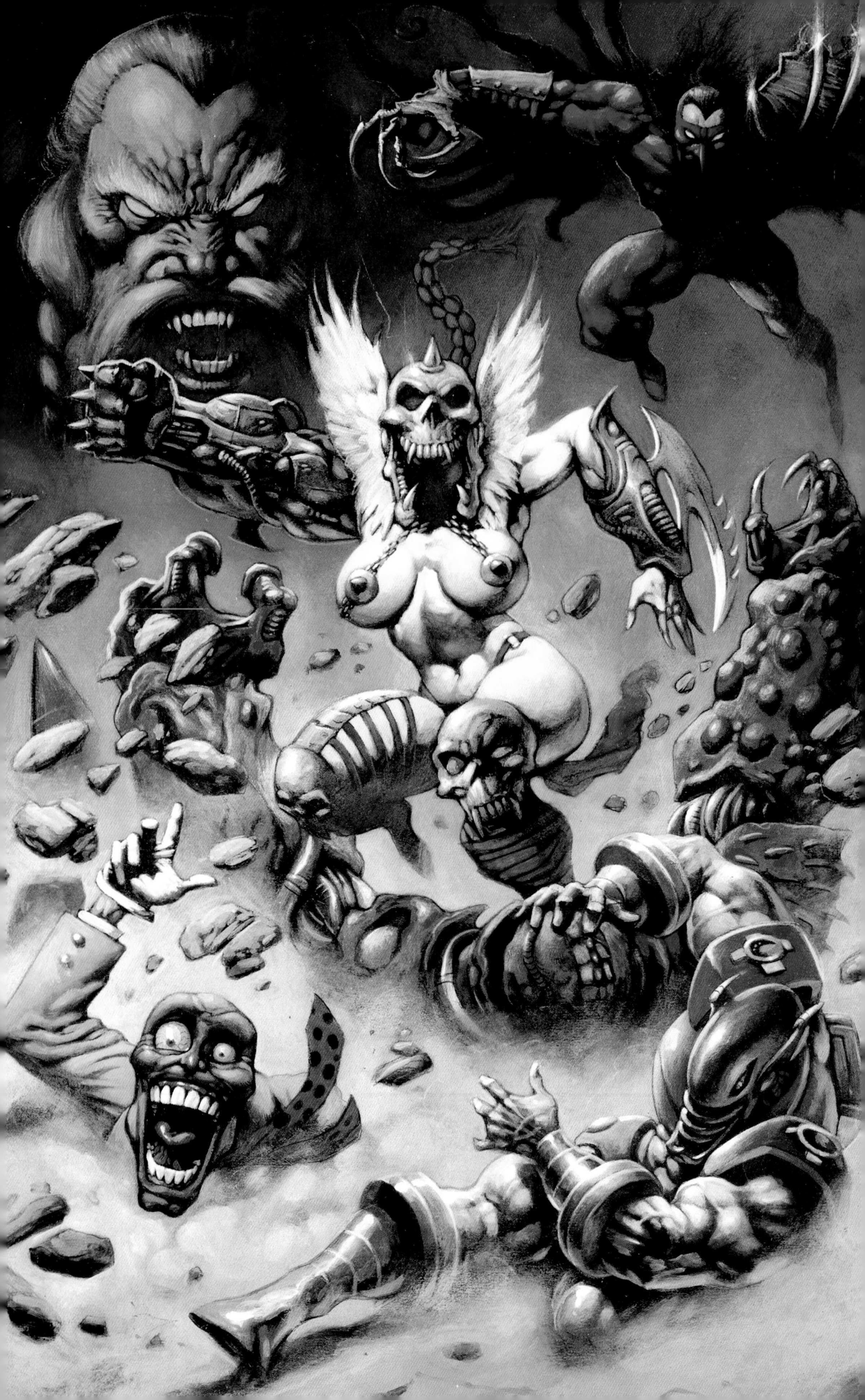

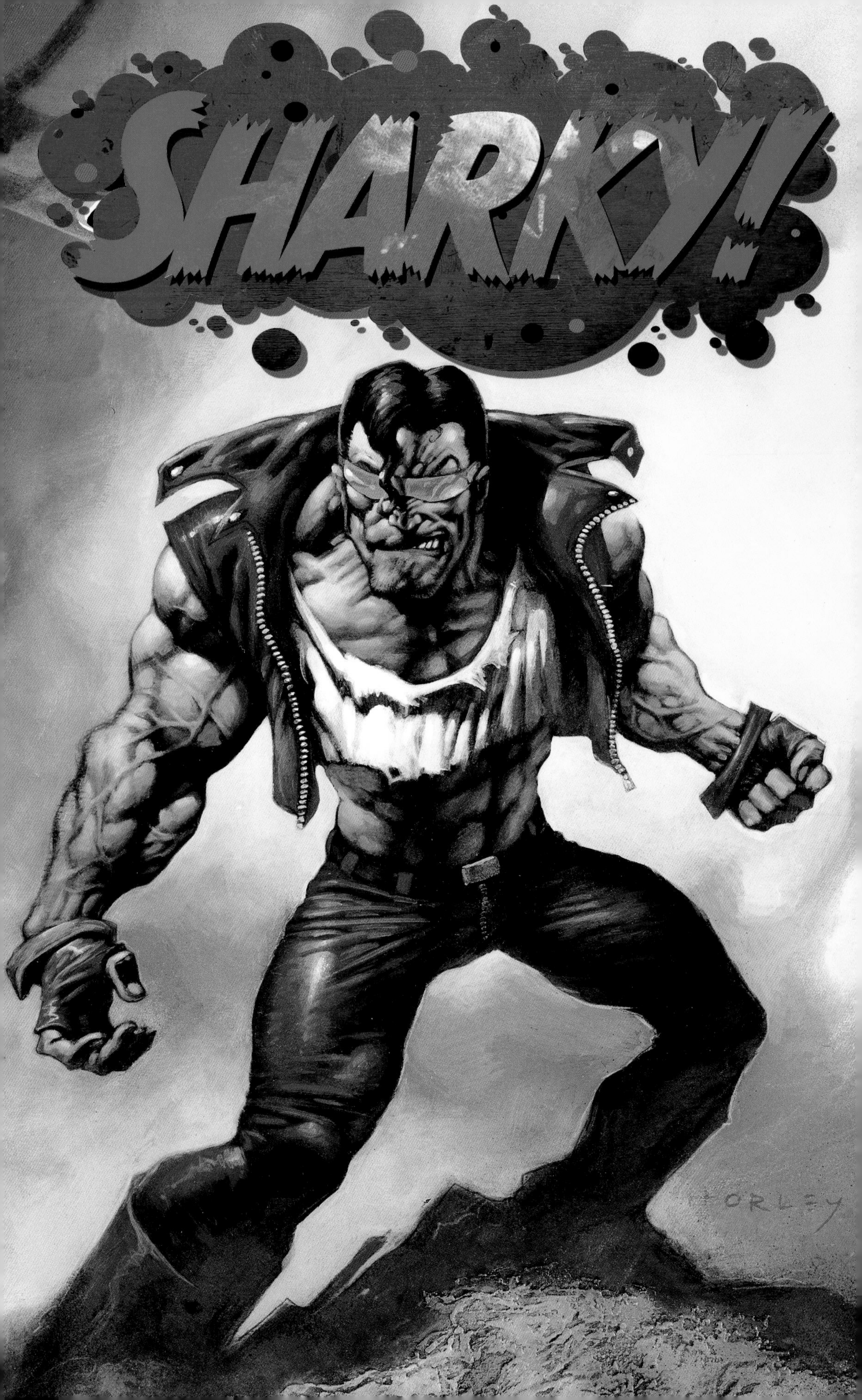
SHARKY!

SHARKY!

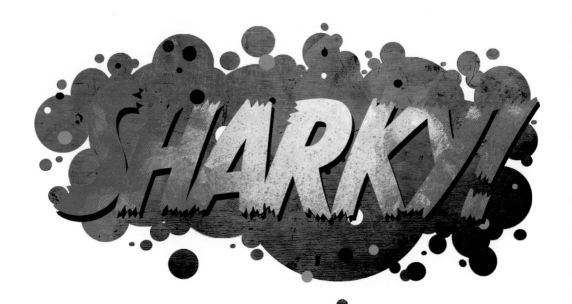

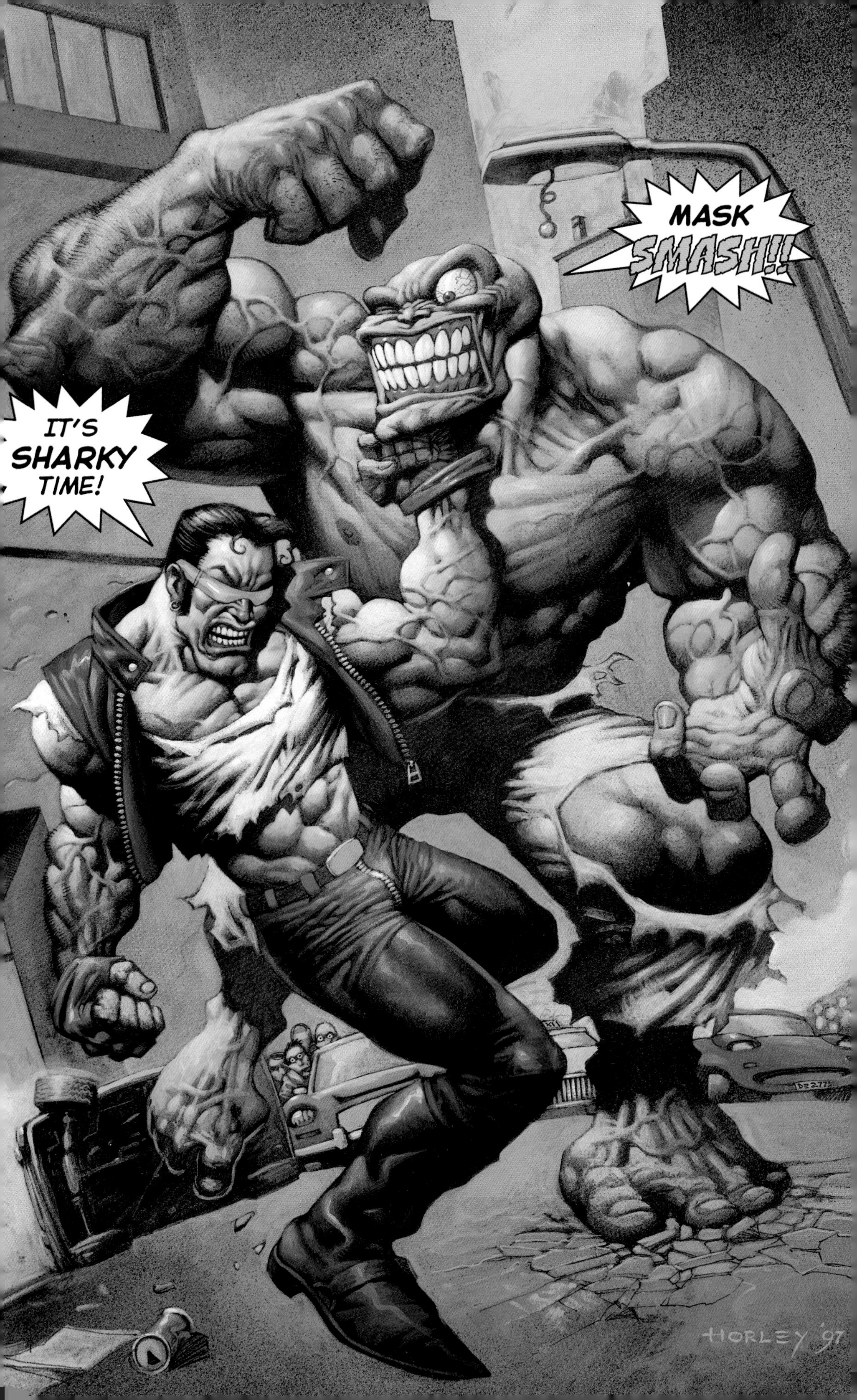
MASK SMASH!!
IT'S SHARKY TIME!
HORLEY '97

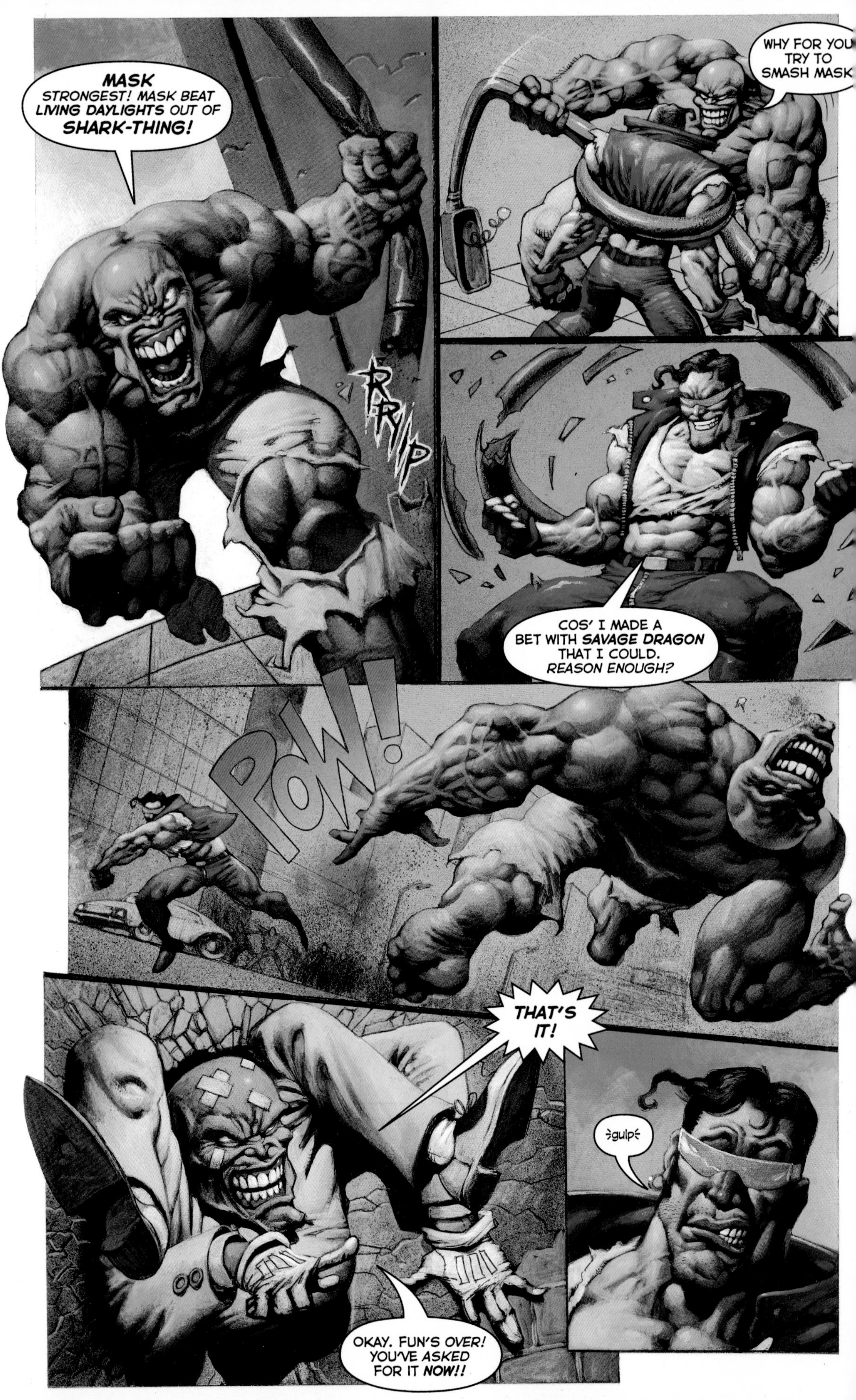
MASK STRONGEST! MASK BEAT LIVING DAYLIGHTS OUT OF SHARK-THING!
RRRIP
WHY FOR YOU TRY TO SMASH MASK
COS' I MADE A BET WITH SAVAGE DRAGON THAT I COULD. REASON ENOUGH?
POW!
THAT'S IT!
gulp
OKAY. FUN'S OVER! YOU'VE ASKED FOR IT NOW!!

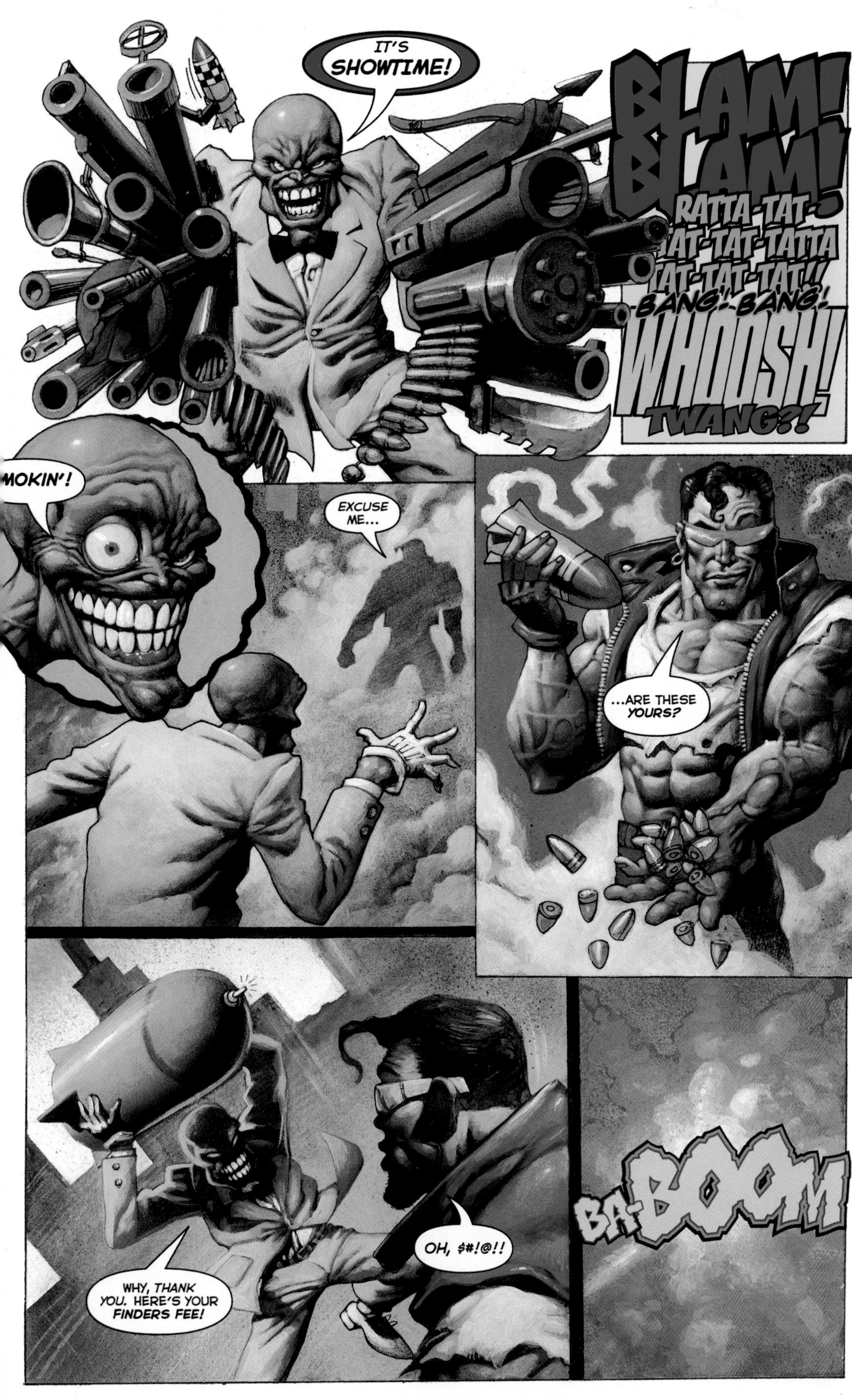
IT'S SHOWTIME!
BLAM! BLAM!
RATTA-TAT-TAT-TAT-TATTA TAT-TAT-TAT!!
BANG! BANG!
WHOOSH!
TWANG?!
MOKIN'!
EXCUSE ME...
...ARE THESE YOURS?
WHY, THANK YOU. HERE'S YOUR FINDERS FEE!
OH, $#!@!!
BA-BOOM

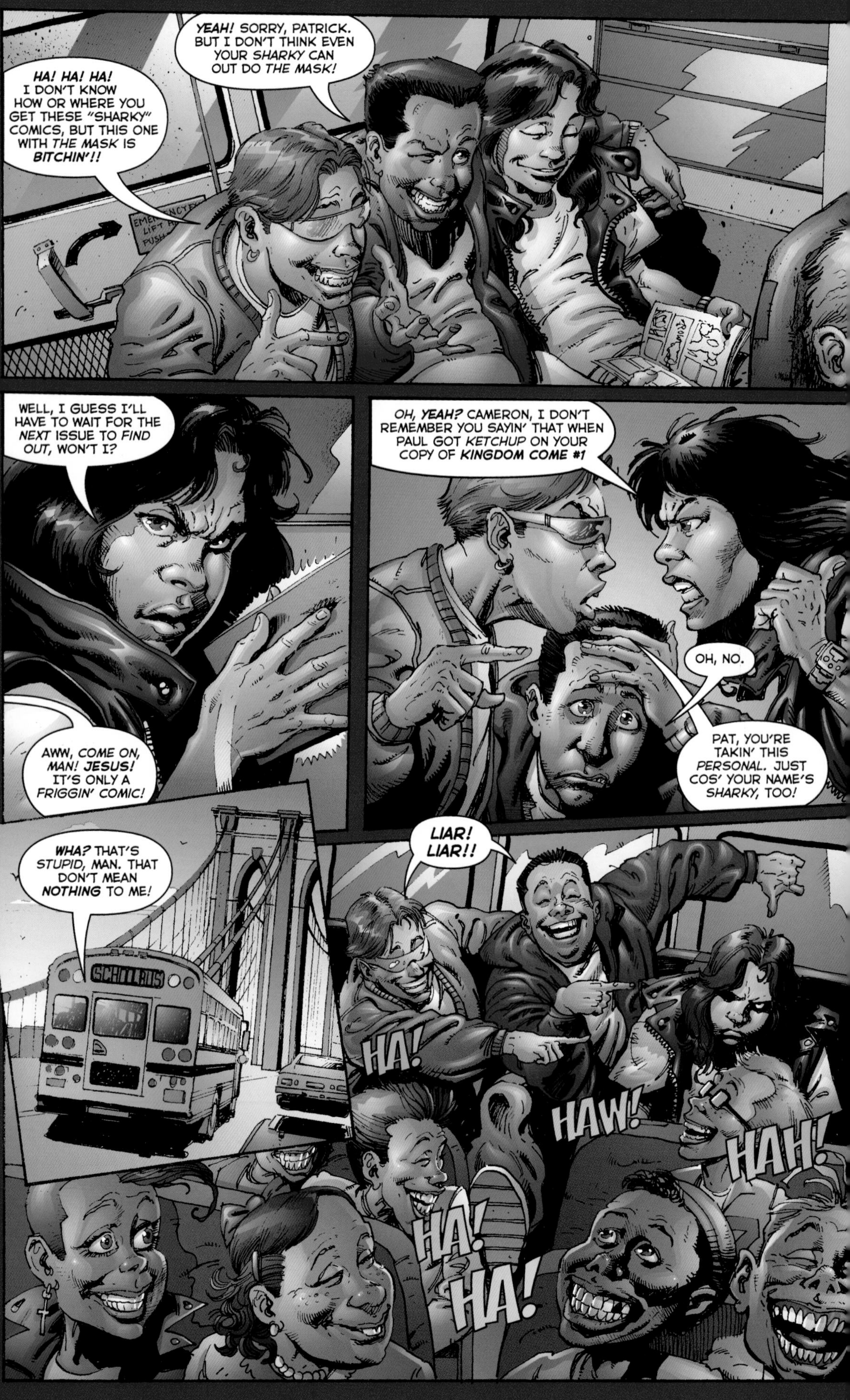

HA! HA! HA! I DON'T KNOW HOW OR WHERE YOU GET THESE "SHARKY" COMICS, BUT THIS ONE WITH *THE MASK* IS ***BITCHIN'!!***
YEAH! SORRY, PATRICK. BUT I DON'T THINK EVEN YOUR *SHARKY* CAN OUT DO *THE MASK!*
WELL, I GUESS I'LL HAVE TO WAIT FOR THE *NEXT* ISSUE TO *FIND OUT*, WON'T I?
AWW, *COME ON, MAN!* ***JESUS!*** IT'S ONLY A *FRIGGIN' COMIC!*
OH, YEAH? CAMERON, I DON'T REMEMBER YOU SAYIN' THAT WHEN PAUL GOT *KETCHUP* ON YOUR COPY OF ***KINGDOM COME #1***
OH, NO.
PAT, YOU'RE TAKIN' THIS *PERSONAL*. JUST COS' YOUR NAME'S *SHARKY*, TOO!
WHA? THAT'S *STUPID*, MAN. THAT DON'T MEAN ***NOTHING*** TO ME!
SCHOOLBUS
LIAR! LIAR!!
HA!
HAW!
HAH!
HA!
HA!

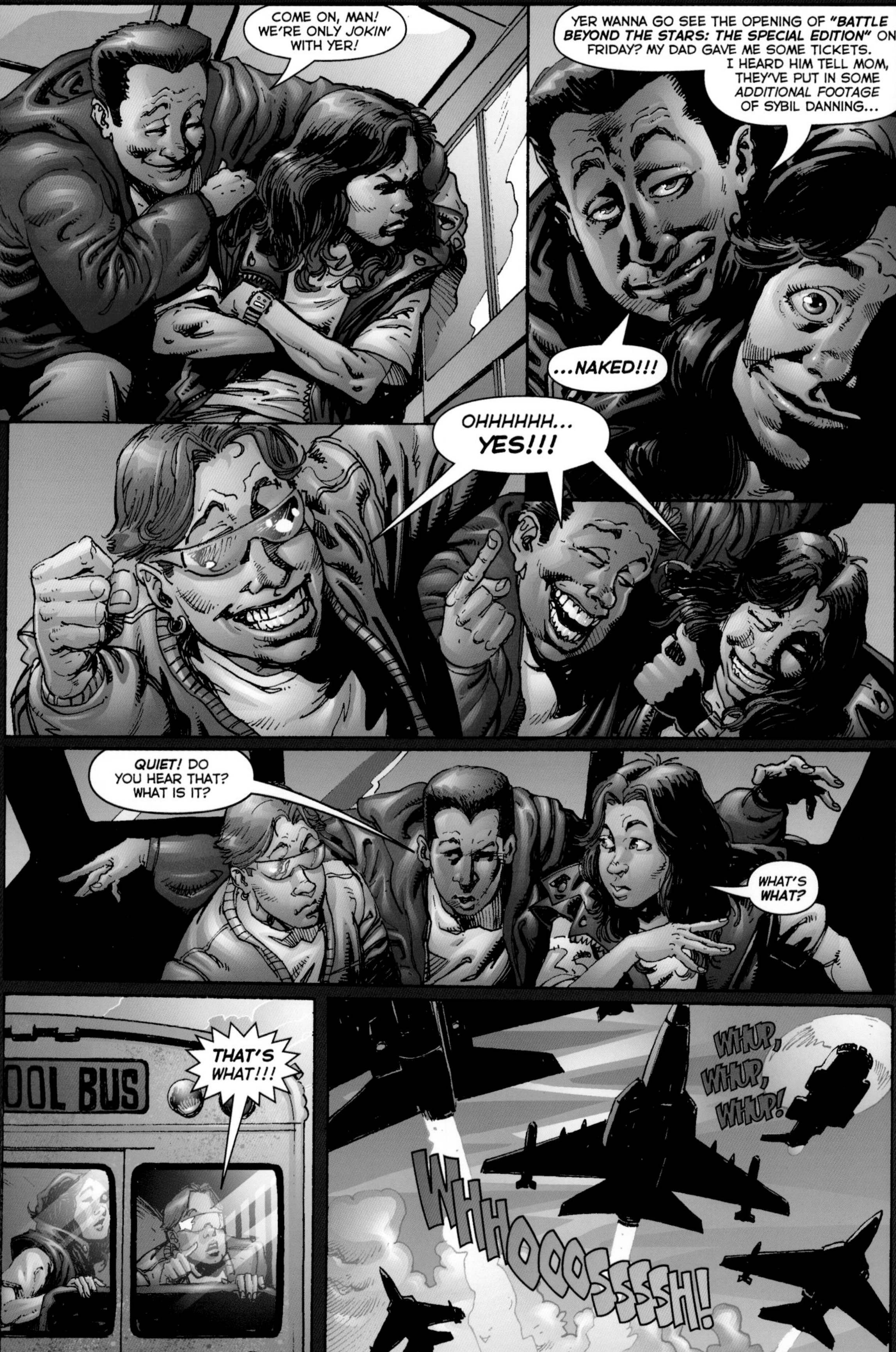

COME ON, MAN! WE'RE ONLY JOKIN' WITH YER!
YER WANNA GO SEE THE OPENING OF "BATTLE BEYOND THE STARS: THE SPECIAL EDITION" ON FRIDAY? MY DAD GAVE ME SOME TICKETS. I HEARD HIM TELL MOM, THEY'VE PUT IN SOME ADDITIONAL FOOTAGE OF SYBIL DANNING...
...NAKED!!!
OHHHHHH... YES!!!
QUIET! DO YOU HEAR THAT? WHAT IS IT?
WHAT'S WHAT?
OOL BUS
THAT'S WHAT!!!
WHUP, WHUP, WHUP!
WHHOOOSSSSH!

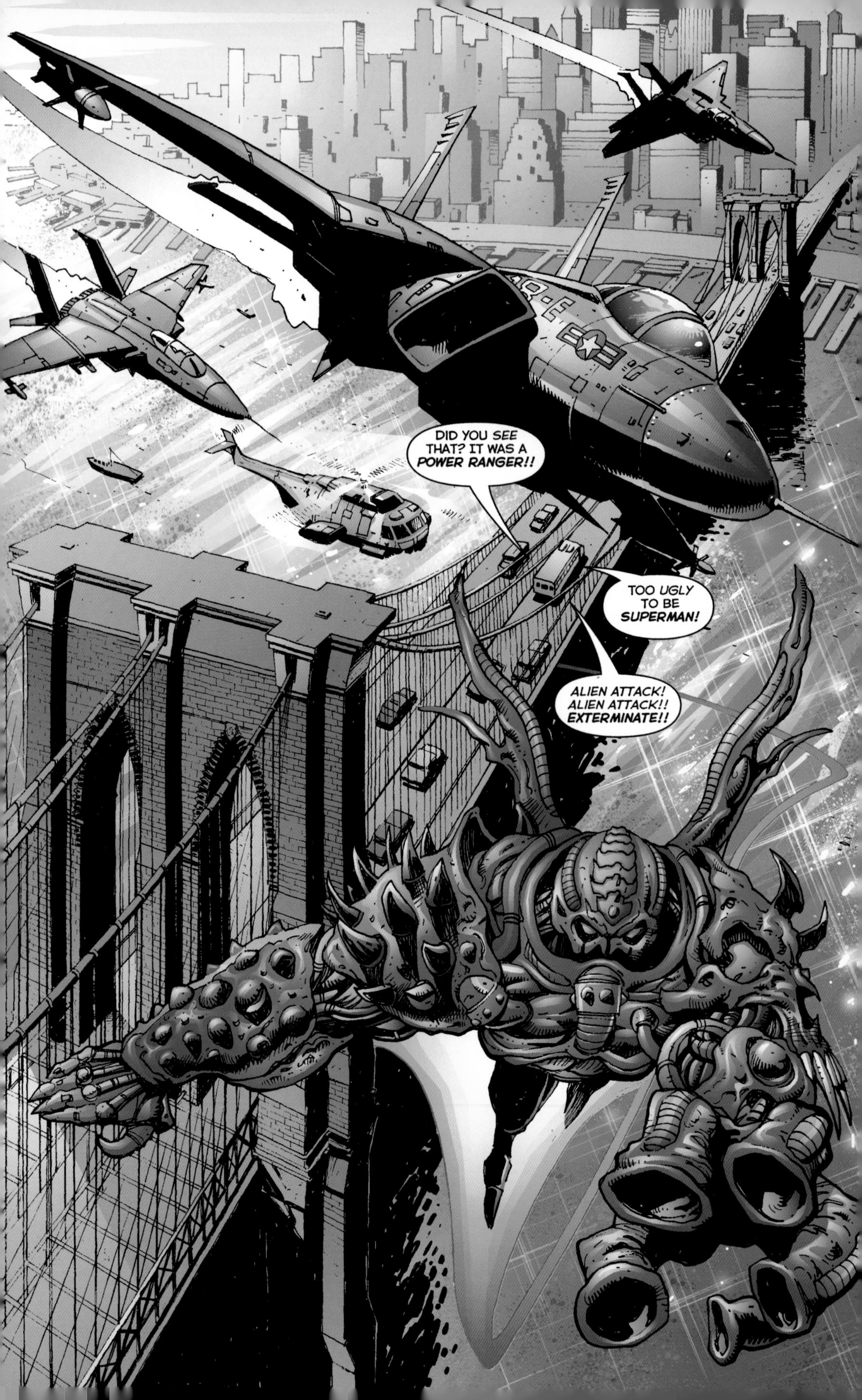
DID YOU SEE THAT? IT WAS A POWER RANGER!!
TOO UGLY TO BE SUPERMAN!
ALIEN ATTACK! ALIEN ATTACK!! EXTERMINATE!!

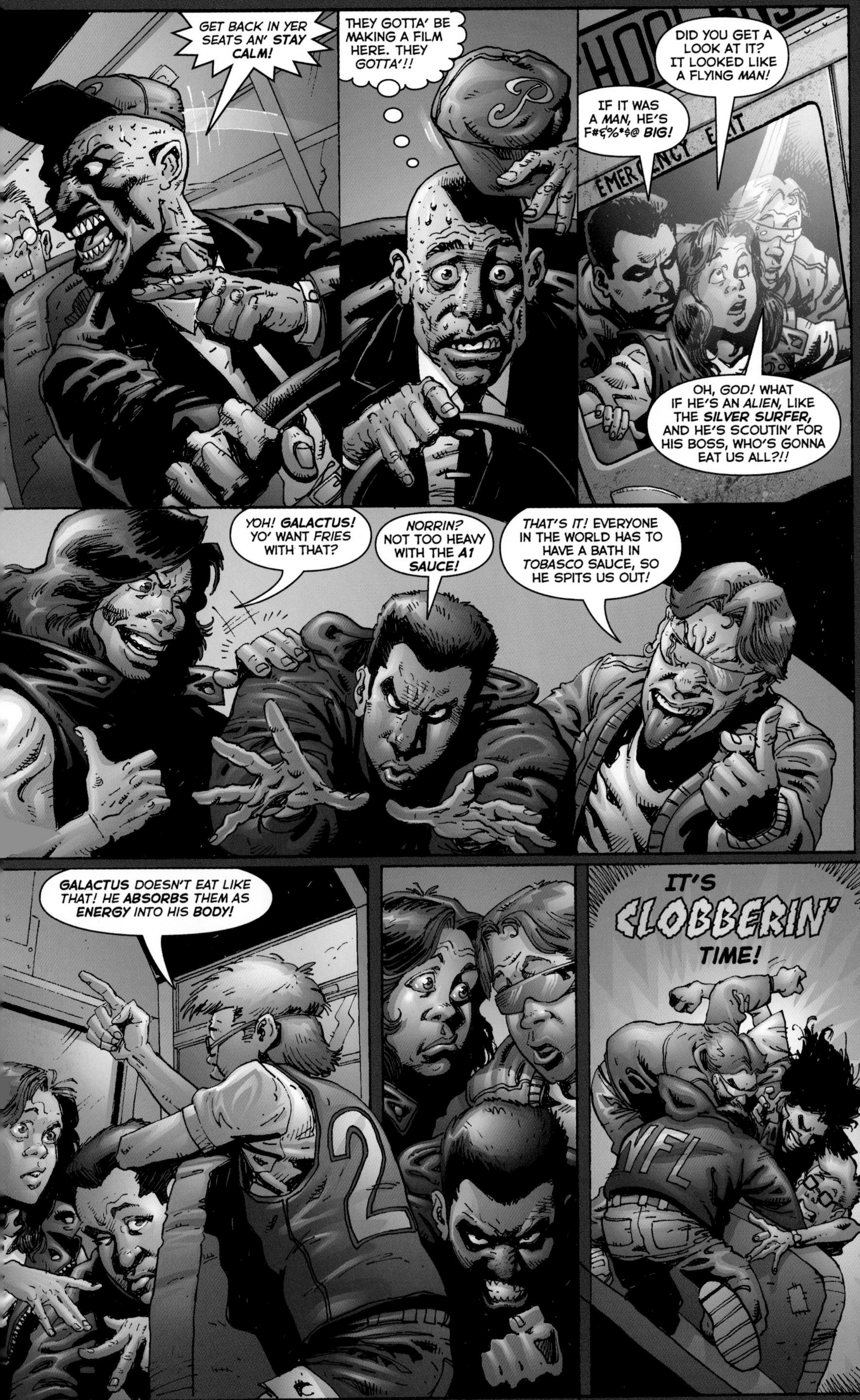
GET BACK IN YER SEATS AN' STAY CALM!
THEY GOTTA' BE MAKING A FILM HERE. THEY GOTTA'!!
DID YOU GET A LOOK AT IT? IT LOOKED LIKE A FLYING MAN!
IF IT WAS A MAN, HE'S F#€%*$@ BIG!
OH, GOD! WHAT IF HE'S AN ALIEN, LIKE THE SILVER SURFER, AND HE'S SCOUTIN' FOR HIS BOSS, WHO'S GONNA EAT US ALL?!!
YOH! GALACTUS! YO' WANT FRIES WITH THAT?
NORRIN? NOT TOO HEAVY WITH THE A1 SAUCE!
THAT'S IT! EVERYONE IN THE WORLD HAS TO HAVE A BATH IN TOBASCO SAUCE, SO HE SPITS US OUT!
GALACTUS DOESN'T EAT LIKE THAT! HE ABSORBS THEM AS ENERGY INTO HIS BODY!
IT'S CLOBBERIN' TIME!

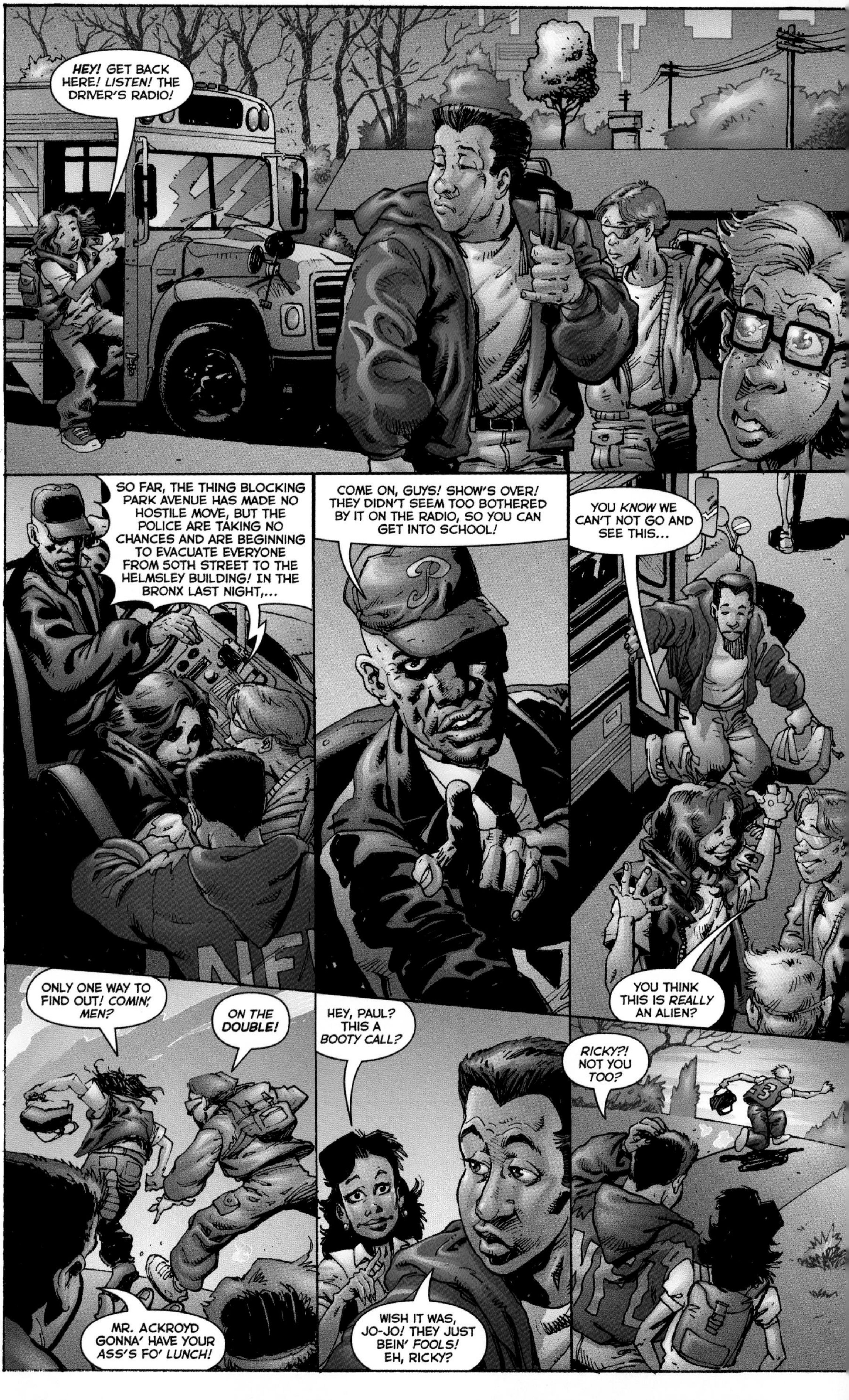
HEY! GET BACK HERE! LISTEN! THE DRIVER'S RADIO!
SO FAR, THE THING BLOCKING PARK AVENUE HAS MADE NO HOSTILE MOVE, BUT THE POLICE ARE TAKING NO CHANCES AND ARE BEGINNING TO EVACUATE EVERYONE FROM 50TH STREET TO THE HELMSLEY BUILDING! IN THE BRONX LAST NIGHT,...
COME ON, GUYS! SHOW'S OVER! THEY DIDN'T SEEM TOO BOTHERED BY IT ON THE RADIO, SO YOU CAN GET INTO SCHOOL!
YOU KNOW WE CAN'T NOT GO AND SEE THIS...
YOU THINK THIS IS REALLY AN ALIEN?
ONLY ONE WAY TO FIND OUT! COMIN', MEN?
ON THE DOUBLE!
MR. ACKROYD GONNA' HAVE YOUR ASS'S FO' LUNCH!
HEY, PAUL? THIS A BOOTY CALL?
WISH IT WAS, JO-JO! THEY JUST BEIN' FOOLS! EH, RICKY?
RICKY?! NOT YOU TOO?

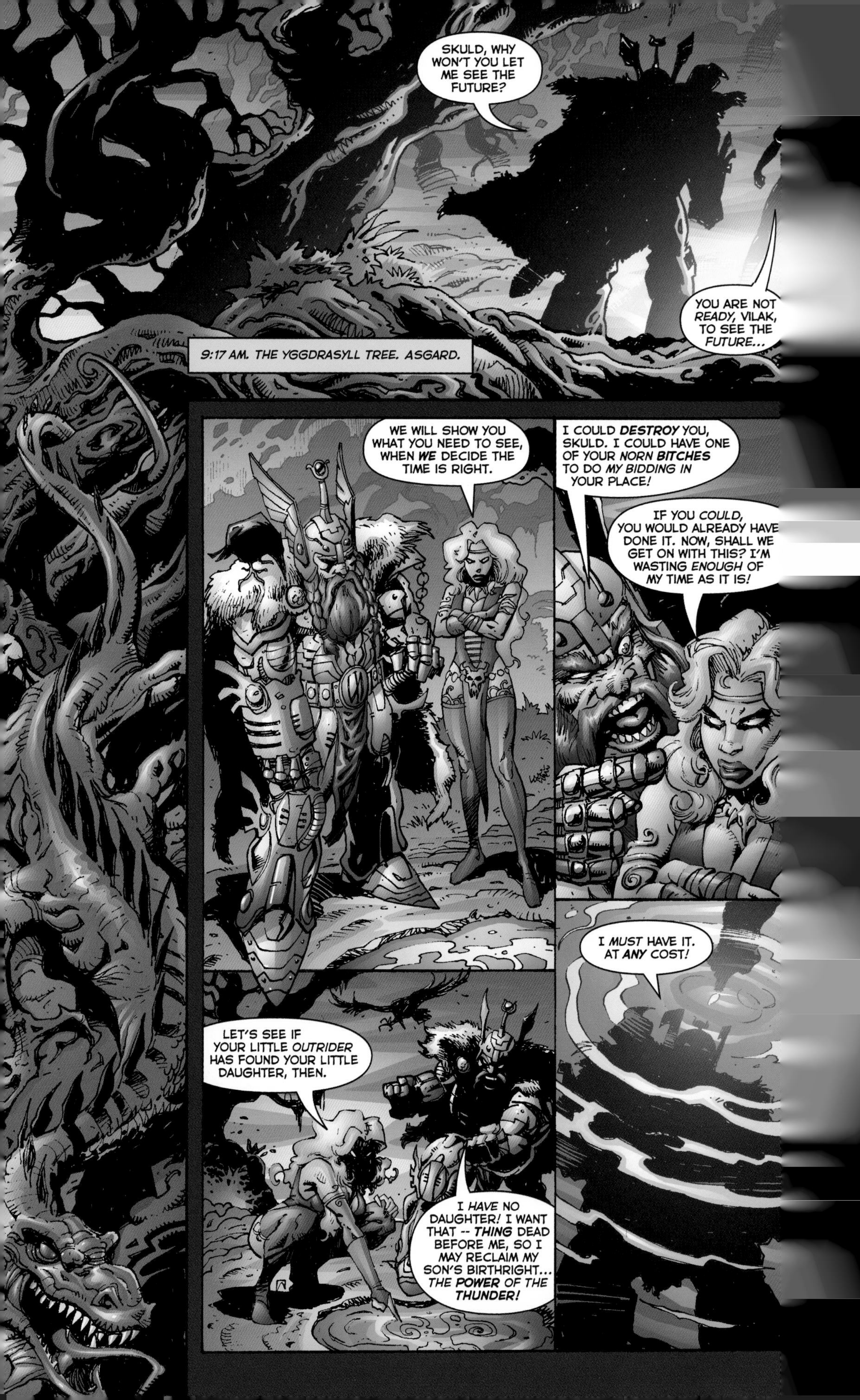
SKULD, WHY WON'T YOU LET ME SEE THE FUTURE?
YOU ARE NOT READY, VILAK, TO SEE THE FUTURE...
9:17 AM. THE YGGDRASYLL TREE. ASGARD.
WE WILL SHOW YOU WHAT YOU NEED TO SEE, WHEN WE DECIDE THE TIME IS RIGHT.
I COULD DESTROY YOU, SKULD. I COULD HAVE ONE OF YOUR NORN BITCHES TO DO MY BIDDING IN YOUR PLACE!
IF YOU COULD, YOU WOULD ALREADY HAVE DONE IT. NOW, SHALL WE GET ON WITH THIS? I'M WASTING ENOUGH OF MY TIME AS IT IS!
LET'S SEE IF YOUR LITTLE OUTRIDER HAS FOUND YOUR LITTLE DAUGHTER, THEN.
I HAVE NO DAUGHTER! I WANT THAT -- THING DEAD BEFORE ME, SO I MAY RECLAIM MY SON'S BIRTHRIGHT... THE POWER OF THE THUNDER!
I MUST HAVE IT. AT ANY COST!

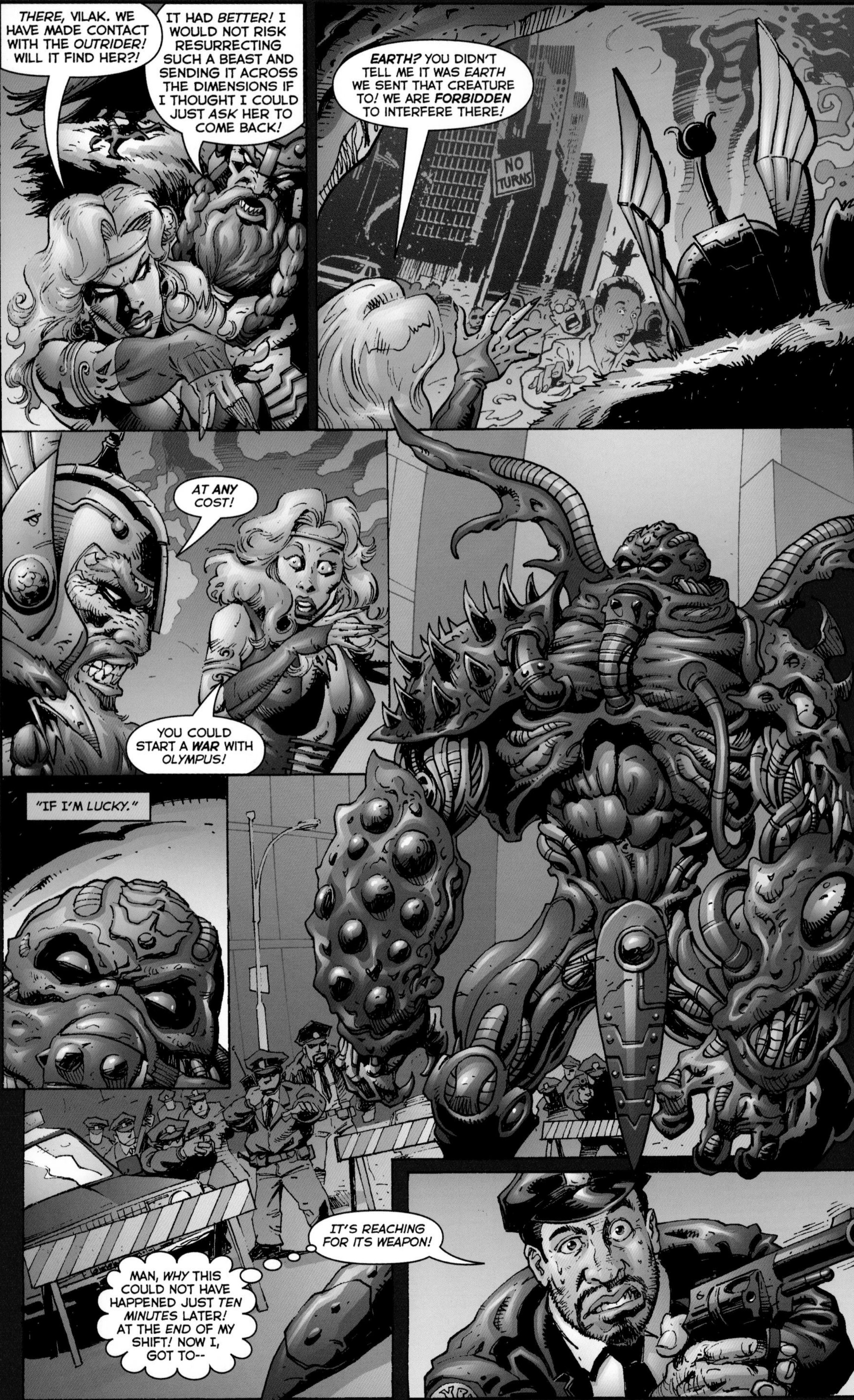
THERE, VILAK. WE HAVE MADE CONTACT WITH THE OUTRIDER! WILL IT FIND HER?!
IT HAD BETTER! I WOULD NOT RISK RESURRECTING SUCH A BEAST AND SENDING IT ACROSS THE DIMENSIONS IF I THOUGHT I COULD JUST ASK HER TO COME BACK!
EARTH? YOU DIDN'T TELL ME IT WAS EARTH WE SENT THAT CREATURE TO! WE ARE FORBIDDEN TO INTERFERE THERE!
NO TURNS
AT ANY COST!
YOU COULD START A WAR WITH OLYMPUS!
"IF I'M LUCKY."
IT'S REACHING FOR ITS WEAPON!
MAN, WHY THIS COULD NOT HAVE HAPPENED JUST TEN MINUTES LATER! AT THE END OF MY SHIFT! NOW I, GOT TO--

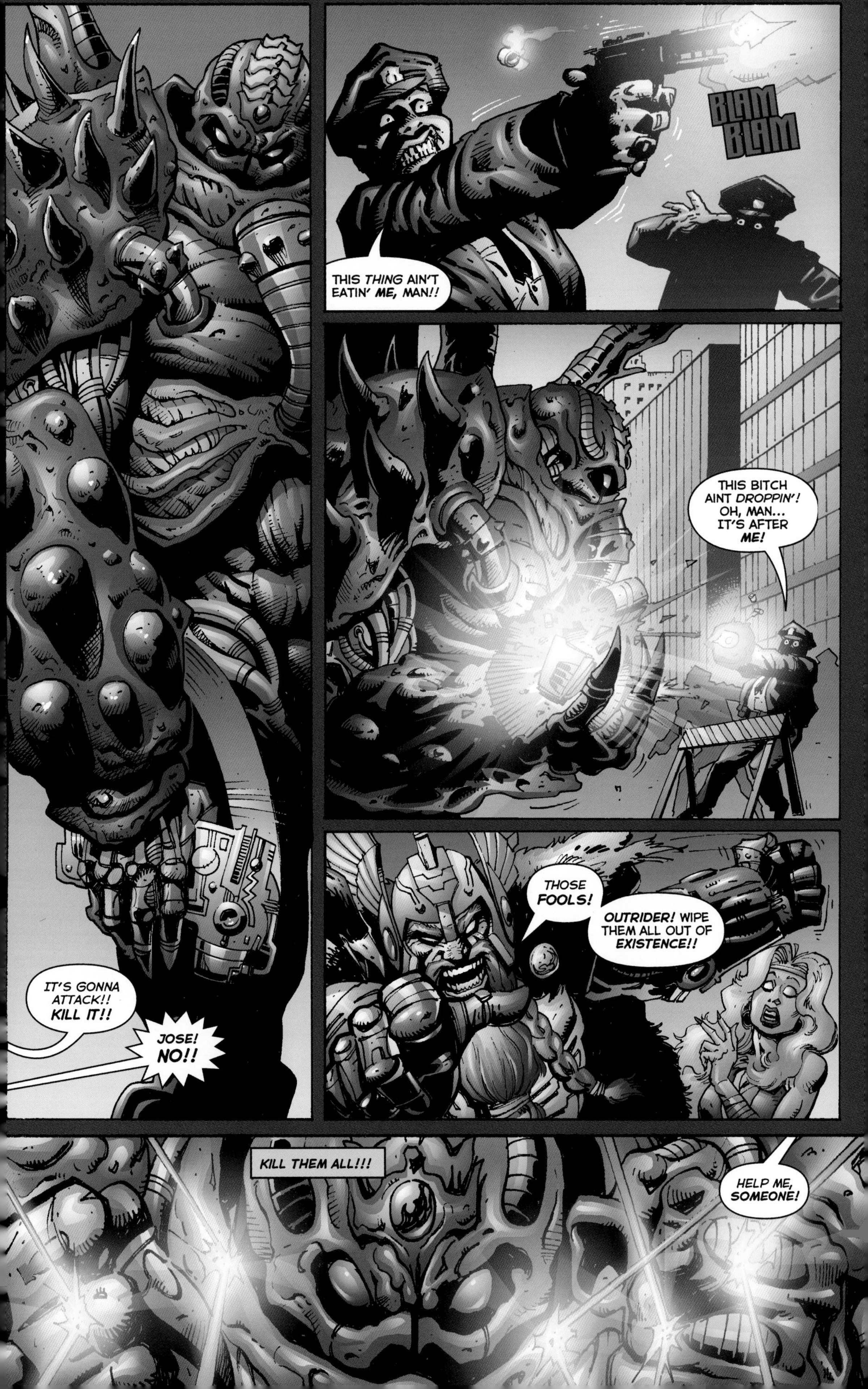
THIS THING AIN'T EATIN' ME, MAN!!
BLAM BLAM
THIS BITCH AINT DROPPIN'! OH, MAN... IT'S AFTER ME!
IT'S GONNA ATTACK!! KILL IT!!
JOSE! NO!!
THOSE FOOLS!
OUTRIDER! WIPE THEM ALL OUT OF EXISTENCE!!
KILL THEM ALL!!!
HELP ME, SOMEONE!

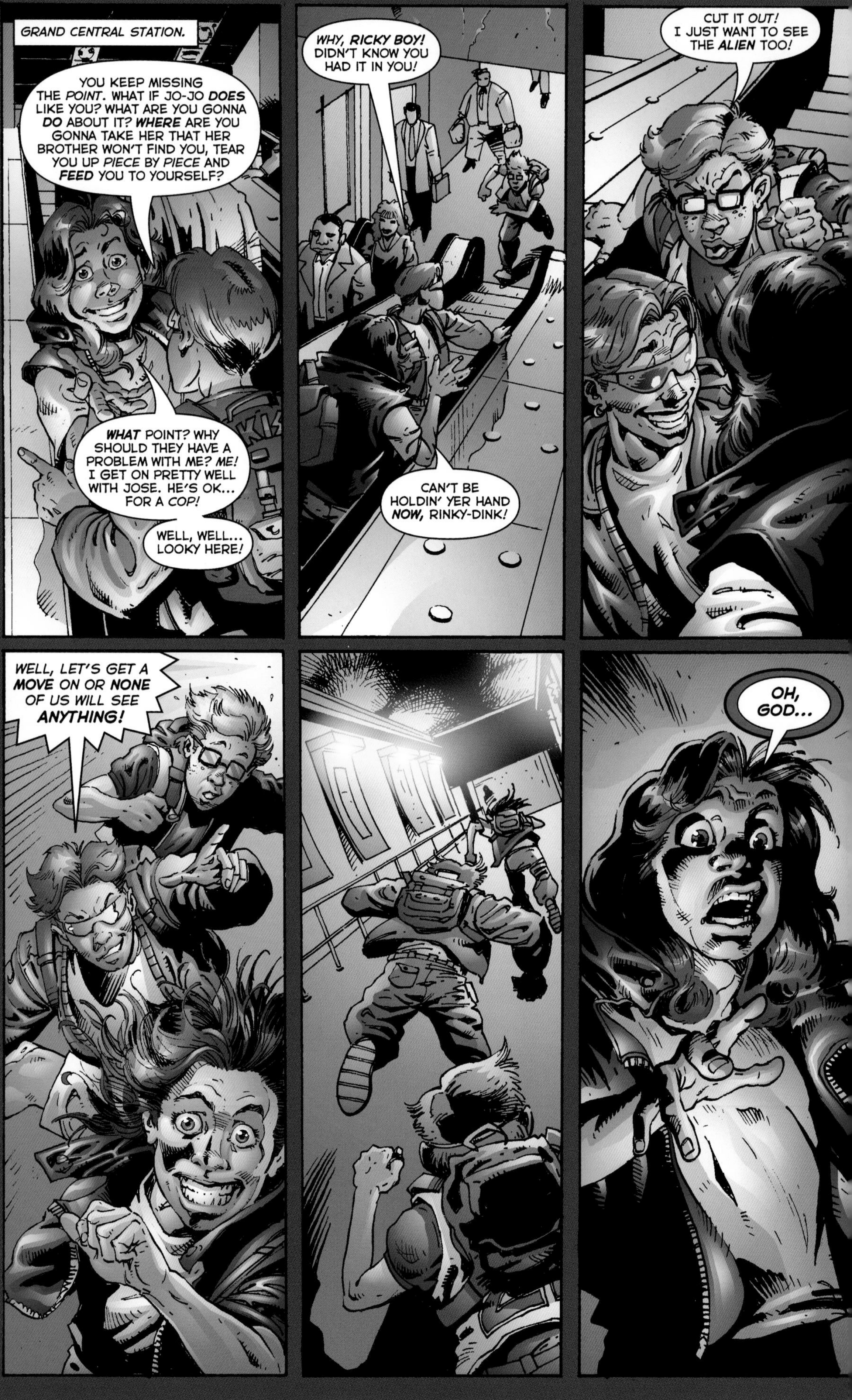
GRAND CENTRAL STATION.
YOU KEEP MISSING THE POINT. WHAT IF JO-JO DOES LIKE YOU? WHAT ARE YOU GONNA DO ABOUT IT? WHERE ARE YOU GONNA TAKE HER THAT HER BROTHER WON'T FIND YOU, TEAR YOU UP PIECE BY PIECE AND FEED YOU TO YOURSELF?
WHAT POINT? WHY SHOULD THEY HAVE A PROBLEM WITH ME? ME! I GET ON PRETTY WELL WITH JOSE. HE'S OK... FOR A COP!
WELL, WELL... LOOKY HERE!
WHY, RICKY BOY! DIDN'T KNOW YOU HAD IT IN YOU!
CAN'T BE HOLDIN' YER HAND NOW, RINKY-DINK!
CUT IT OUT! I JUST WANT TO SEE THE ALIEN TOO!
WELL, LET'S GET A MOVE ON OR NONE OF US WILL SEE ANYTHING!
OH, GOD...

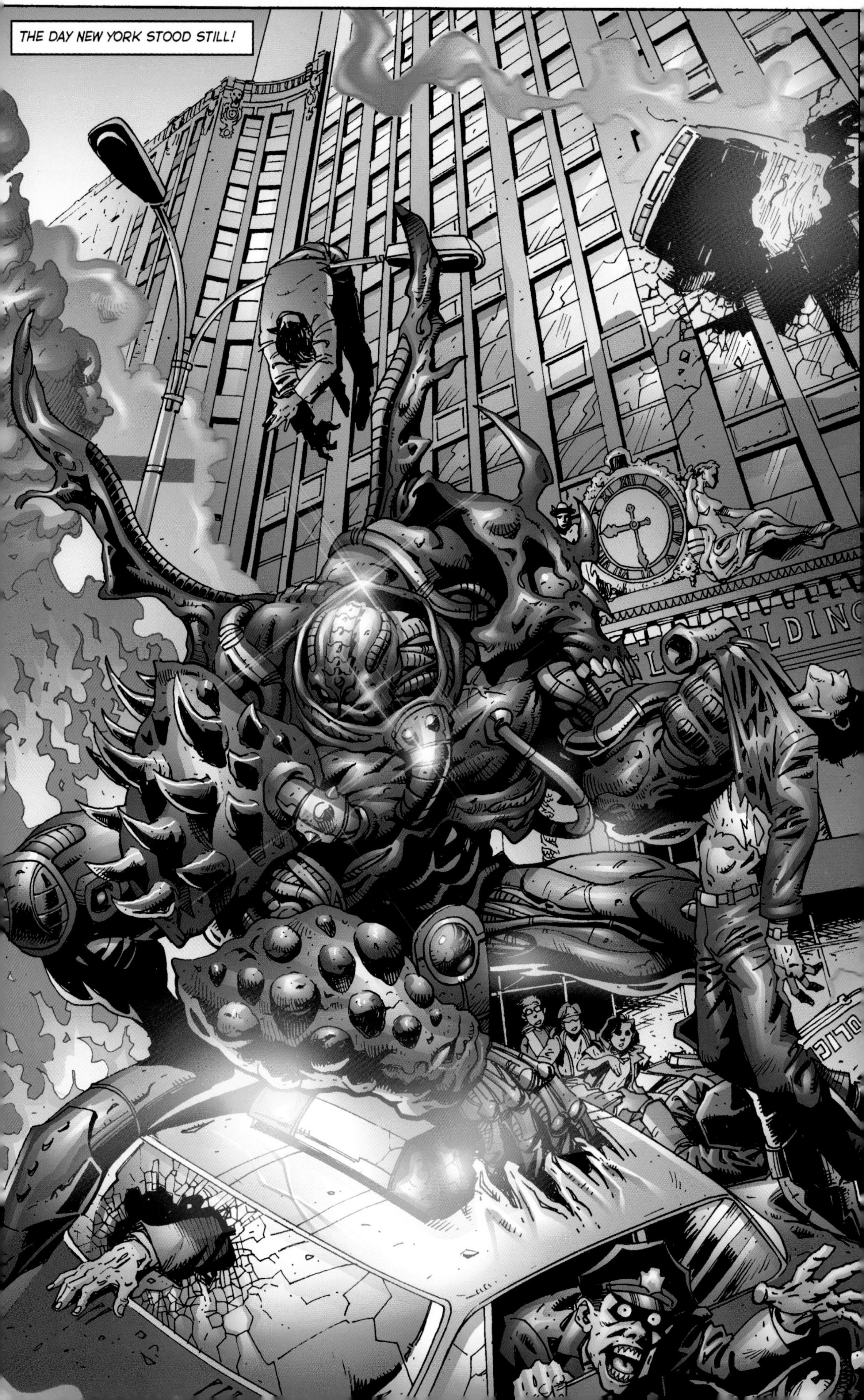
THE DAY NEW YORK STOOD STILL!

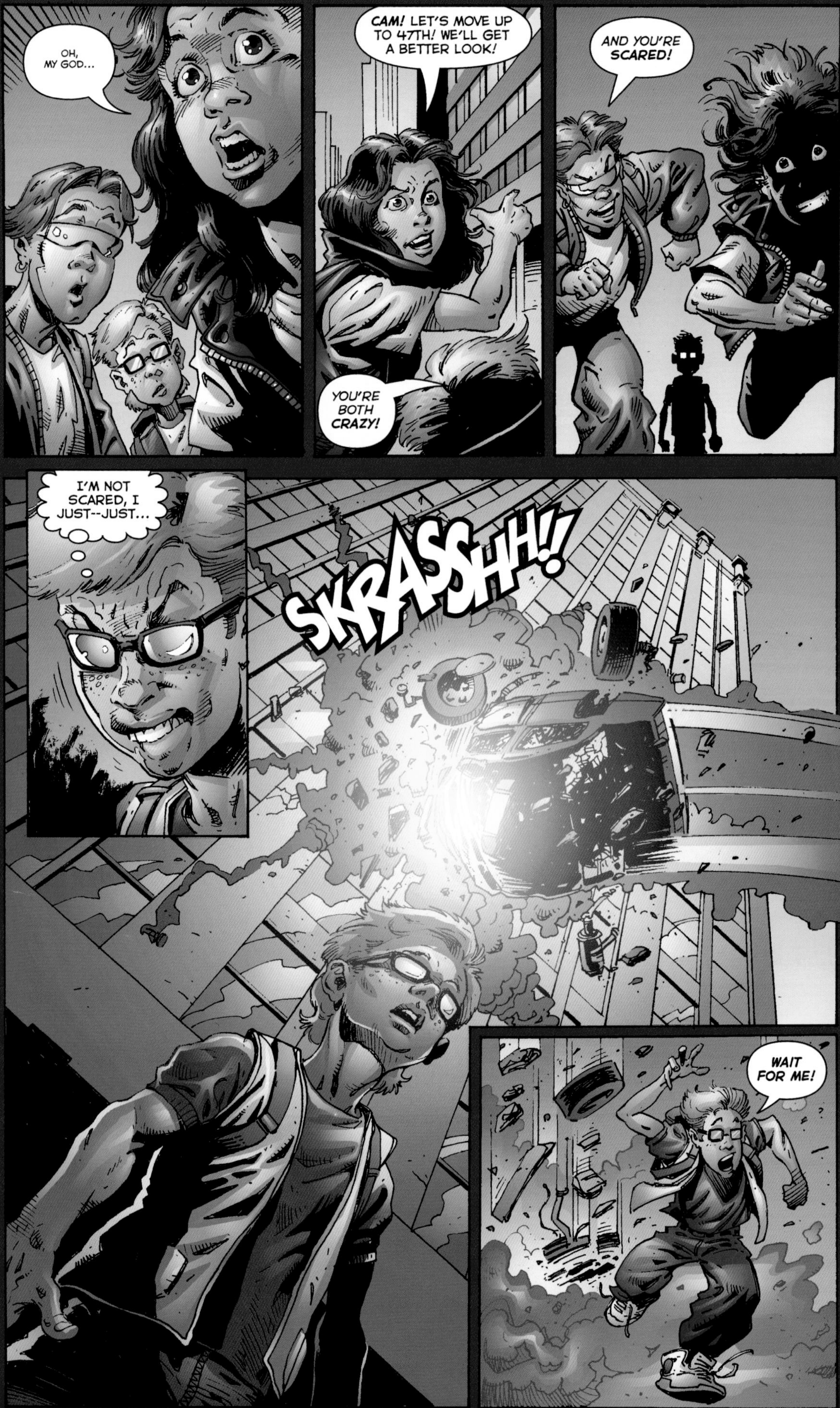
OH, MY GOD...
CAM! LET'S MOVE UP TO 47TH! WE'LL GET A BETTER LOOK!
YOU'RE BOTH CRAZY!
AND YOU'RE SCARED!
I'M NOT SCARED, I JUST--JUST...
SKRASSHH!!
WAIT FOR ME!

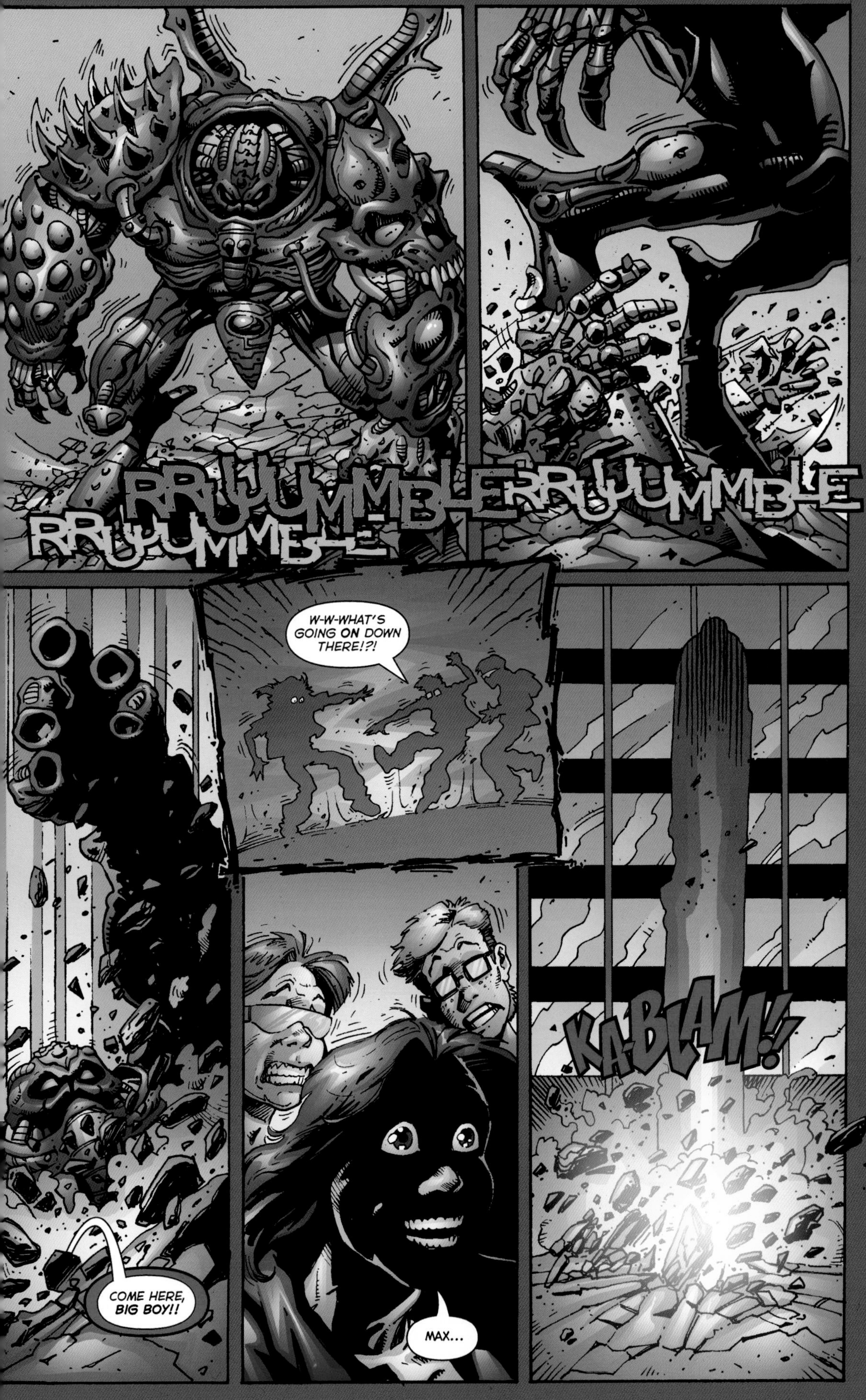
RRUUUMMBLE
RRUUUMMBLE
RRUUUMMBLE
W-W-WHAT'S GOING ON DOWN THERE!?!
COME HERE, BIG BOY!!
MAX...
KA-BLAM!!

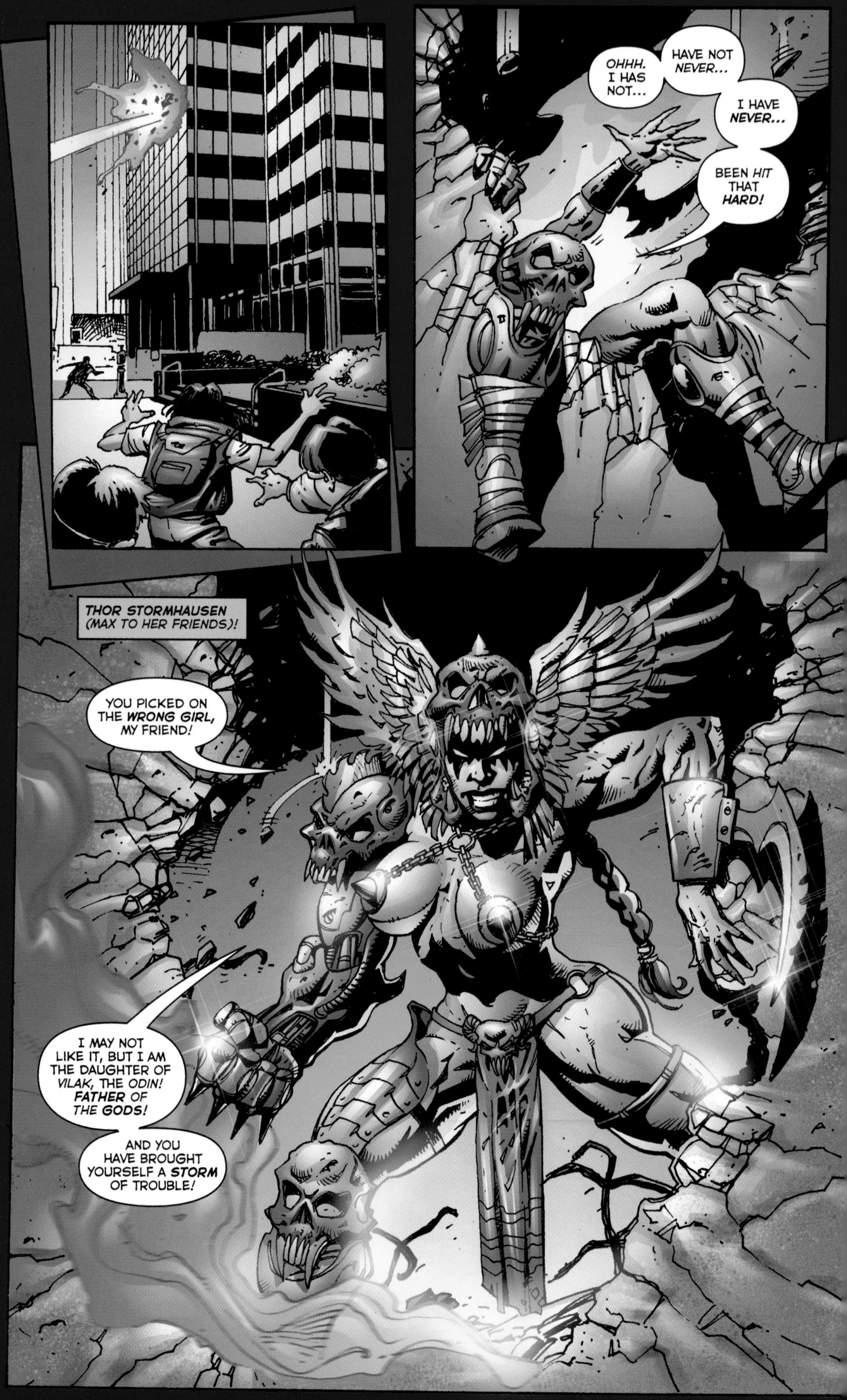
OHHH. I HAS NOT...
HAVE NOT NEVER...
I HAVE NEVER...
BEEN HIT THAT HARD!
THOR STORMHAUSEN (MAX TO HER FRIENDS)!
YOU PICKED ON THE WRONG GIRL, MY FRIEND!
I MAY NOT LIKE IT, BUT I AM THE DAUGHTER OF VILAK, THE ODIN! FATHER OF THE GODS!
AND YOU HAVE BROUGHT YOURSELF A STORM OF TROUBLE!

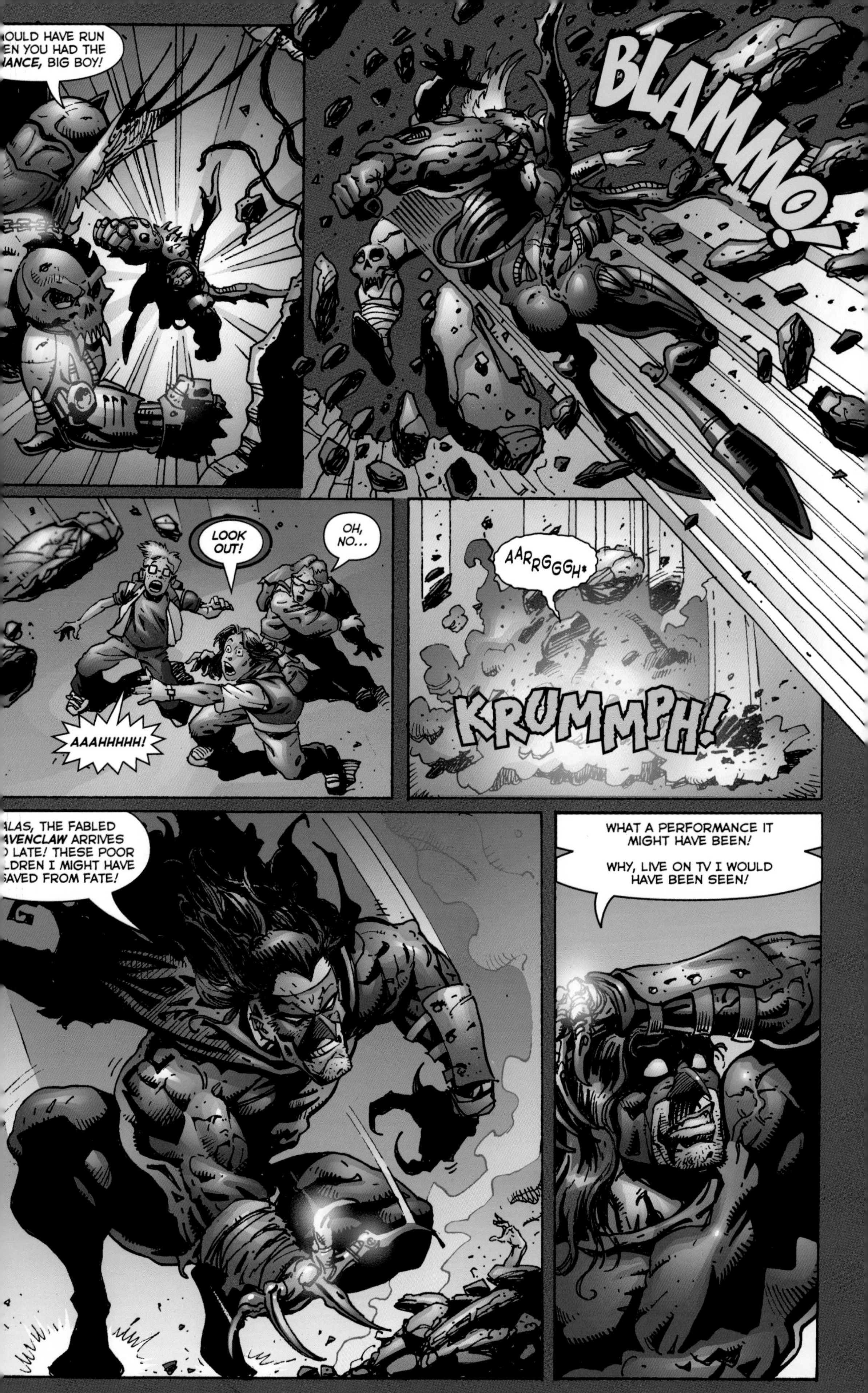
OULD HAVE RUN EN YOU HAD THE ANCE, BIG BOY!
BLAMMO!
LOOK OUT!
OH, NO...
AAAHHHHH!
AARRGGGH*
KRUMMPH!
ALAS, THE FABLED AVENCLAW ARRIVES LATE! THESE POOR LDREN I MIGHT HAVE SAVED FROM FATE!
WHAT A PERFORMANCE IT MIGHT HAVE BEEN!
WHY, LIVE ON TV I WOULD HAVE BEEN SEEN!

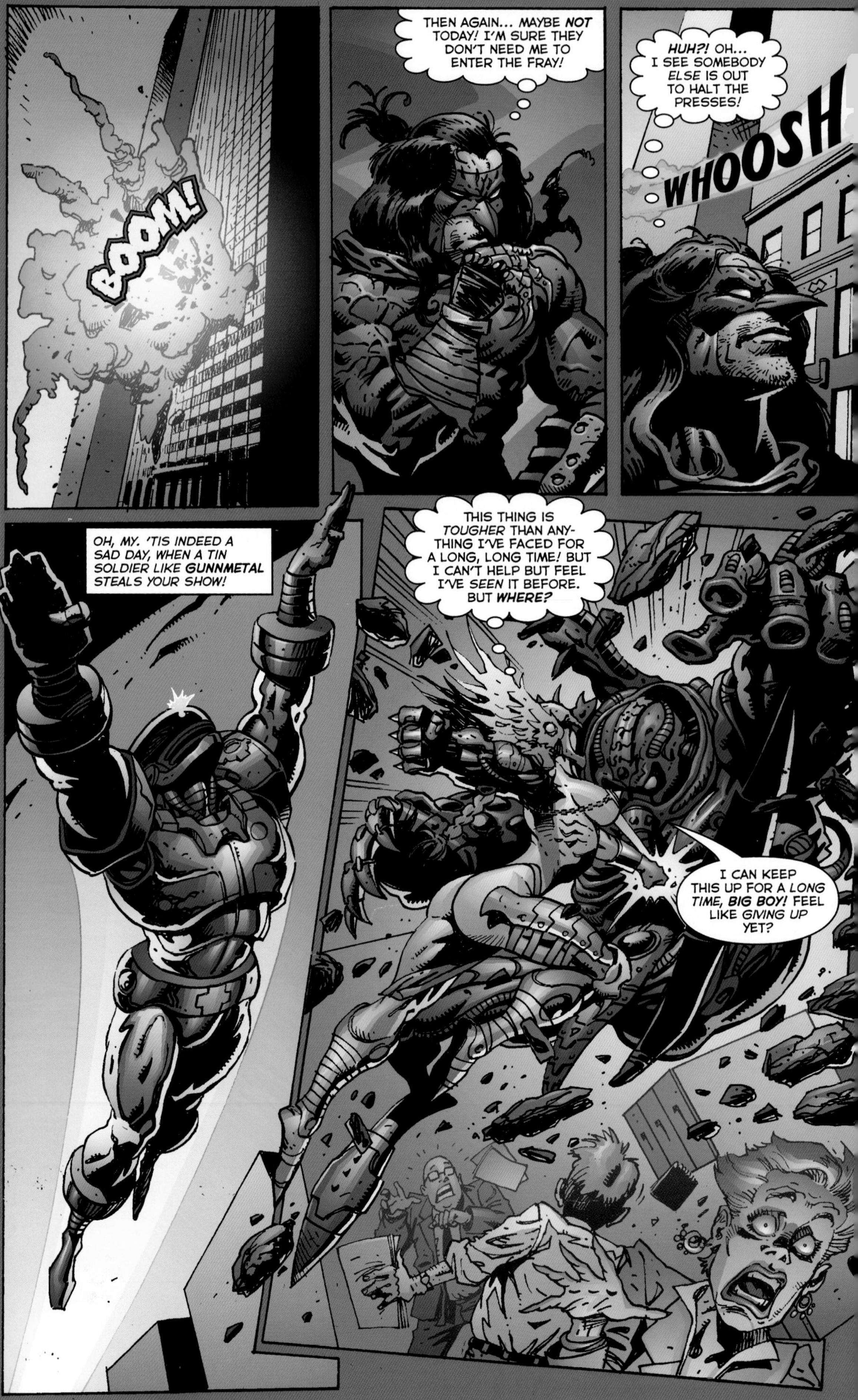
BOOM!
THEN AGAIN... MAYBE NOT TODAY! I'M SURE THEY DON'T NEED ME TO ENTER THE FRAY!
HUH?! OH... I SEE SOMEBODY ELSE IS OUT TO HALT THE PRESSES!
WHOOSH
OH, MY. 'TIS INDEED A SAD DAY, WHEN A TIN SOLDIER LIKE GUNNMETAL STEALS YOUR SHOW!
THIS THING IS TOUGHER THAN ANY-THING I'VE FACED FOR A LONG, LONG TIME! BUT I CAN'T HELP BUT FEEL I'VE SEEN IT BEFORE. BUT WHERE?
I CAN KEEP THIS UP FOR A LONG TIME, BIG BOY! FEEL LIKE GIVING UP YET?

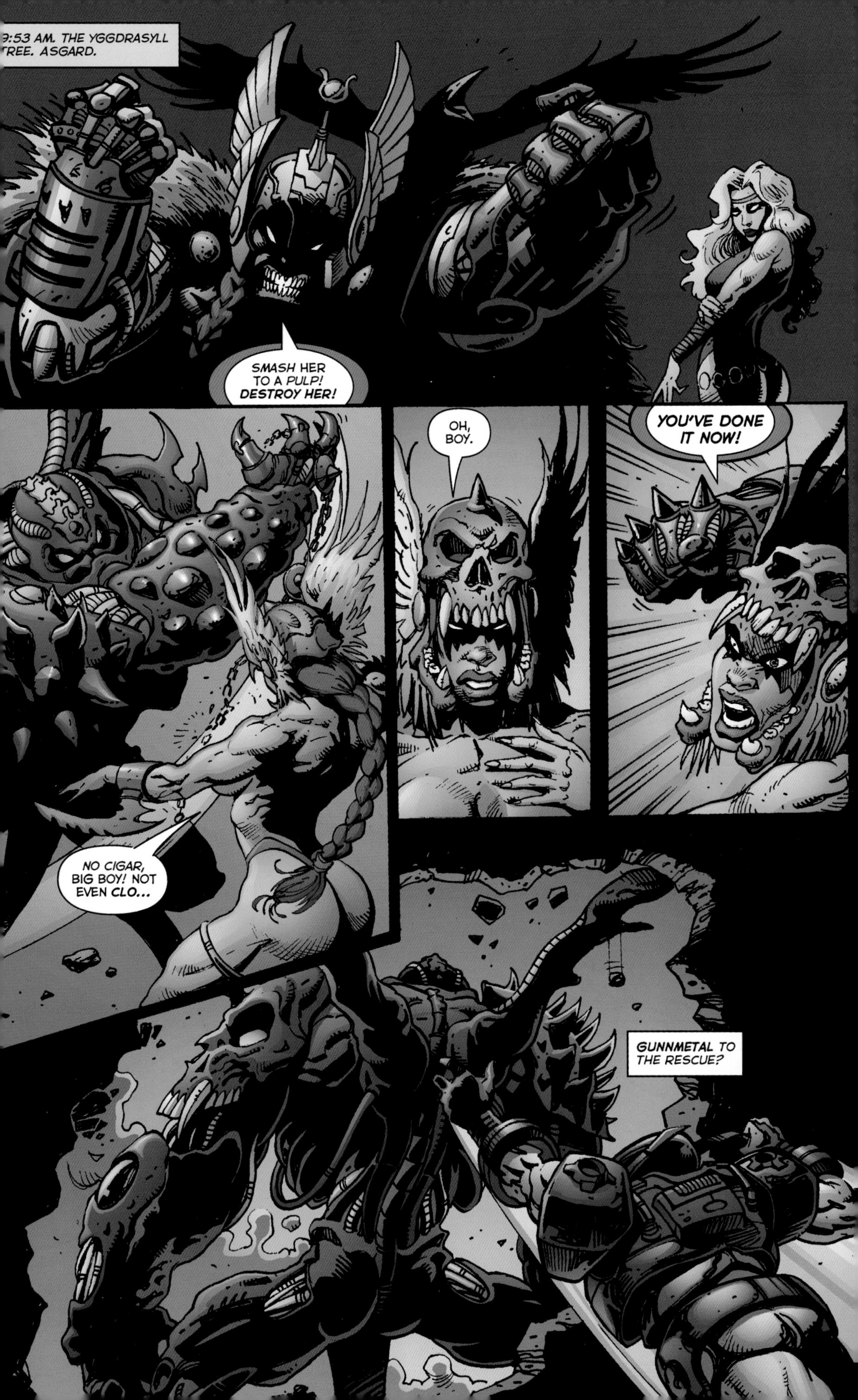
9:53 AM. THE YGGDRASYLL TREE. ASGARD.
SMASH HER TO A PULP! DESTROY HER!
NO CIGAR, BIG BOY! NOT EVEN CLO...
OH, BOY.
YOU'VE DONE IT NOW!
GUNNMETAL TO THE RESCUE?

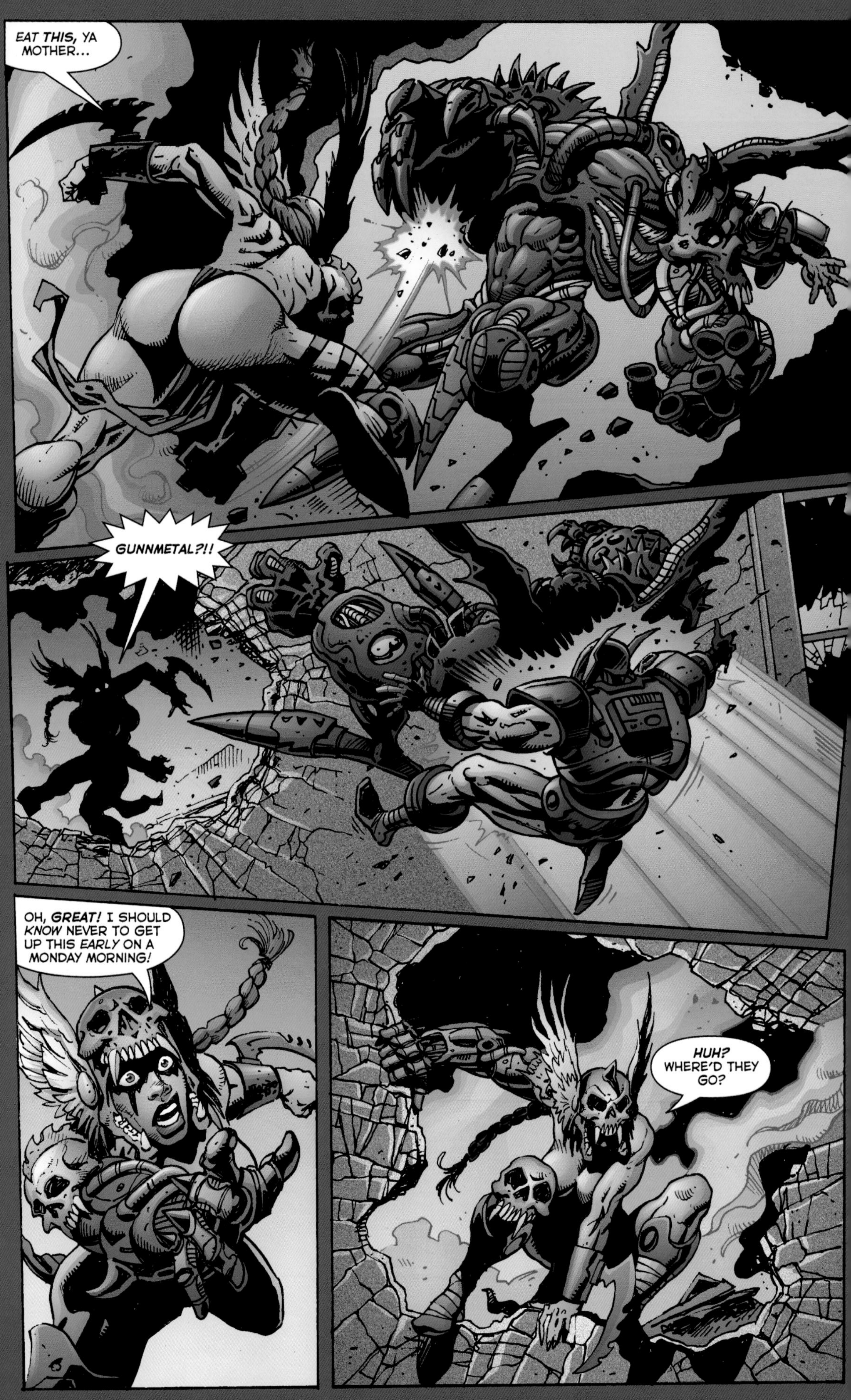
EAT THIS, YA MOTHER...
GUNNMETAL?!!
OH, GREAT! I SHOULD KNOW NEVER TO GET UP THIS EARLY ON A MONDAY MORNING!
HUH? WHERE'D THEY GO?

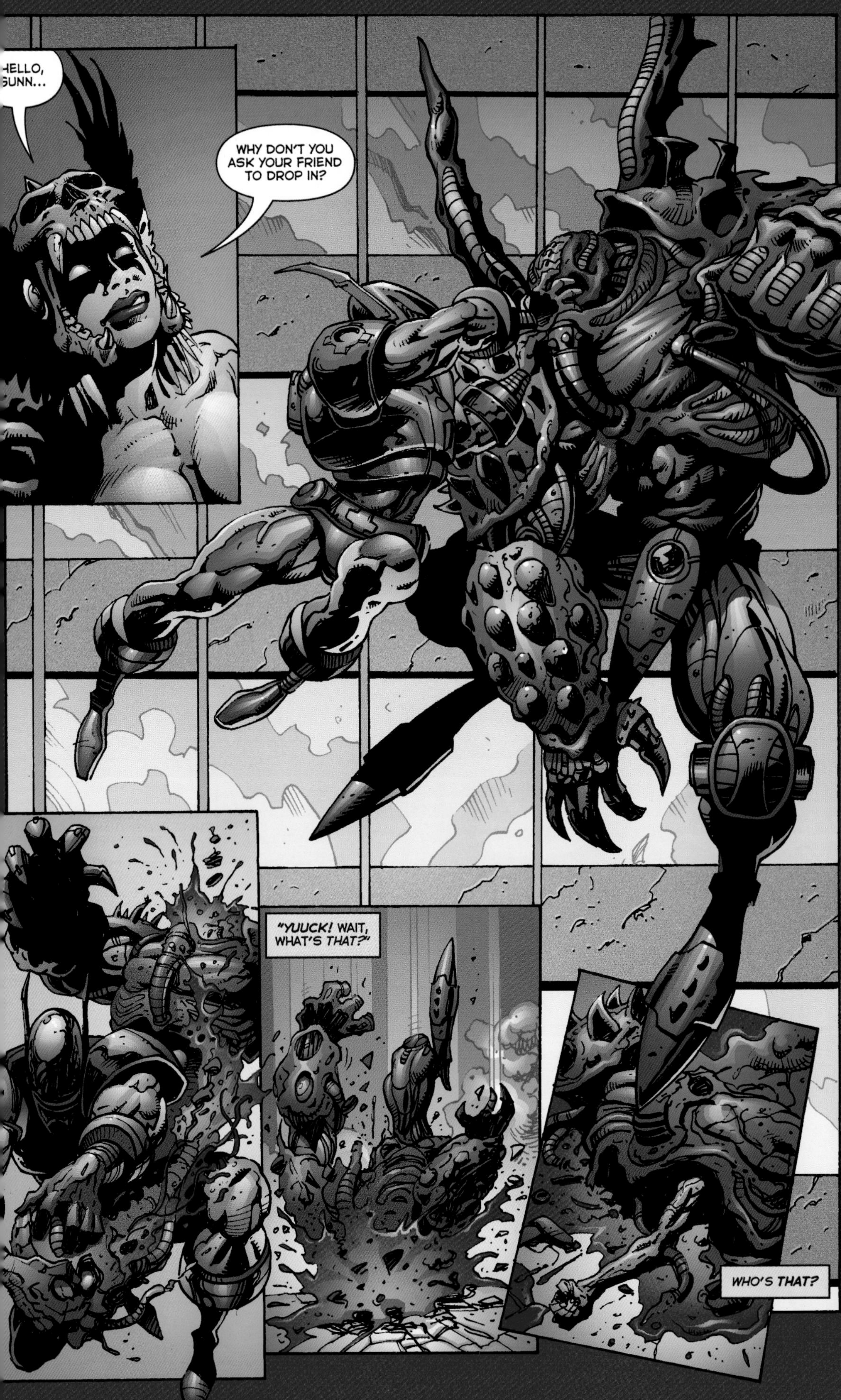
HELLO, GUNN...
WHY DON'T YOU ASK YOUR FRIEND TO DROP IN?
"YUUCK! WAIT, WHAT'S THAT?"
WHO'S THAT?

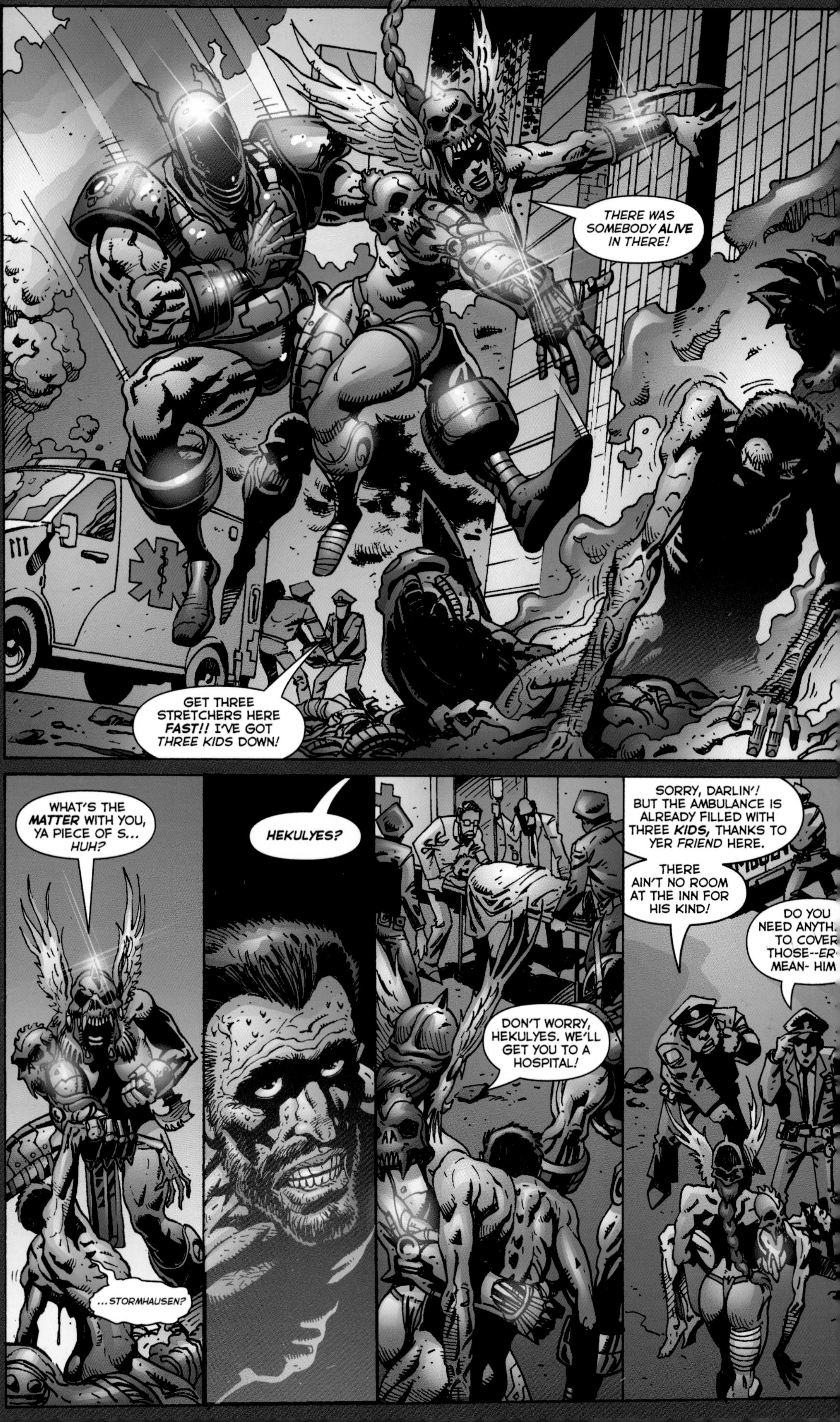
THERE WAS SOMEBODY ALIVE IN THERE!
GET THREE STRETCHERS HERE FAST!! I'VE GOT THREE KIDS DOWN!
WHAT'S THE MATTER WITH YOU, YA PIECE OF S... HUH?
...STORMHAUSEN?
HEKULYES?
DON'T WORRY, HEKULYES. WE'LL GET YOU TO A HOSPITAL!
SORRY, DARLIN'! BUT THE AMBULANCE IS ALREADY FILLED WITH THREE KIDS, THANKS TO YER FRIEND HERE.
THERE AIN'T NO ROOM AT THE INN FOR HIS KIND!
DO YOU NEED ANYTH. TO COVER THOSE--ER MEAN- HIM

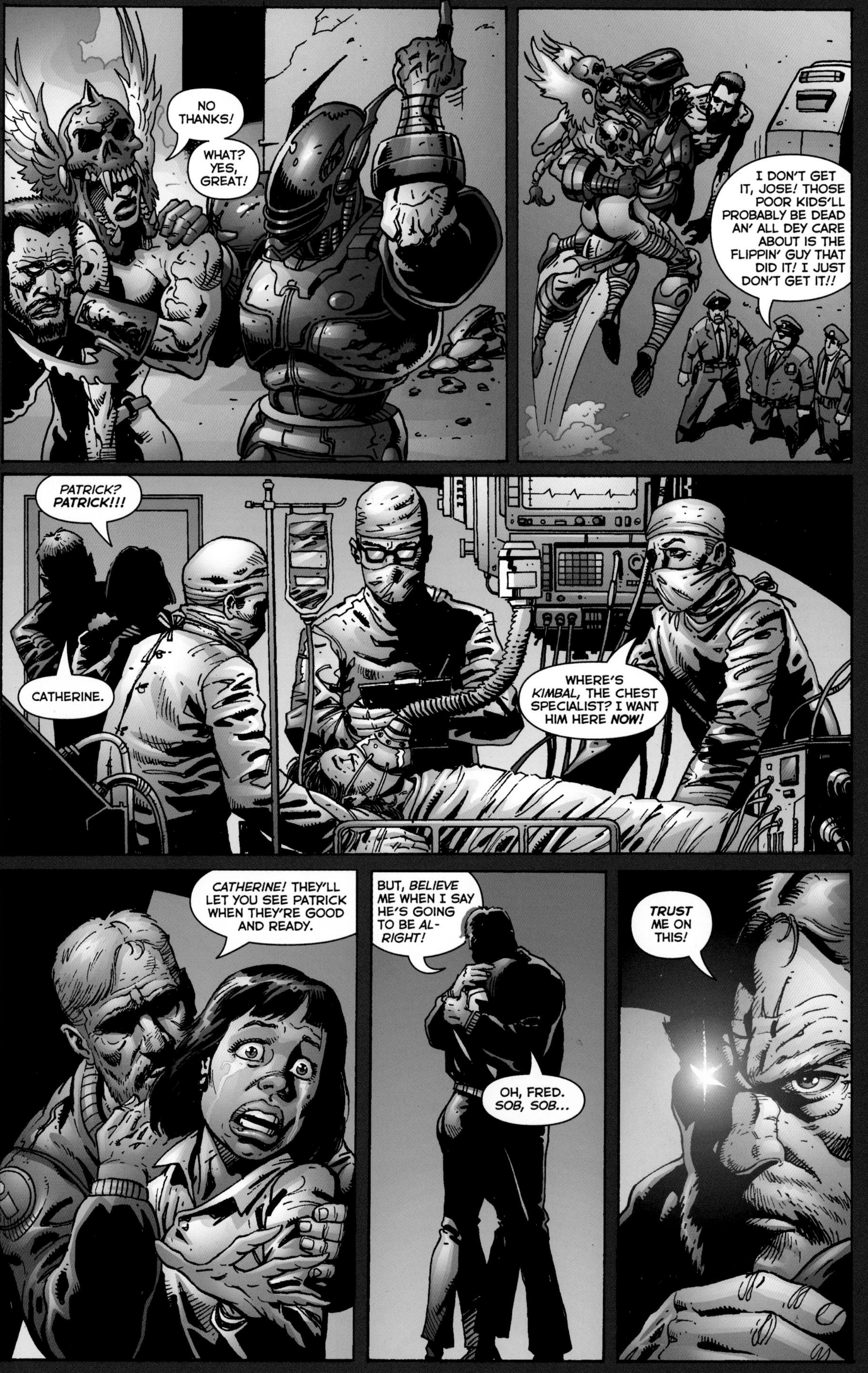
NO THANKS!
WHAT? YES, GREAT!
I DON'T GET IT, JOSE! THOSE POOR KIDS'LL PROBABLY BE DEAD AN' ALL DEY CARE ABOUT IS THE FLIPPIN' GUY THAT DID IT! I JUST DON'T GET IT!!
PATRICK? PATRICK!!!
CATHERINE.
WHERE'S KIMBAL, THE CHEST SPECIALIST? I WANT HIM HERE NOW!
CATHERINE! THEY'LL LET YOU SEE PATRICK WHEN THEY'RE GOOD AND READY.
BUT, BELIEVE ME WHEN I SAY HE'S GOING TO BE AL-RIGHT!
OH, FRED. SOB, SOB...
TRUST ME ON THIS!

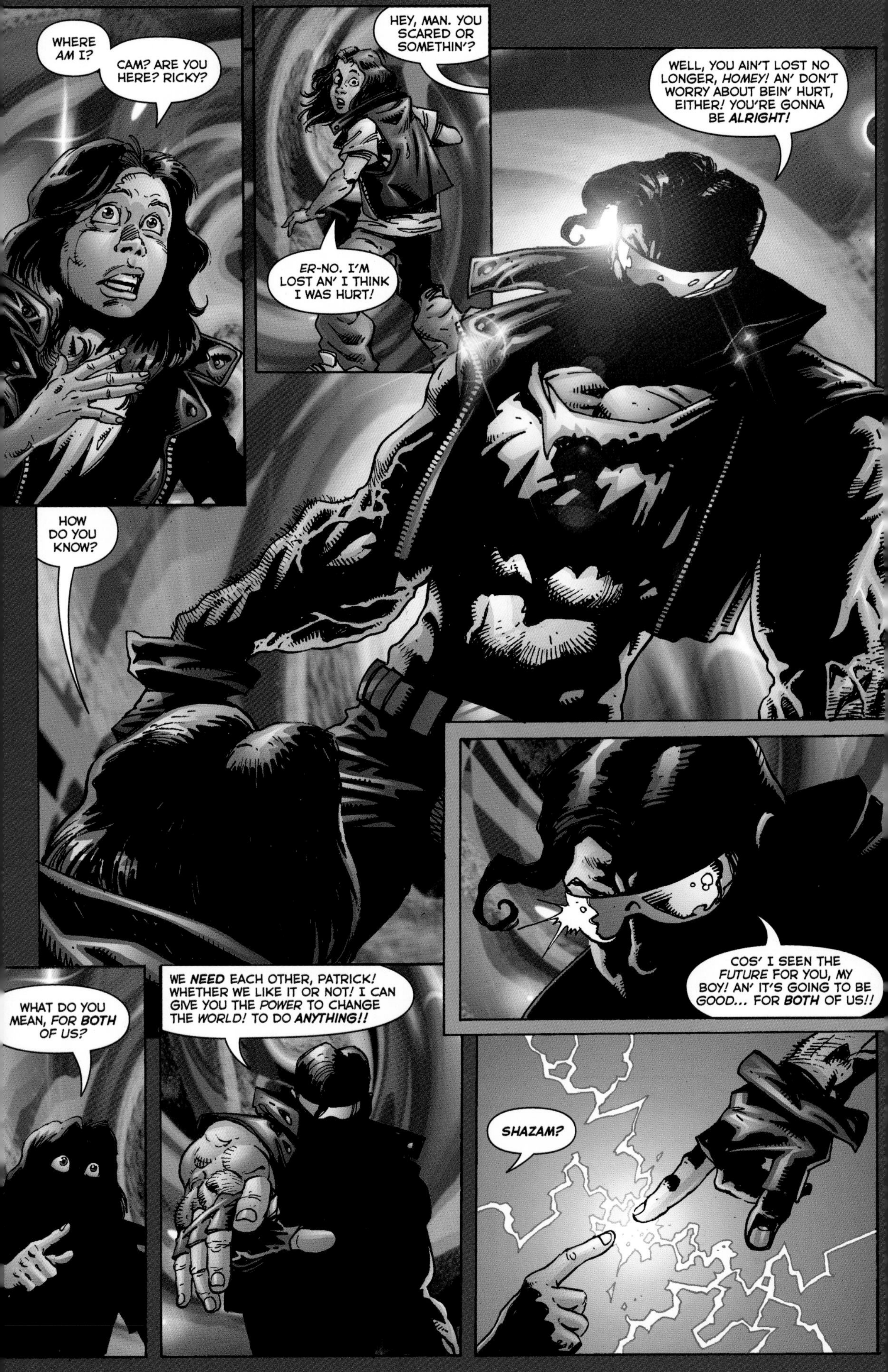
WHERE AM I?
CAM? ARE YOU HERE? RICKY?
HEY, MAN. YOU SCARED OR SOMETHIN'?
ER-NO. I'M LOST AN' I THINK I WAS HURT!
WELL, YOU AIN'T LOST NO LONGER, HOMEY! AN' DON'T WORRY ABOUT BEIN' HURT, EITHER! YOU'RE GONNA BE ALRIGHT!
HOW DO YOU KNOW?
COS' I SEEN THE FUTURE FOR YOU, MY BOY! AN' IT'S GOING TO BE GOOD... FOR BOTH OF US!!
WHAT DO YOU MEAN, FOR BOTH OF US?
WE NEED EACH OTHER, PATRICK! WHETHER WE LIKE IT OR NOT! I CAN GIVE YOU THE POWER TO CHANGE THE WORLD! TO DO ANYTHING!!
SHAZAM?

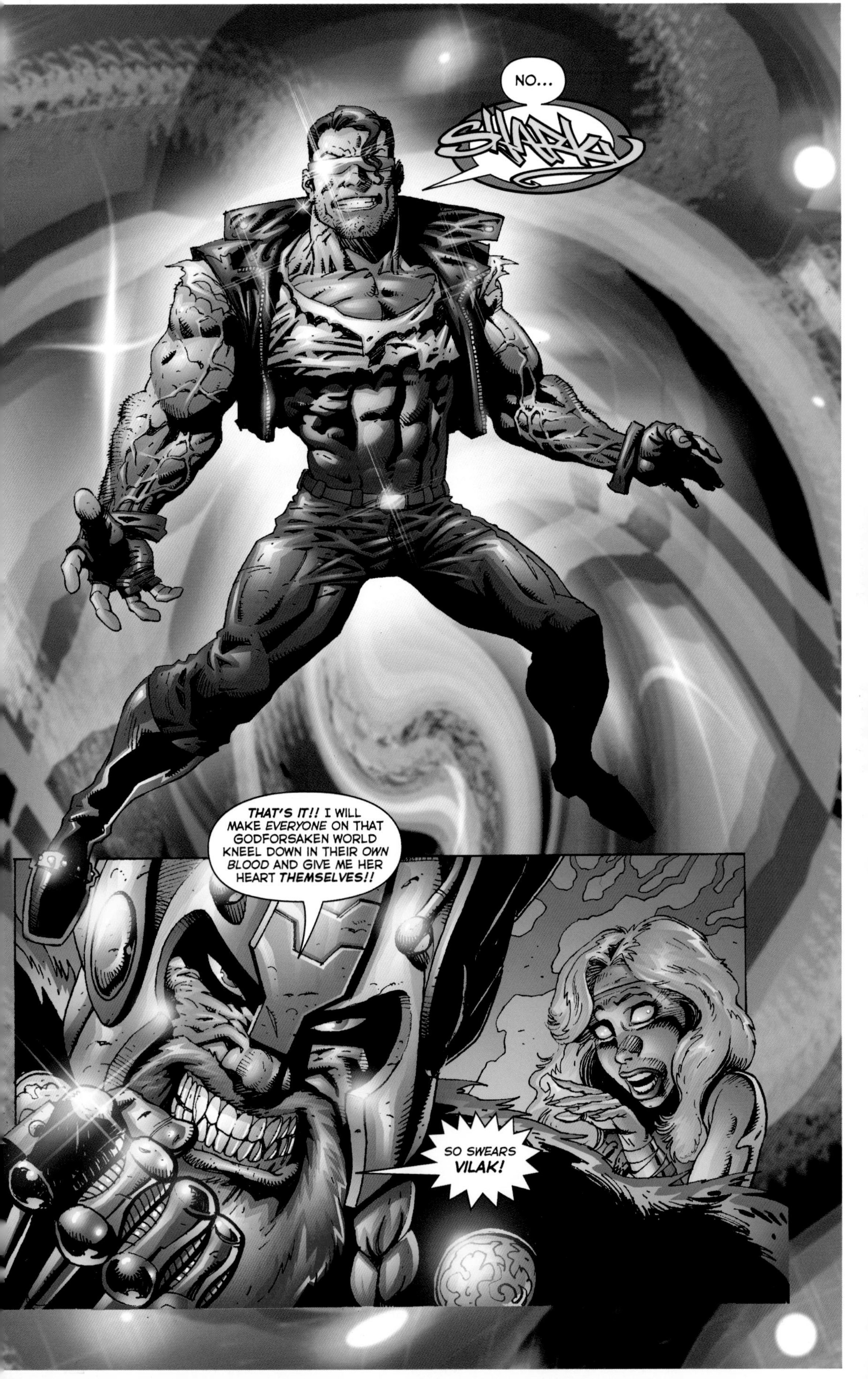
NO...
THAT'S IT!! I WILL MAKE EVERYONE ON THAT GODFORSAKEN WORLD KNEEL DOWN IN THEIR OWN BLOOD AND GIVE ME HER HEART THEMSELVES!!
SO SWEARS VILAK!

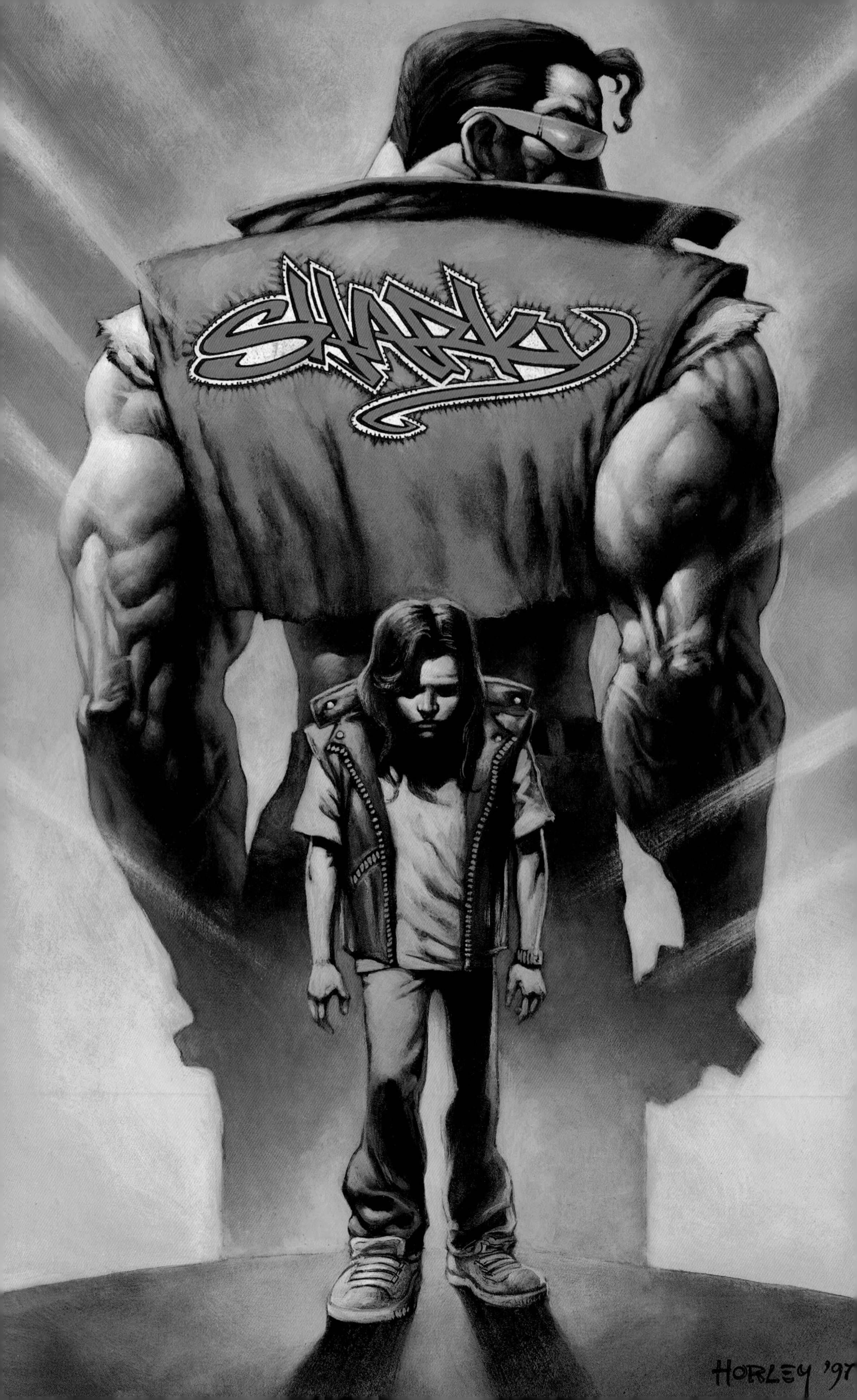
HORLEY '97

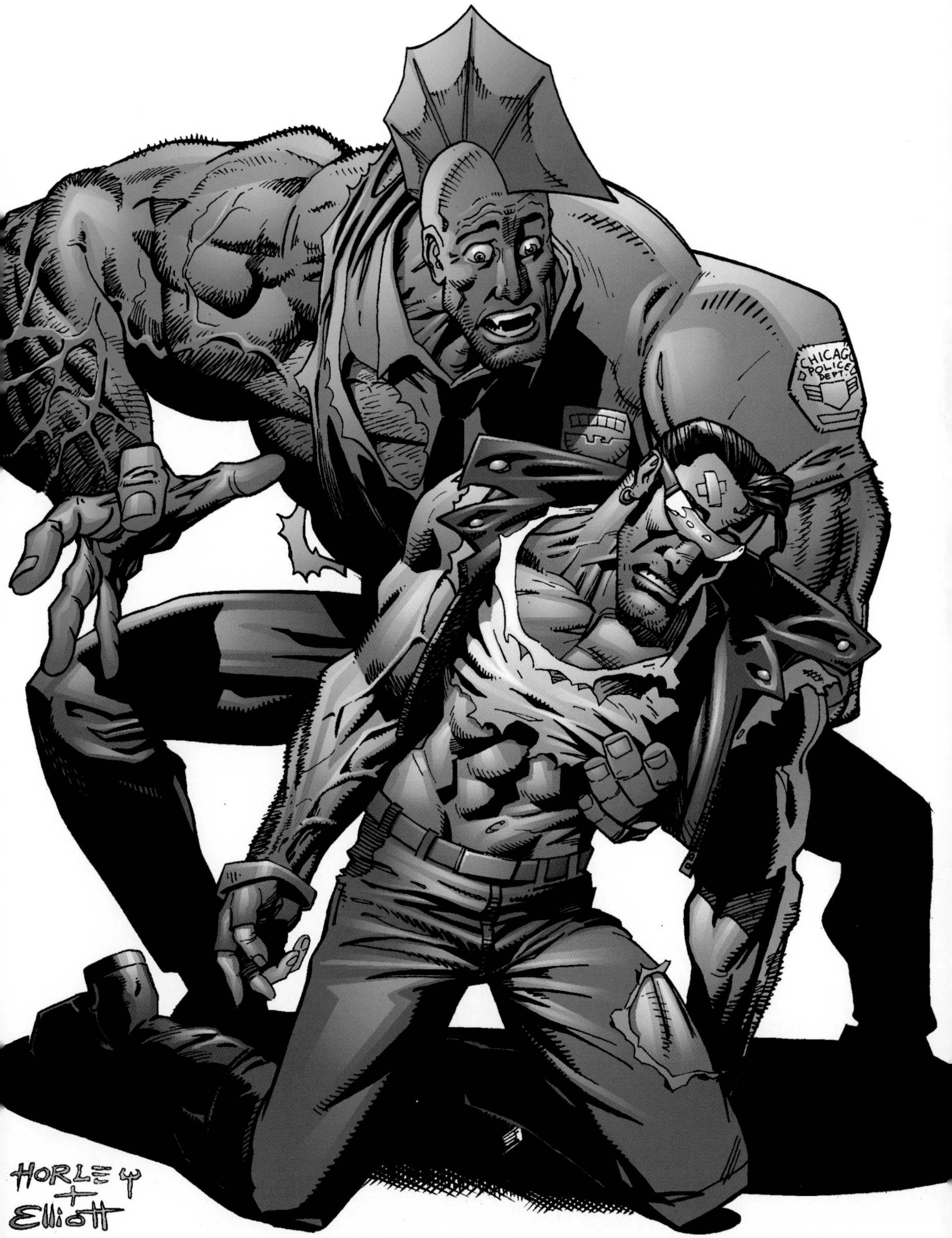
CHICAGO POLICE DEPT.
HORLEY + ELLIOTT

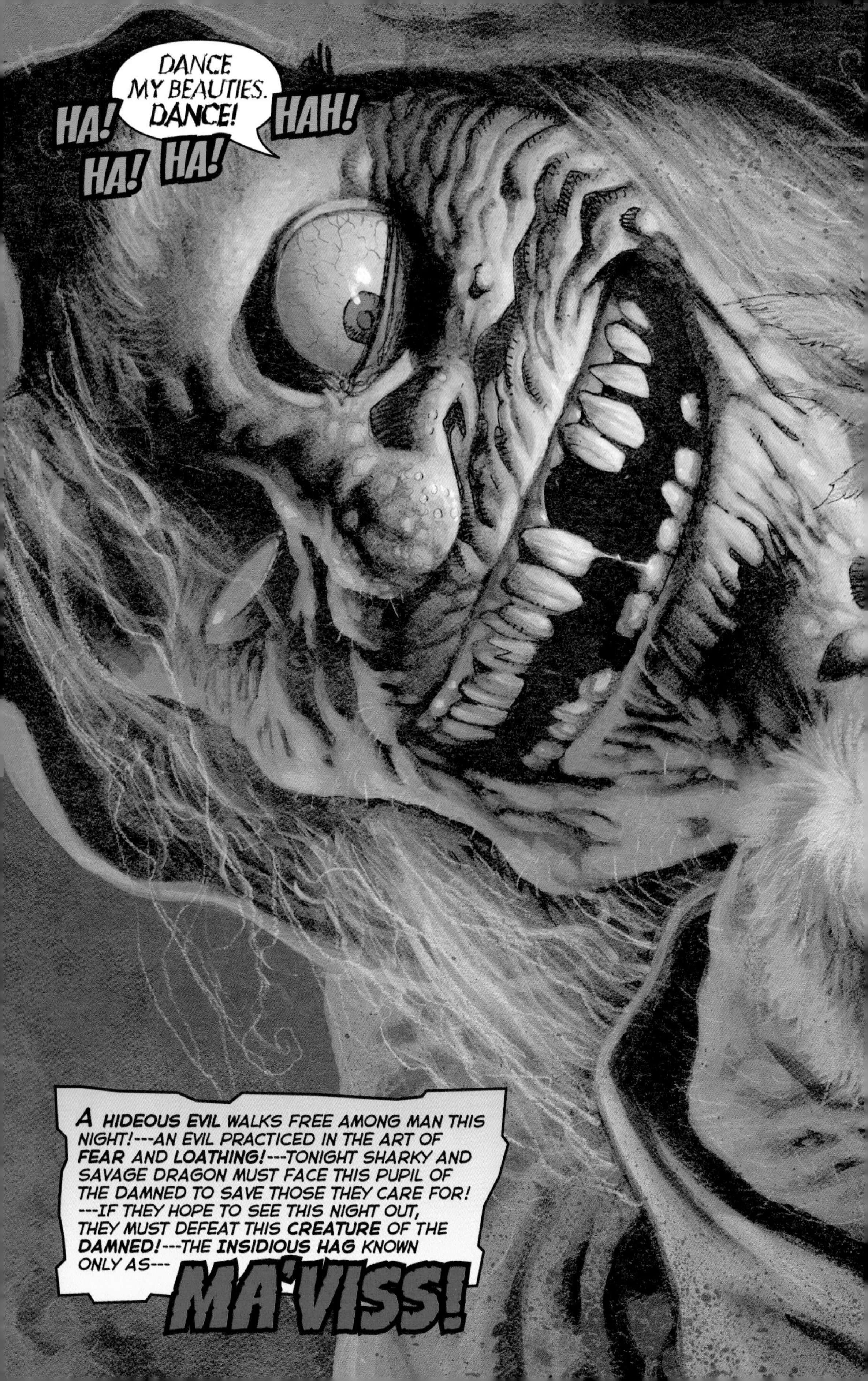

HA!
DANCE MY BEAUTIES. DANCE!
HAH!
HA! HA!
A HIDEOUS EVIL WALKS FREE AMONG MAN THIS NIGHT!---AN EVIL PRACTICED IN THE ART OF FEAR AND LOATHING!---TONIGHT SHARKY AND SAVAGE DRAGON MUST FACE THIS PUPIL OF THE DAMNED TO SAVE THOSE THEY CARE FOR! ---IF THEY HOPE TO SEE THIS NIGHT OUT, THEY MUST DEFEAT THIS CREATURE OF THE DAMNED!---THE INSIDIOUS HAG KNOWN ONLY AS---
MA'VISS!

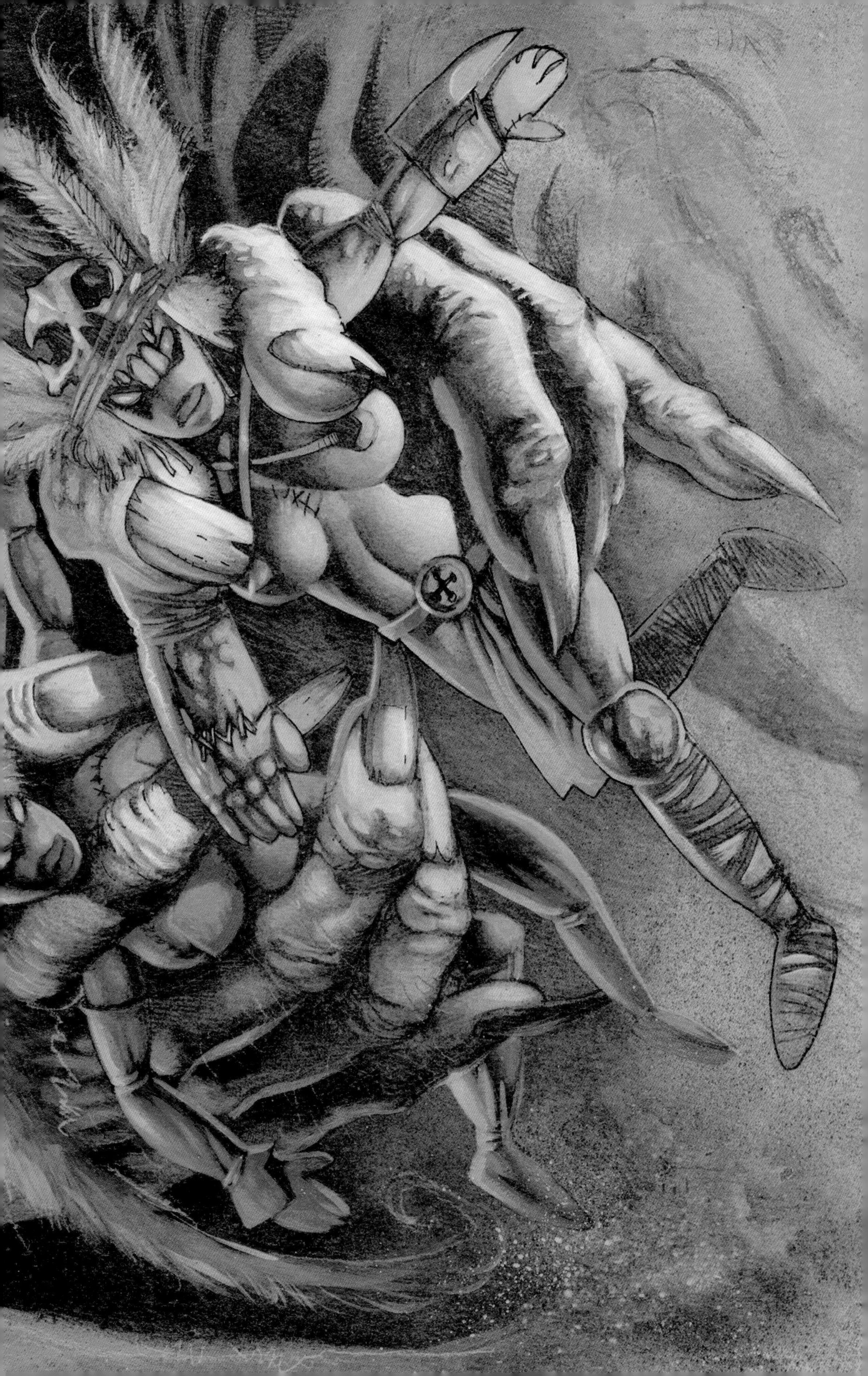

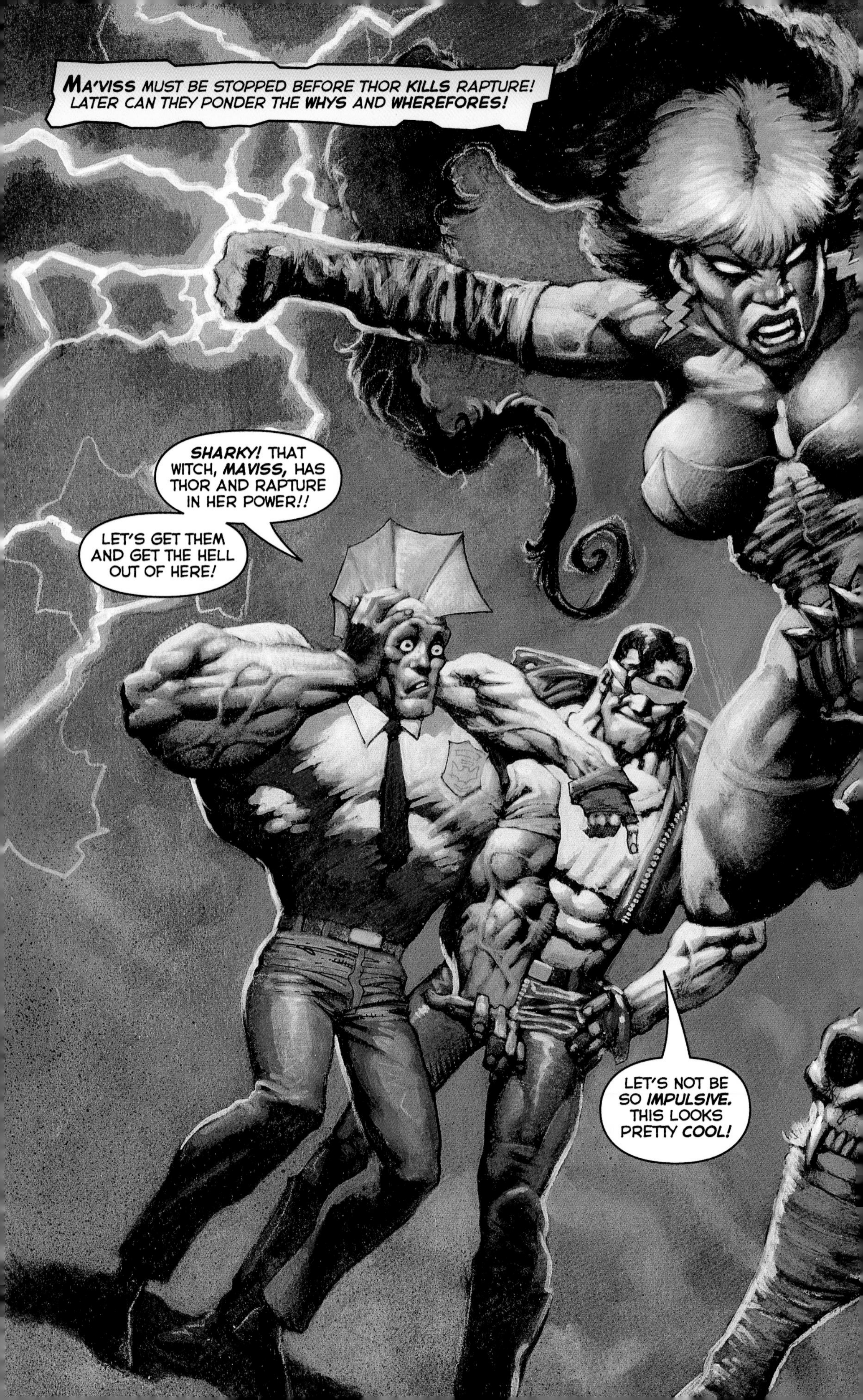
MA'VISS MUST BE STOPPED BEFORE THOR KILLS RAPTURE! LATER CAN THEY PONDER THE WHYS AND WHEREFORES!
SHARKY! THAT WITCH, MAVISS, HAS THOR AND RAPTURE IN HER POWER!!
LET'S GET THEM AND GET THE HELL OUT OF HERE!
LET'S NOT BE SO IMPULSIVE. THIS LOOKS PRETTY COOL!

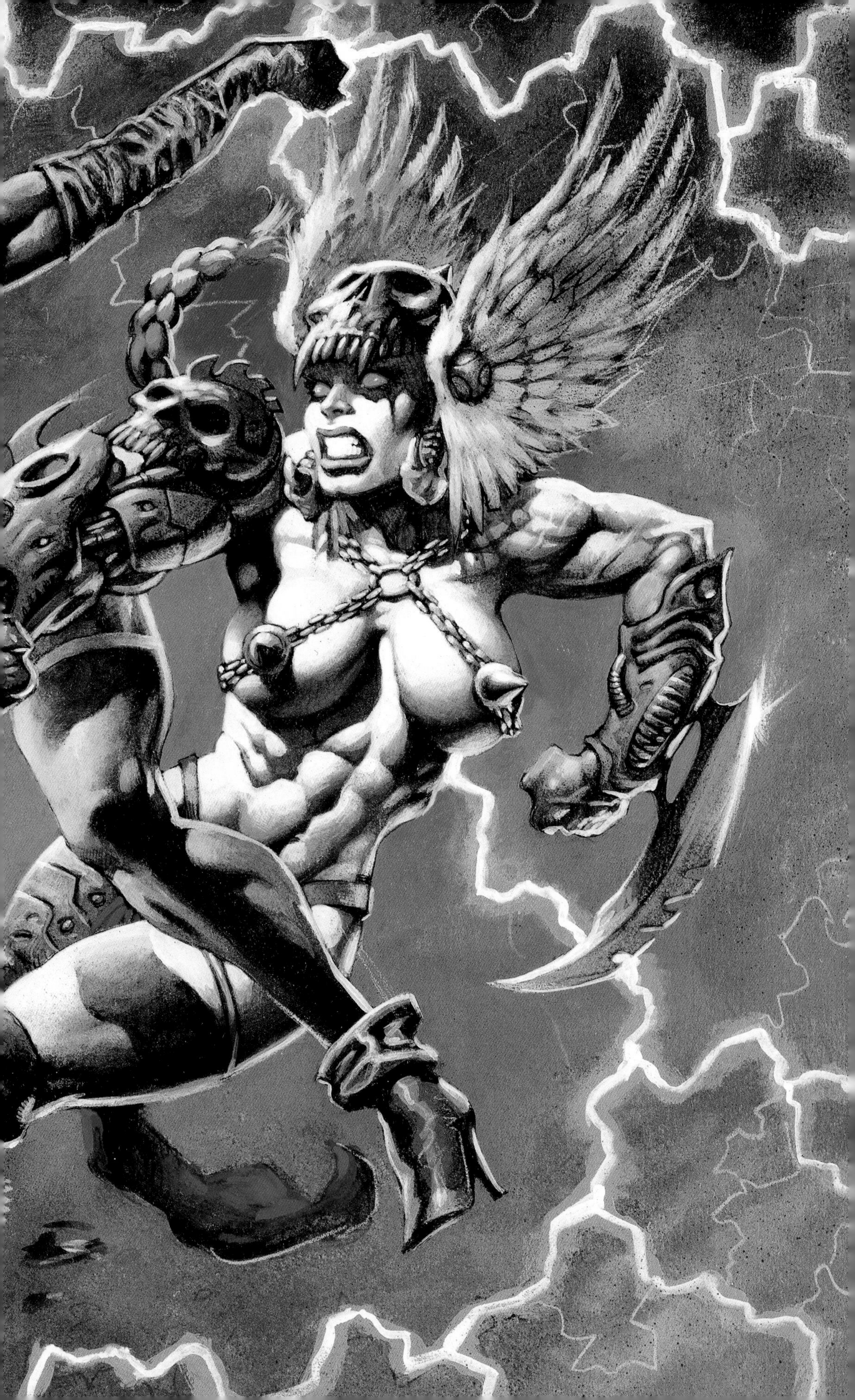

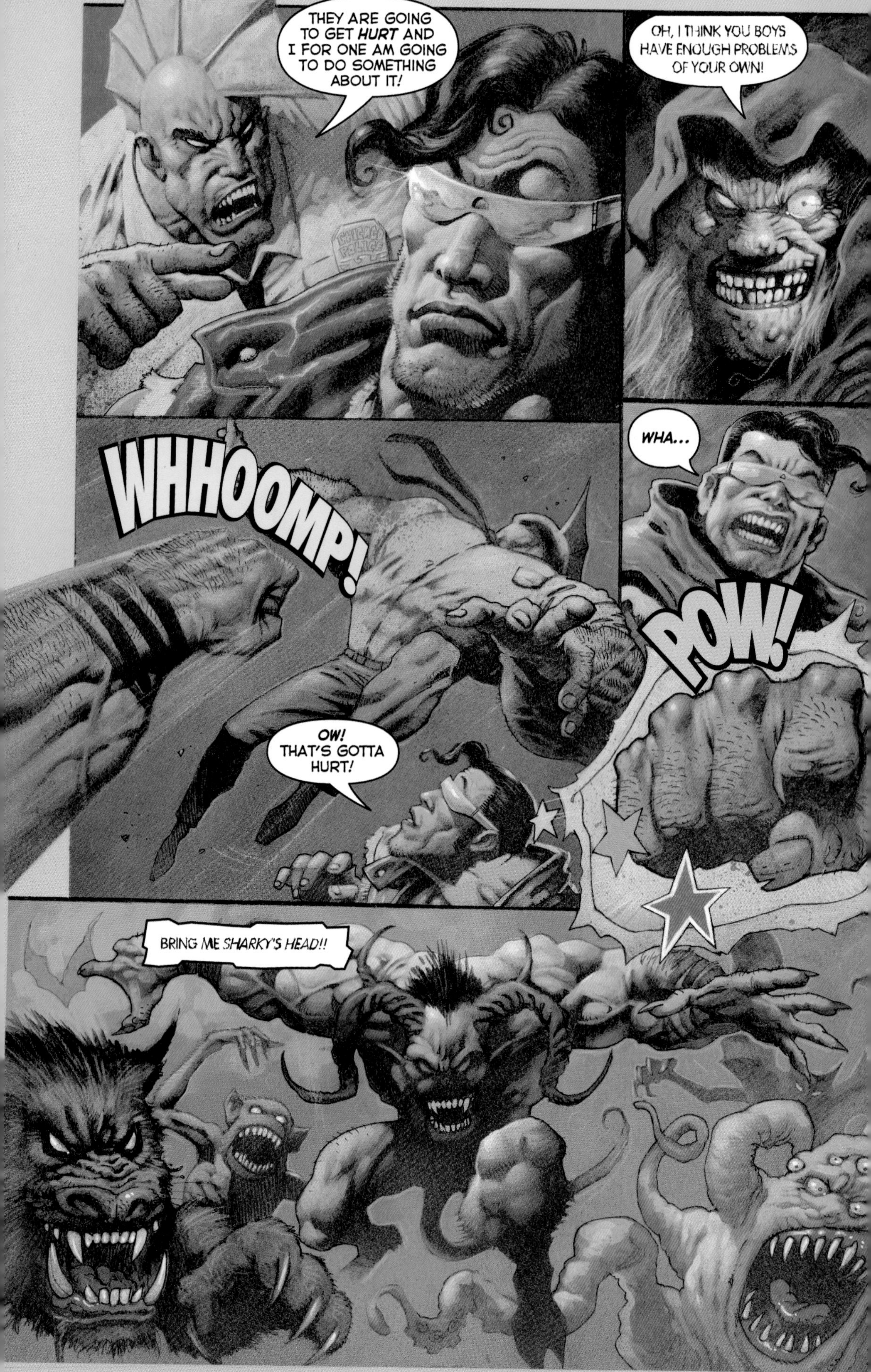
THEY ARE GOING TO GET *HURT* AND I FOR ONE AM GOING TO DO SOMETHING ABOUT IT!
OH, I THINK YOU BOYS HAVE ENOUGH PROBLEMS OF YOUR OWN!
WHHOOMP!
WHA...
POW!
OW! THAT'S GOTTA HURT!
BRING ME *SHARKY'S HEAD!!*

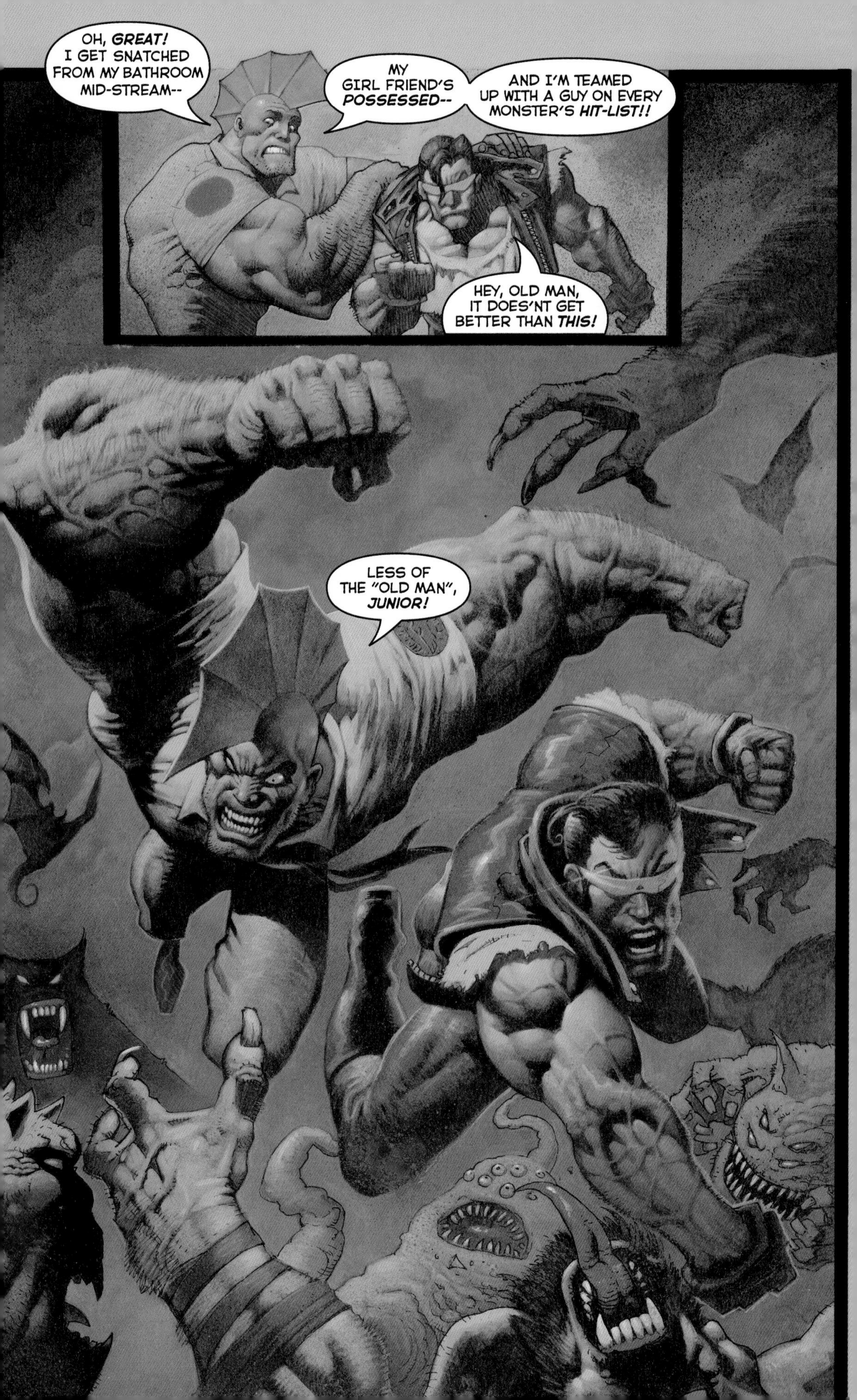
OH, GREAT! I GET SNATCHED FROM MY BATHROOM MID-STREAM--
MY GIRL FRIEND'S POSSESSED--
AND I'M TEAMED UP WITH A GUY ON EVERY MONSTER'S HIT-LIST!!
HEY, OLD MAN, IT DOES'NT GET BETTER THAN THIS!
LESS OF THE "OLD MAN", JUNIOR!

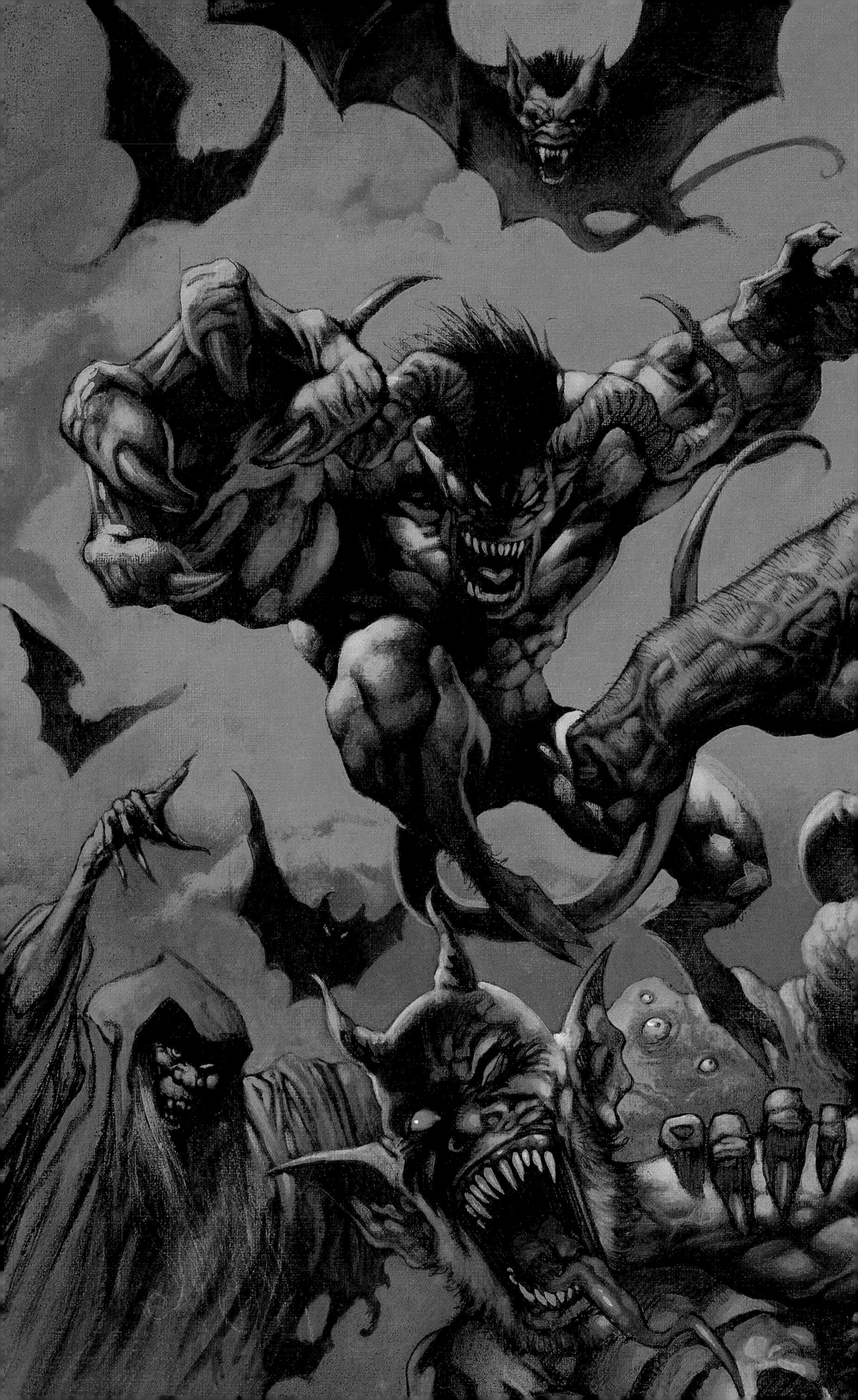

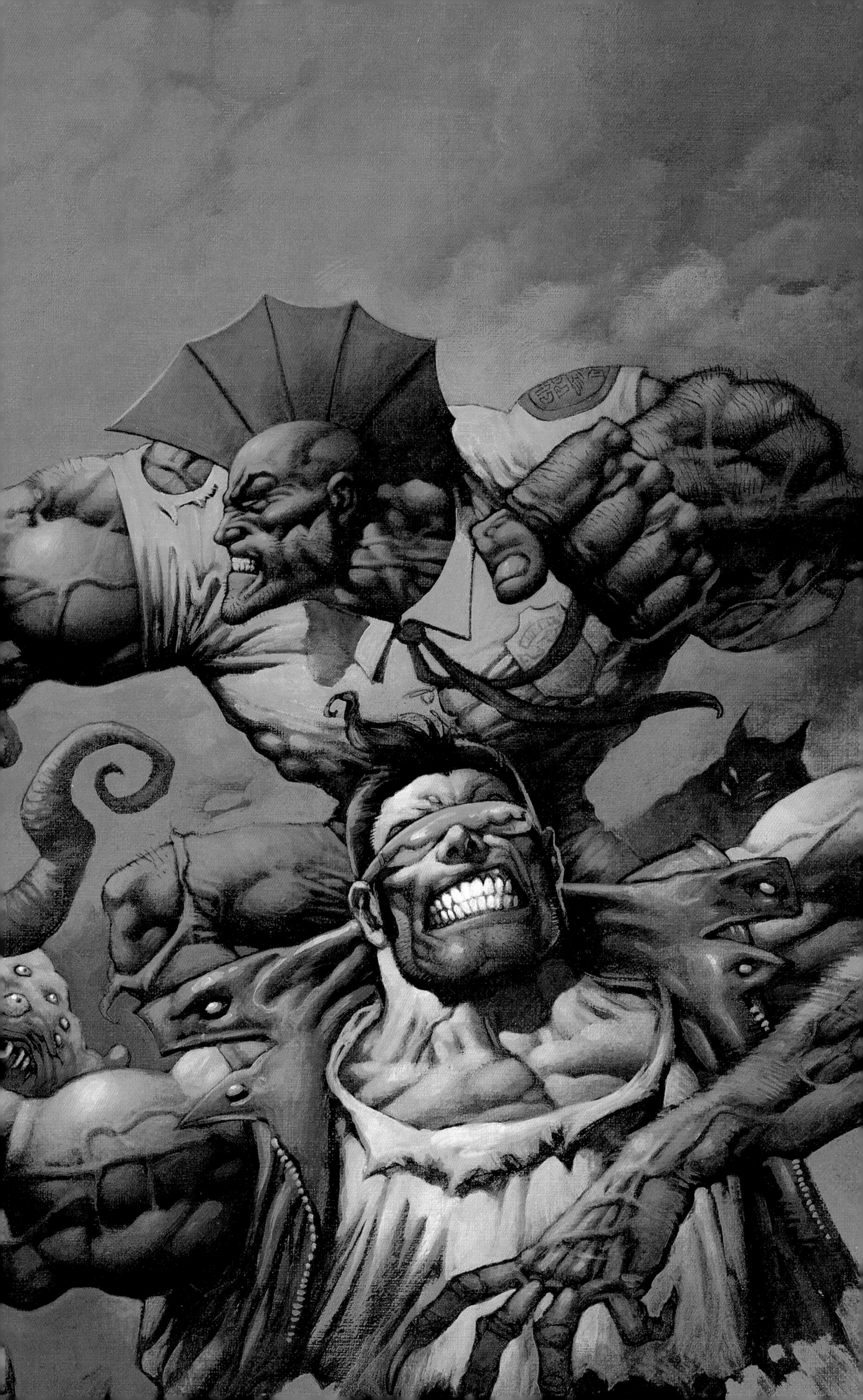

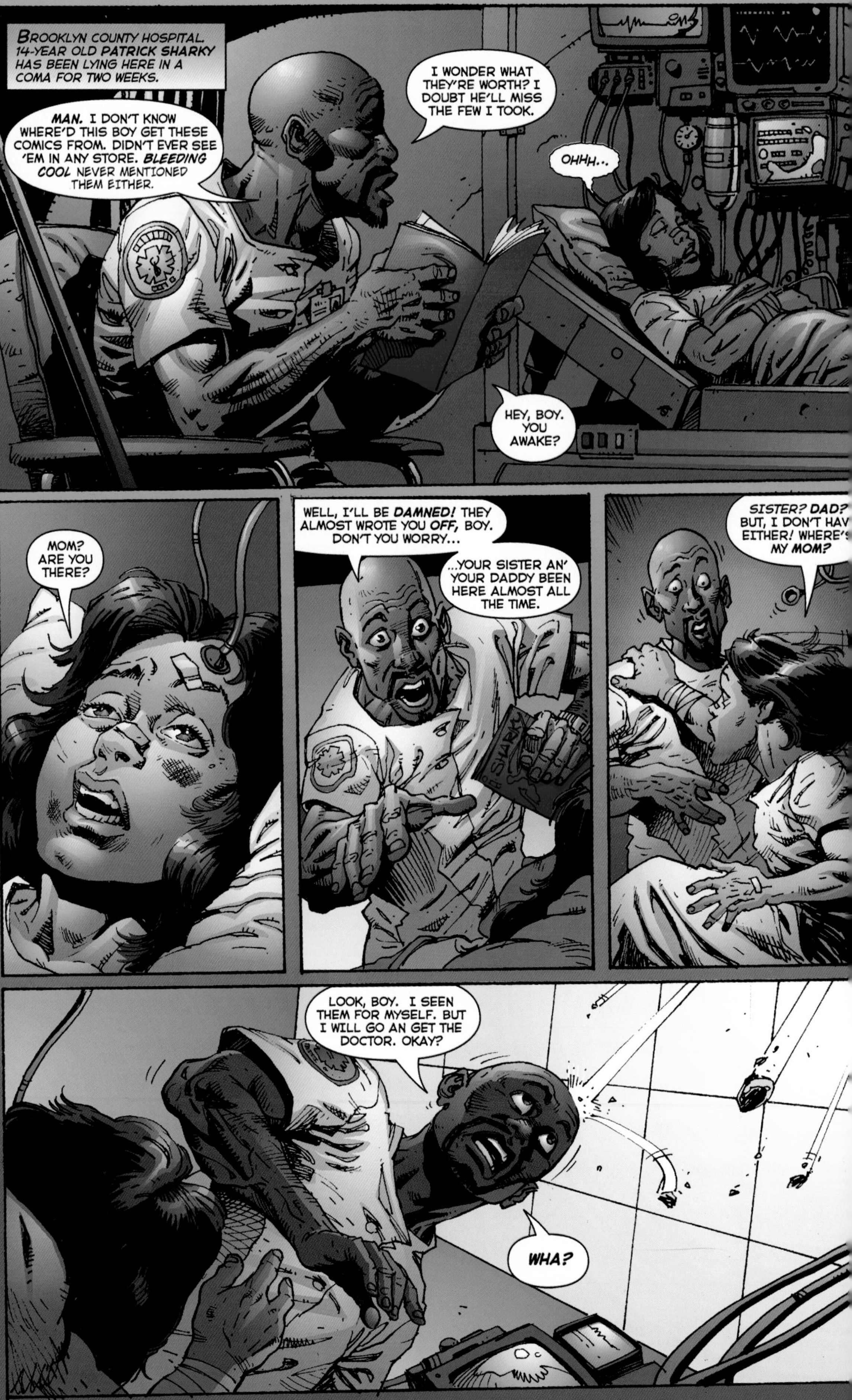
BROOKLYN COUNTY HOSPITAL. 14-YEAR OLD PATRICK SHARKY HAS BEEN LYING HERE IN A COMA FOR TWO WEEKS.
MAN. I DON'T KNOW WHERE'D THIS BOY GET THESE COMICS FROM. DIDN'T EVER SEE 'EM IN ANY STORE. BLEEDING COOL NEVER MENTIONED THEM EITHER.
I WONDER WHAT THEY'RE WORTH? I DOUBT HE'LL MISS THE FEW I TOOK.
OHHH...
HEY, BOY. YOU AWAKE?
MOM? ARE YOU THERE?
WELL, I'LL BE DAMNED! THEY ALMOST WROTE YOU OFF, BOY. DON'T YOU WORRY...
...YOUR SISTER AN' YOUR DADDY BEEN HERE ALMOST ALL THE TIME.
SHARK
SISTER? DAD? BUT, I DON'T HAV EITHER! WHERE'S MY MOM?
LOOK, BOY. I SEEN THEM FOR MYSELF. BUT I WILL GO AN GET THE DOCTOR. OKAY?
WHA?

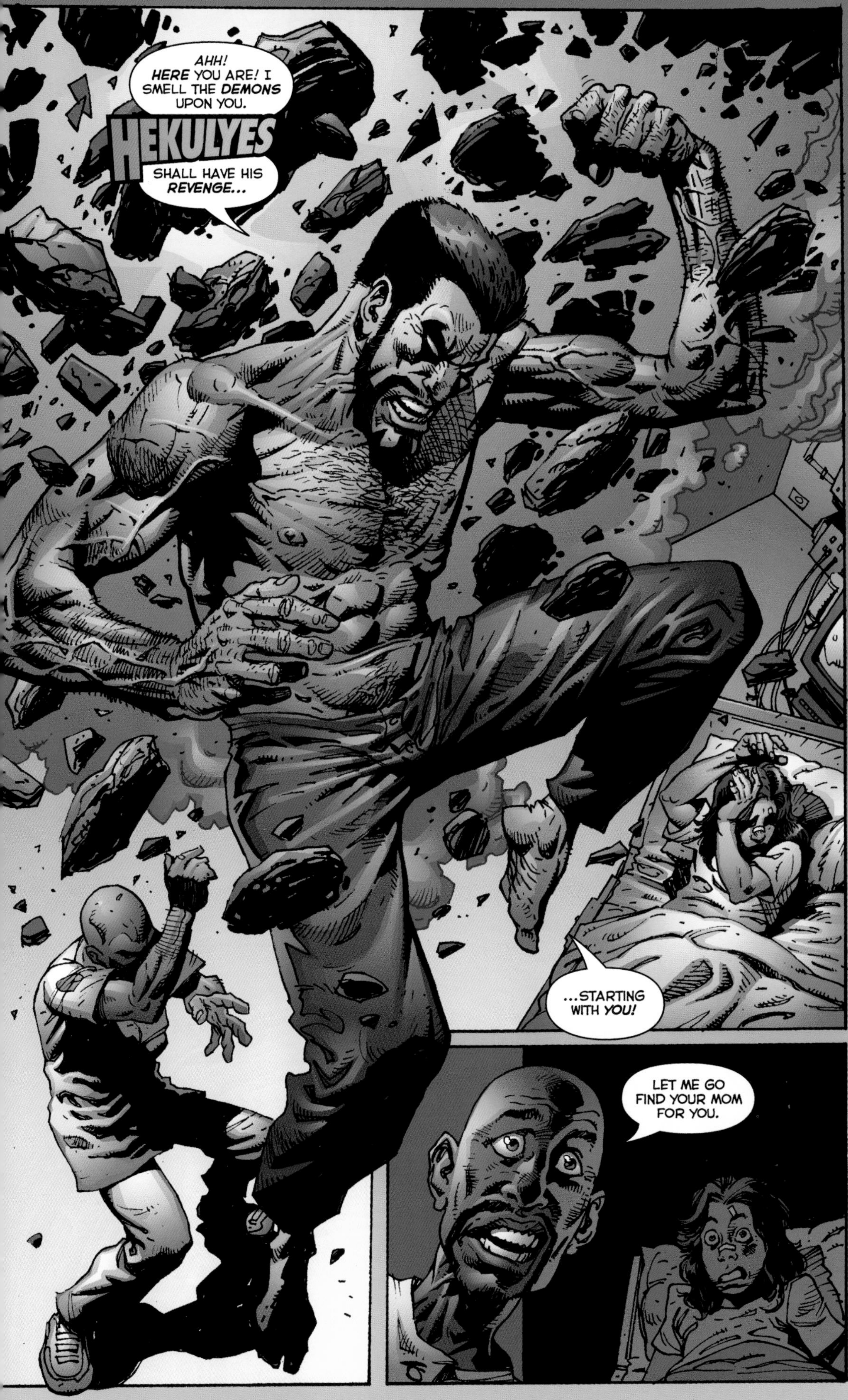
AHH! HERE YOU ARE! I SMELL THE DEMONS UPON YOU.
HEKULYES
SHALL HAVE HIS REVENGE...
...STARTING WITH YOU!
LET ME GO FIND YOUR MOM FOR YOU.

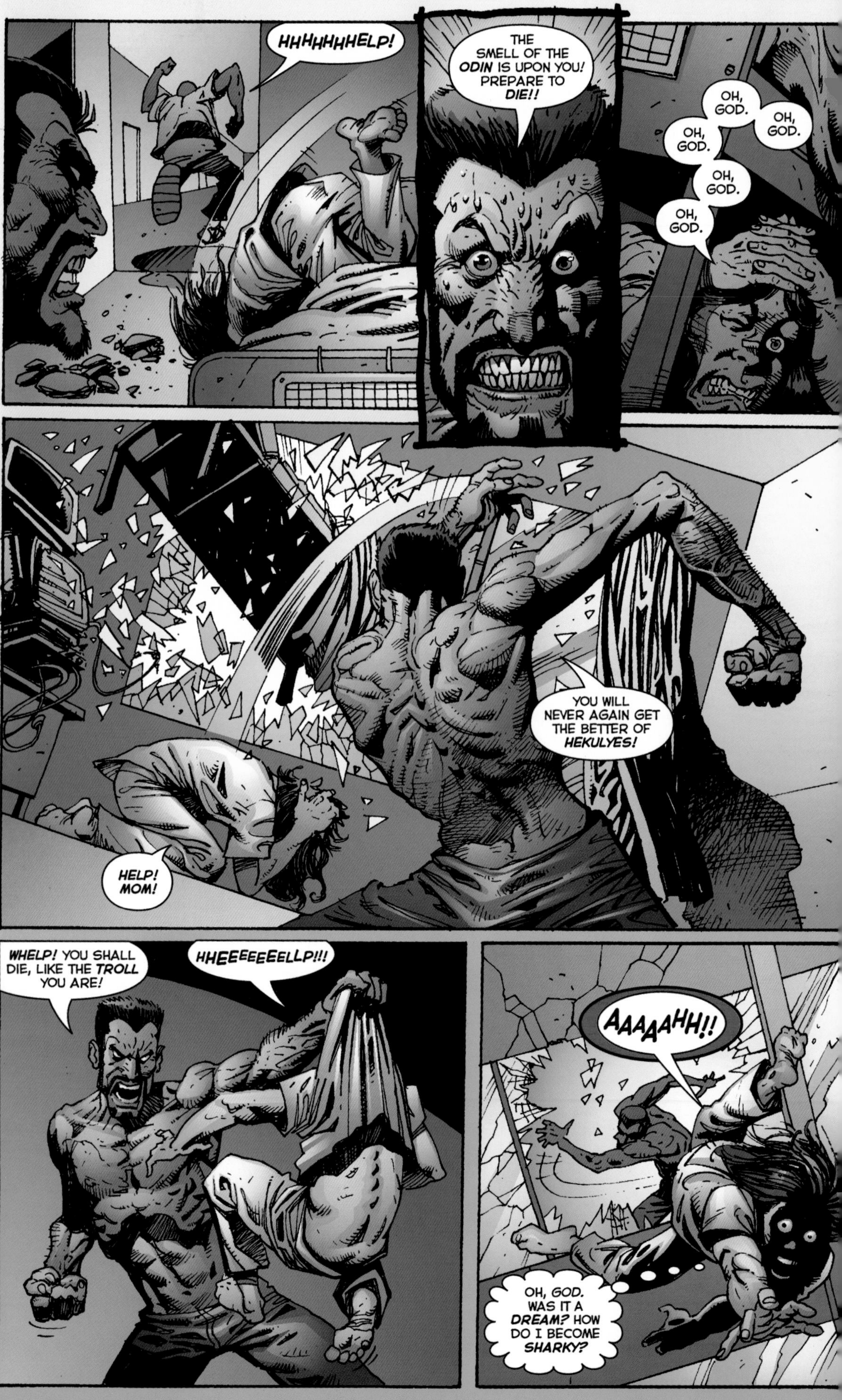
HHHHHHHELP!
THE SMELL OF THE ODIN IS UPON YOU! PREPARE TO DIE!!
OH, GOD.
OH, GOD.
OH, GOD.
OH, GOD.
OH, GOD.
YOU WILL NEVER AGAIN GET THE BETTER OF HEKULYES!
HELP! MOM!
WHELP! YOU SHALL DIE, LIKE THE TROLL YOU ARE!
HHEEEEEEELLP!!!
AAAAAHH!!
OH, GOD. WAS IT A DREAM? HOW DO I BECOME SHARKY?

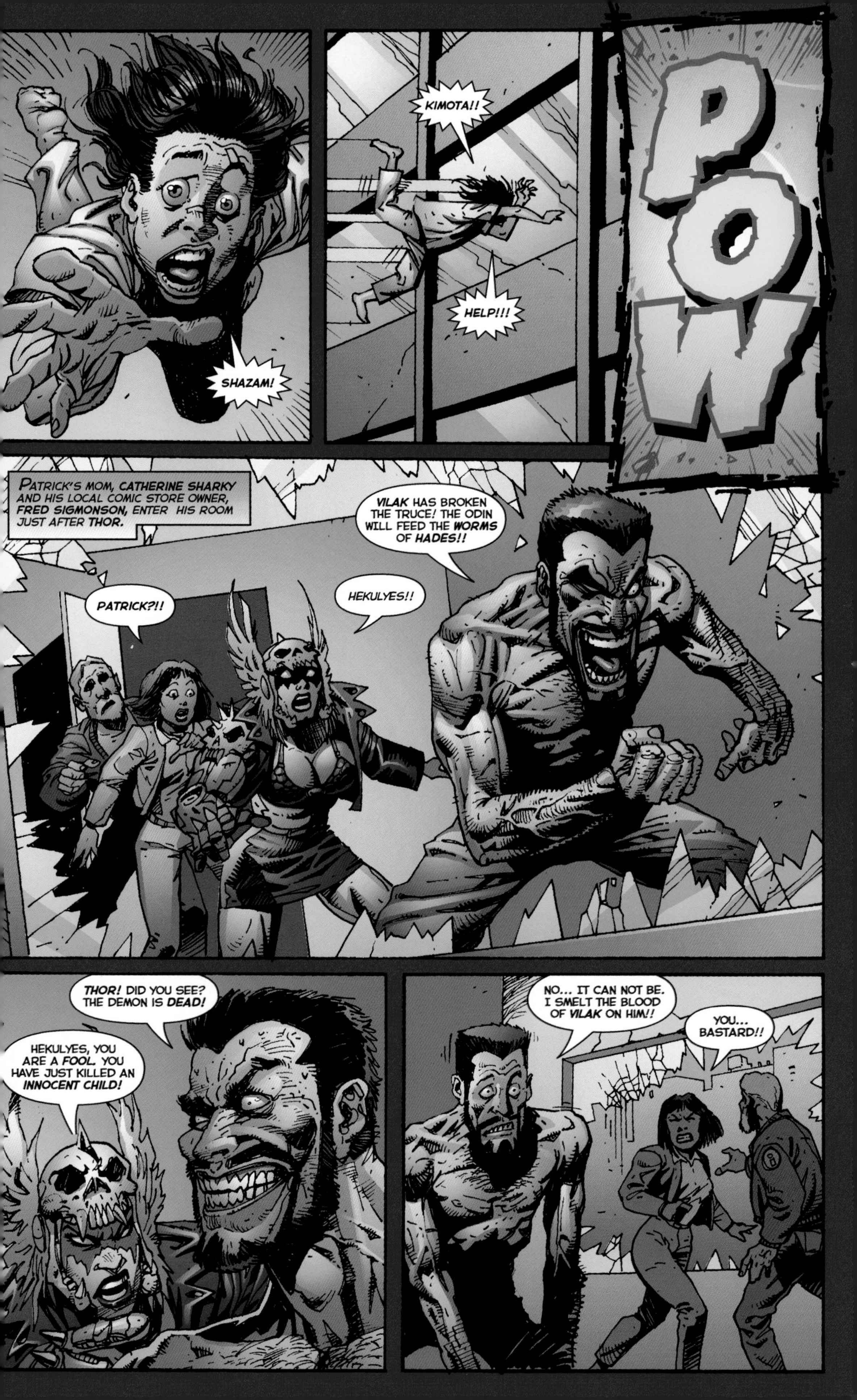
SHAZAM!
KIMOTA!!
HELP!!!
POW
PATRICK'S MOM, CATHERINE SHARKY AND HIS LOCAL COMIC STORE OWNER, FRED SIGMONSON, ENTER HIS ROOM JUST AFTER THOR.
VILAK HAS BROKEN THE TRUCE! THE ODIN WILL FEED THE WORMS OF HADES!!
PATRICK?!!
HEKULYES!!
THOR! DID YOU SEE? THE DEMON IS DEAD!
HEKULYES, YOU ARE A FOOL. YOU HAVE JUST KILLED AN INNOCENT CHILD!
NO... IT CAN NOT BE. I SMELT THE BLOOD OF VILAK ON HIM!!
YOU... BASTARD!!

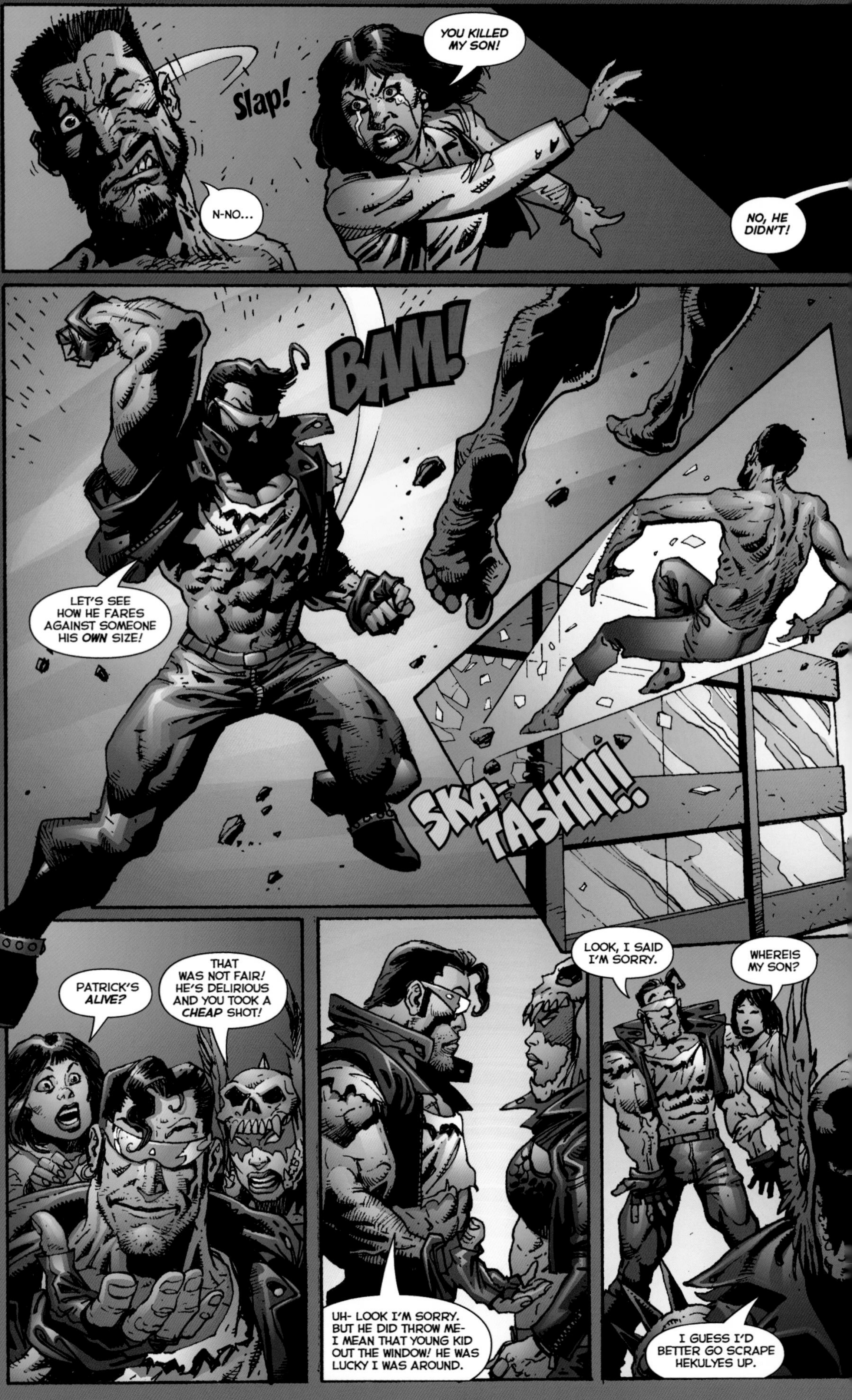

Slap!
YOU KILLED MY SON!
N-NO...
NO, HE DIDN'T!
BAM!
LET'S SEE HOW HE FARES AGAINST SOMEONE HIS OWN SIZE!
SKA-TASHH!!
PATRICK'S ALIVE?
THAT WAS NOT FAIR! HE'S DELIRIOUS AND YOU TOOK A CHEAP SHOT!
UH- LOOK I'M SORRY. BUT HE DID THROW ME- I MEAN THAT YOUNG KID OUT THE WINDOW! HE WAS LUCKY I WAS AROUND.
LOOK, I SAID I'M SORRY.
WHEREIS MY SON?
I GUESS I'D BETTER GO SCRAPE HEKULYES UP.

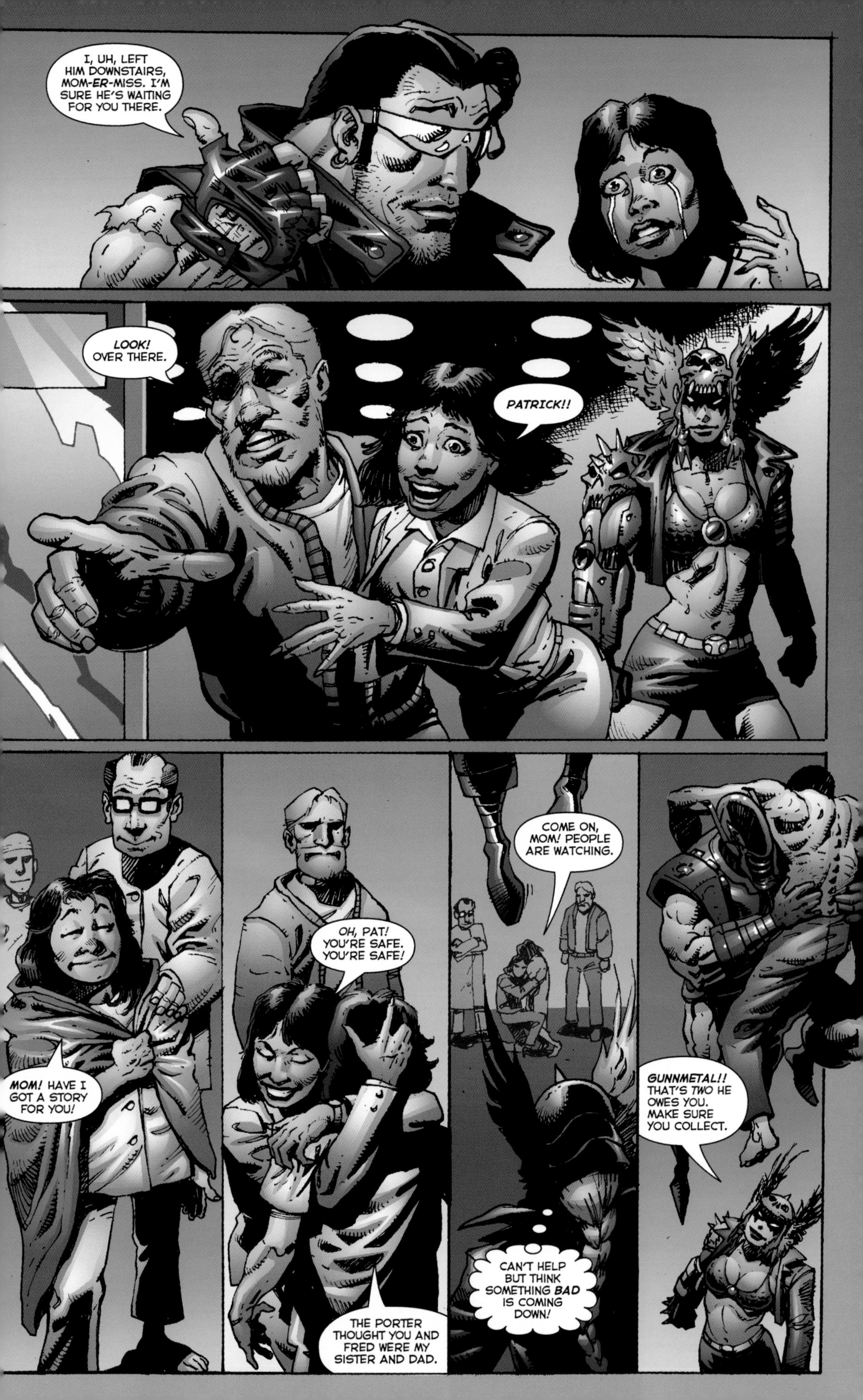
I, UH, LEFT HIM DOWNSTAIRS, MOM-ER-MISS. I'M SURE HE'S WAITING FOR YOU THERE.
LOOK! OVER THERE.
PATRICK!!
MOM! HAVE I GOT A STORY FOR YOU!
OH, PAT! YOU'RE SAFE. YOU'RE SAFE!
THE PORTER THOUGHT YOU AND FRED WERE MY SISTER AND DAD.
COME ON, MOM! PEOPLE ARE WATCHING.
CAN'T HELP BUT THINK SOMETHING BAD IS COMING DOWN!
GUNNMETAL!! THAT'S TWO HE OWES YOU. MAKE SURE YOU COLLECT.

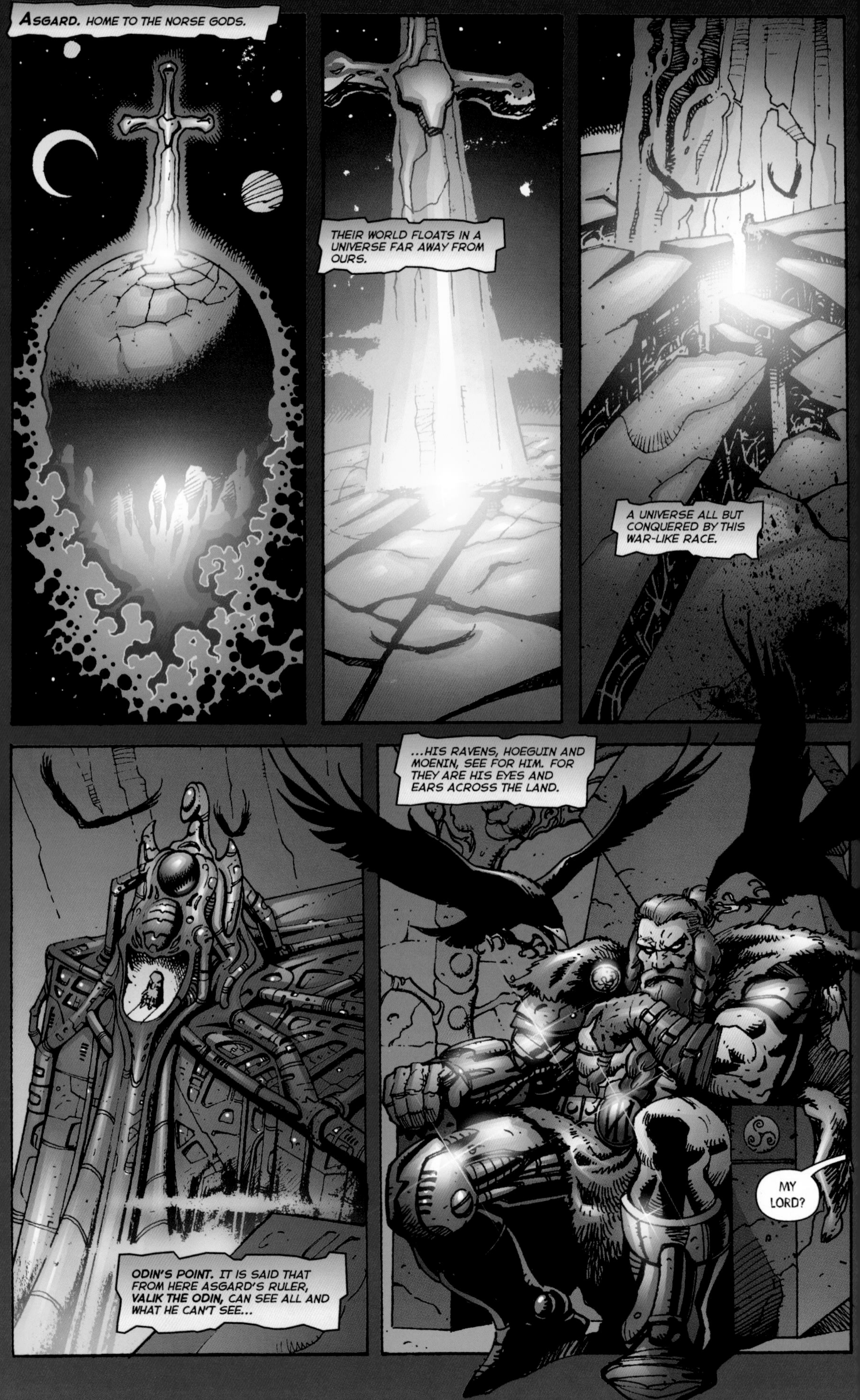
ASGARD. HOME TO THE NORSE GODS.
THEIR WORLD FLOATS IN A UNIVERSE FAR AWAY FROM OURS.
A UNIVERSE ALL BUT CONQUERED BY THIS WAR-LIKE RACE.
ODIN'S POINT. IT IS SAID THAT FROM HERE ASGARD'S RULER, VALIK THE ODIN, CAN SEE ALL AND WHAT HE CAN'T SEE...
...HIS RAVENS, HOEGUIN AND MOENIN, SEE FOR HIM. FOR THEY ARE HIS EYES AND EARS ACROSS THE LAND.
MY LORD?

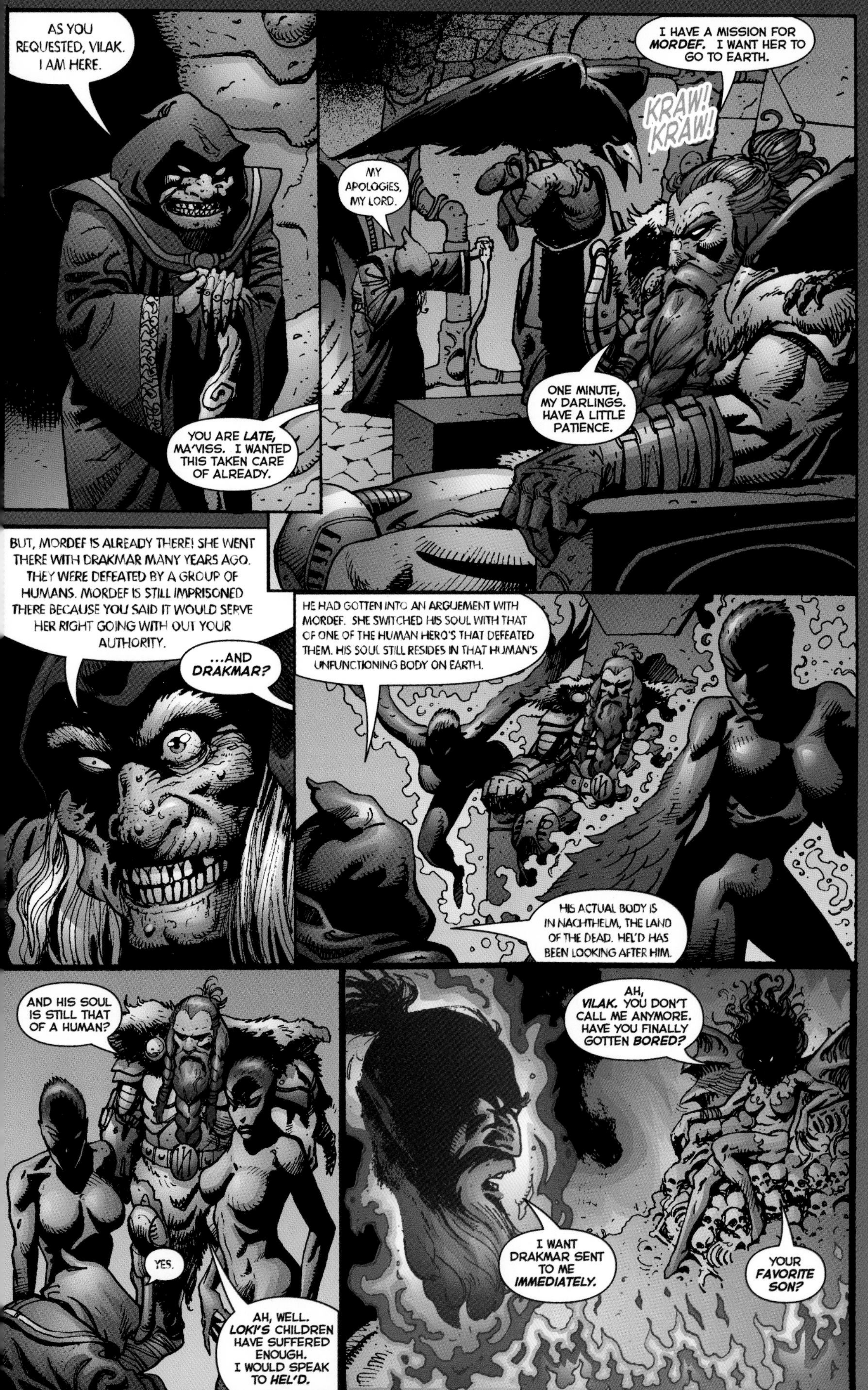
AS YOU REQUESTED, VILAK. I AM HERE.
I HAVE A MISSION FOR MORDEF. I WANT HER TO GO TO EARTH.
KRAW! KRAW!
MY APOLOGIES, MY LORD.
ONE MINUTE, MY DARLINGS. HAVE A LITTLE PATIENCE.
YOU ARE LATE, MA'VISS. I WANTED THIS TAKEN CARE OF ALREADY.
BUT, MORDEF IS ALREADY THERE! SHE WENT THERE WITH DRAKMAR MANY YEARS AGO. THEY WERE DEFEATED BY A GROUP OF HUMANS. MORDEF IS STILL IMPRISONED THERE BECAUSE YOU SAID IT WOULD SERVE HER RIGHT GOING WITH OUT YOUR AUTHORITY.
...AND DRAKMAR?
HE HAD GOTTEN INTO AN ARGUEMENT WITH MORDEF. SHE SWITCHED HIS SOUL WITH THAT OF ONE OF THE HUMAN HERO'S THAT DEFEATED THEM. HIS SOUL STILL RESIDES IN THAT HUMAN'S UNFUNCTIONING BODY ON EARTH.
HIS ACTUAL BODY IS IN NACHTHELM, THE LAND OF THE DEAD. HEL'D HAS BEEN LOOKING AFTER HIM.
AND HIS SOUL IS STILL THAT OF A HUMAN?
YES.
AH, WELL. LOKI'S CHILDREN HAVE SUFFERED ENOUGH. I WOULD SPEAK TO HEL'D.
AH, VILAK. YOU DON'T CALL ME ANYMORE. HAVE YOU FINALLY GOTTEN BORED?
I WANT DRAKMAR SENT TO ME IMMEDIATELY.
YOUR FAVORITE SON?

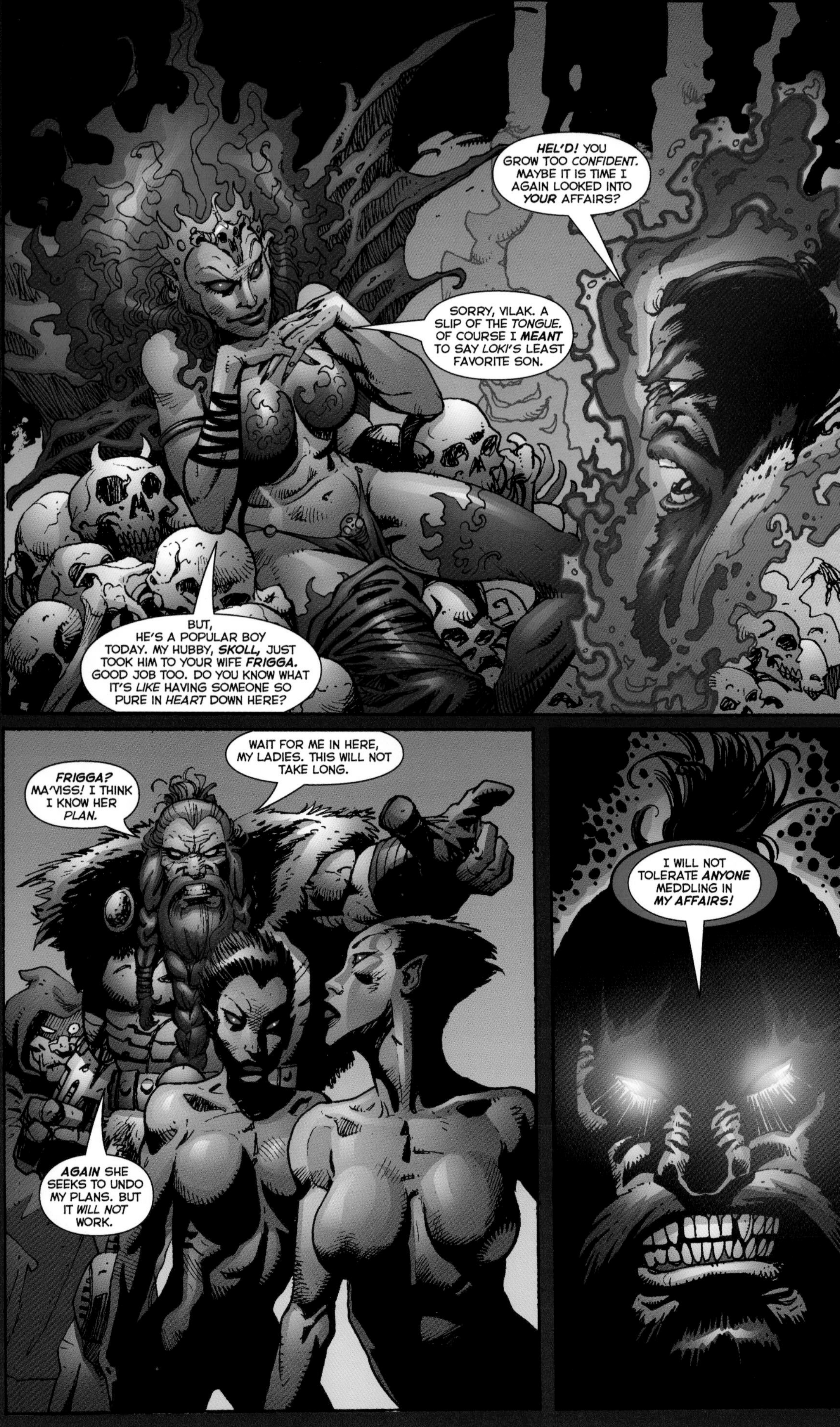
HEL'D! YOU GROW TOO CONFIDENT. MAYBE IT IS TIME I AGAIN LOOKED INTO YOUR AFFAIRS?
SORRY, VILAK. A SLIP OF THE TONGUE. OF COURSE I MEANT TO SAY LOKI'S LEAST FAVORITE SON.
BUT, HE'S A POPULAR BOY TODAY. MY HUBBY, SKOLL, JUST TOOK HIM TO YOUR WIFE FRIGGA. GOOD JOB TOO. DO YOU KNOW WHAT IT'S LIKE HAVING SOMEONE SO PURE IN HEART DOWN HERE?
FRIGGA? MA'VISS! I THINK I KNOW HER PLAN.
WAIT FOR ME IN HERE, MY LADIES. THIS WILL NOT TAKE LONG.
AGAIN SHE SEEKS TO UNDO MY PLANS. BUT IT WILL NOT WORK.
I WILL NOT TOLERATE ANYONE MEDDLING IN MY AFFAIRS!

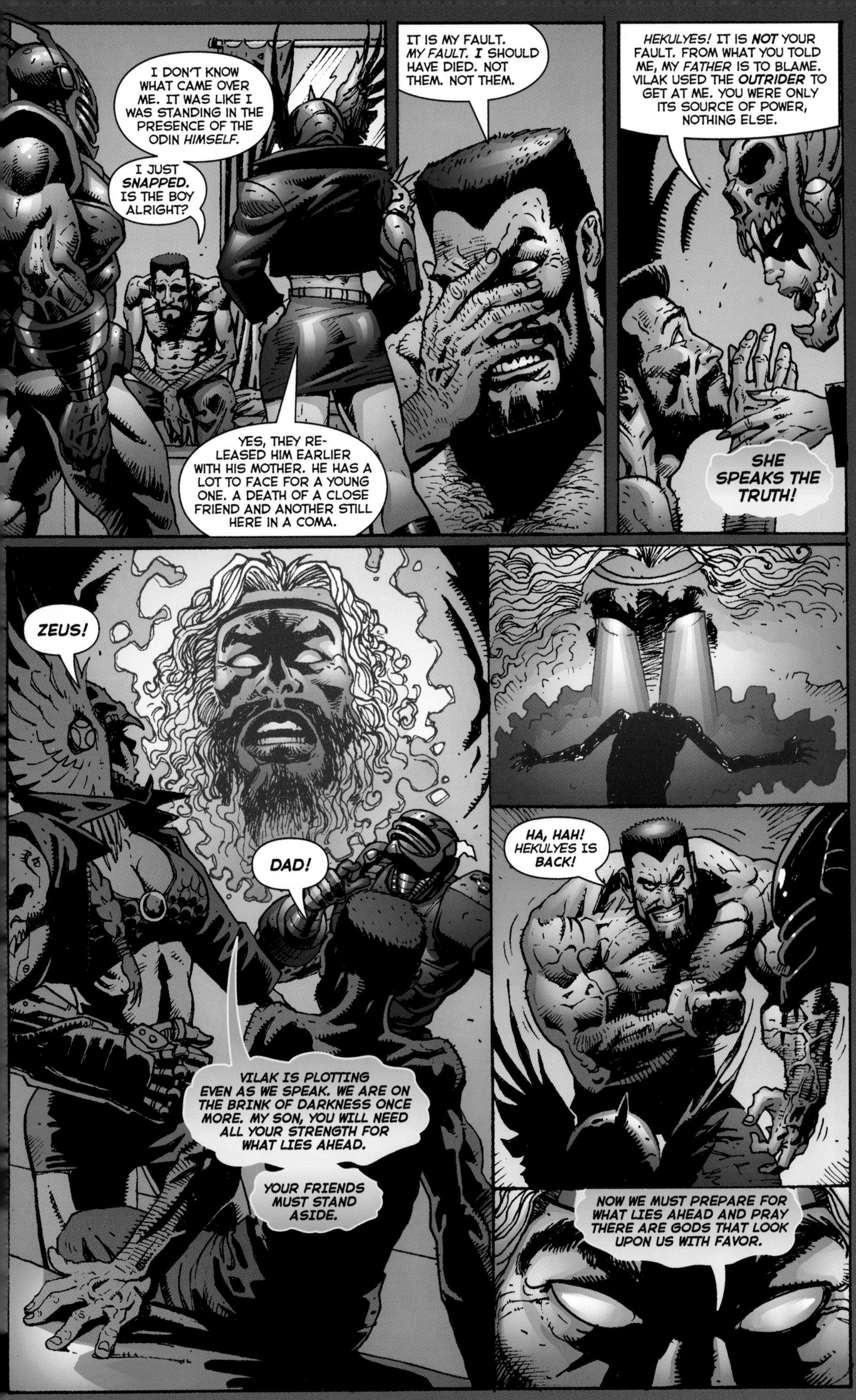
I DON'T KNOW WHAT CAME OVER ME. IT WAS LIKE I WAS STANDING IN THE PRESENCE OF THE ODIN *HIMSELF.*
I JUST *SNAPPED.* IS THE BOY ALRIGHT?
YES, THEY RELEASED HIM EARLIER WITH HIS MOTHER. HE HAS A LOT TO FACE FOR A YOUNG ONE. A DEATH OF A CLOSE FRIEND AND ANOTHER STILL HERE IN A COMA.
IT IS MY FAULT. *MY FAULT. I* SHOULD HAVE DIED. NOT THEM. NOT THEM.
HEKULYES! IT IS *NOT* YOUR FAULT. FROM WHAT YOU TOLD ME, MY *FATHER* IS TO BLAME. VILAK USED THE *OUTRIDER* TO GET AT ME. YOU WERE ONLY ITS SOURCE OF POWER, NOTHING ELSE.
SHE SPEAKS THE TRUTH!
ZEUS!
DAD!
VILAK IS PLOTTING EVEN AS WE SPEAK. WE ARE ON THE BRINK OF DARKNESS ONCE MORE. MY SON, YOU WILL NEED ALL YOUR STRENGTH FOR WHAT LIES AHEAD.
YOUR FRIENDS MUST STAND ASIDE.
HA, HAH! HEKULYES IS BACK!
NOW WE MUST PREPARE FOR WHAT LIES AHEAD AND PRAY THERE ARE GODS THAT LOOK UPON US WITH FAVOR.

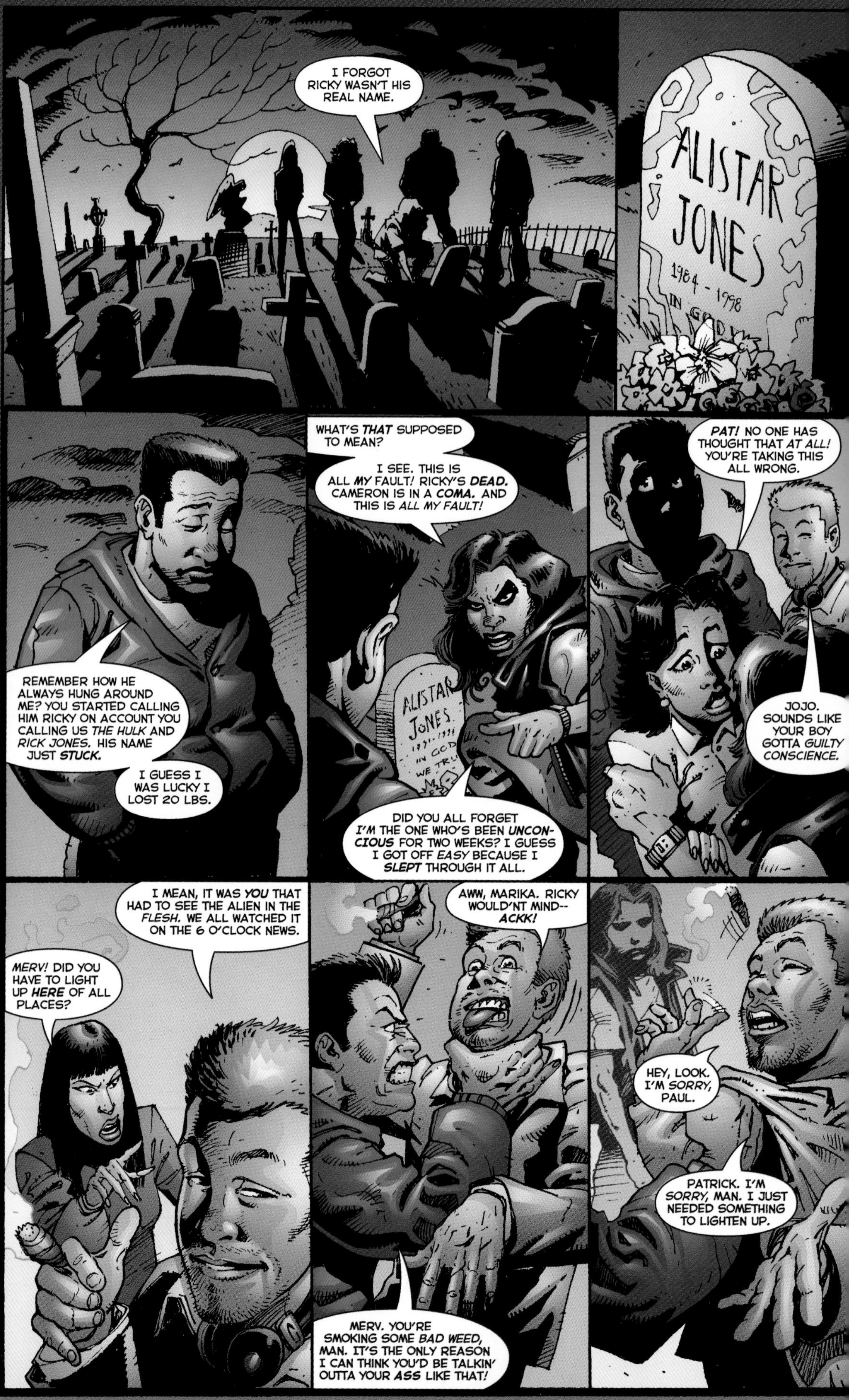
I FORGOT RICKY WASN'T HIS REAL NAME.
ALISTAR JONES 1984 - 1998 IN GOD
REMEMBER HOW HE ALWAYS HUNG AROUND ME? YOU STARTED CALLING HIM RICKY ON ACCOUNT YOU CALLING US *THE HULK* AND *RICK JONES*. HIS NAME JUST **STUCK**.
I GUESS I WAS LUCKY I LOST 20 LBS.
WHAT'S ***THAT*** SUPPOSED TO MEAN?
I SEE. THIS IS ALL *MY* FAULT! RICKY'S ***DEAD***. CAMERON IS IN A ***COMA***. AND THIS IS *ALL MY FAULT!*
DID YOU ALL FORGET ***I'M*** THE ONE WHO'S BEEN ***UNCONCIOUS*** FOR TWO WEEKS? I GUESS I GOT OFF *EASY* BECAUSE I ***SLEPT*** THROUGH IT ALL.
PAT! NO ONE HAS THOUGHT THAT *AT ALL!* YOU'RE TAKING THIS ALL WRONG.
JOJO. SOUNDS LIKE YOUR BOY GOTTA *GUILTY CONSCIENCE*.
I MEAN, IT WAS *YOU* THAT HAD TO SEE THE ALIEN IN THE *FLESH*. WE ALL WATCHED IT ON THE 6 O'CLOCK NEWS.
MERV! DID YOU HAVE TO LIGHT UP ***HERE*** OF ALL PLACES?
AWW, MARIKA. RICKY WOULD'NT MIND-- ***ACKK!***
MERV. YOU'RE SMOKING SOME *BAD WEED*, MAN. IT'S THE ONLY REASON I CAN THINK YOU'D BE TALKIN' OUTTA YOUR ***ASS*** LIKE THAT!
HEY, LOOK. I'M *SORRY*, PAUL.
PATRICK. I'M *SORRY*, MAN. I JUST NEEDED SOMETHING TO LIGHTEN UP.

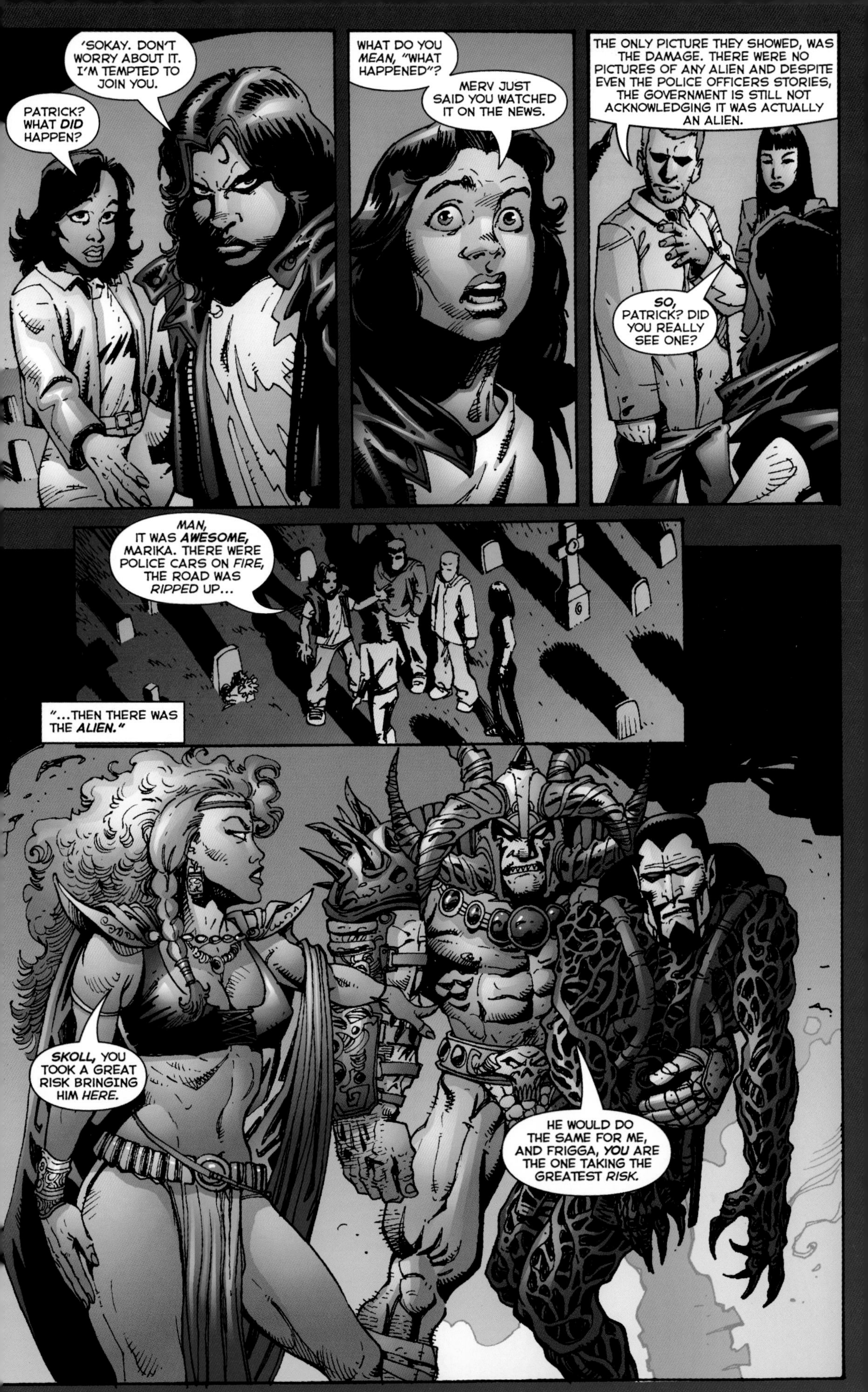
PATRICK? WHAT DID HAPPEN?
'SOKAY. DON'T WORRY ABOUT IT. I'M TEMPTED TO JOIN YOU.
WHAT DO YOU MEAN, "WHAT HAPPENED"?
MERV JUST SAID YOU WATCHED IT ON THE NEWS.
THE ONLY PICTURE THEY SHOWED, WAS THE DAMAGE. THERE WERE NO PICTURES OF ANY ALIEN AND DESPITE EVEN THE POLICE OFFICERS STORIES, THE GOVERNMENT IS STILL NOT ACKNOWLEDGING IT WAS ACTUALLY AN ALIEN.
SO, PATRICK? DID YOU REALLY SEE ONE?
MAN, IT WAS AWESOME, MARIKA. THERE WERE POLICE CARS ON FIRE, THE ROAD WAS RIPPED UP...
"...THEN THERE WAS THE ALIEN."
SKOLL, YOU TOOK A GREAT RISK BRINGING HIM HERE.
HE WOULD DO THE SAME FOR ME, AND FRIGGA, YOU ARE THE ONE TAKING THE GREATEST RISK.

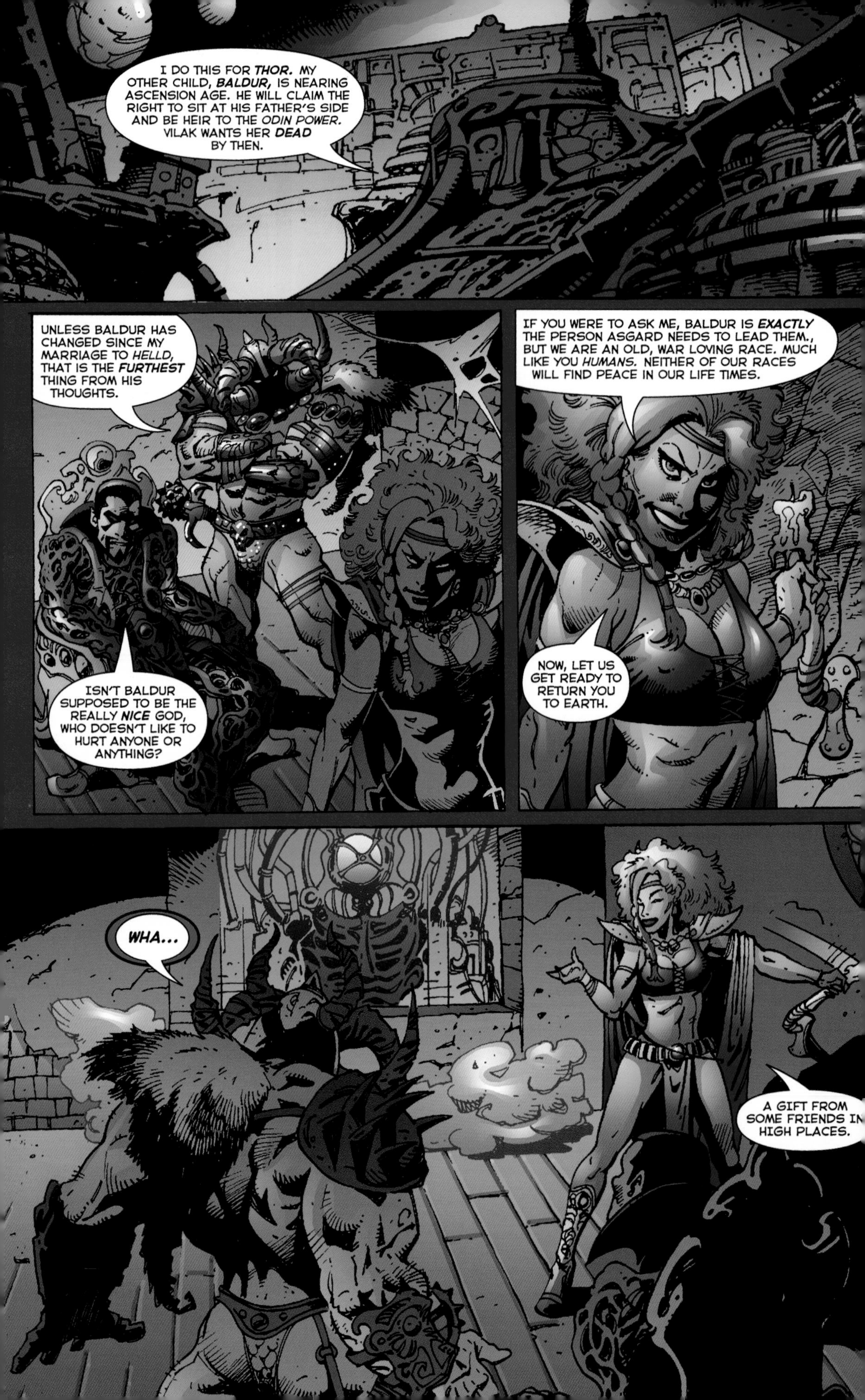
I DO THIS FOR THOR. MY OTHER CHILD, BALDUR, IS NEARING ASCENSION AGE. HE WILL CLAIM THE RIGHT TO SIT AT HIS FATHER'S SIDE AND BE HEIR TO THE ODIN POWER. VILAK WANTS HER DEAD BY THEN.
UNLESS BALDUR HAS CHANGED SINCE MY MARRIAGE TO HELLD, THAT IS THE FURTHEST THING FROM HIS THOUGHTS.
ISN'T BALDUR SUPPOSED TO BE THE REALLY NICE GOD, WHO DOESN'T LIKE TO HURT ANYONE OR ANYTHING?
IF YOU WERE TO ASK ME, BALDUR IS EXACTLY THE PERSON ASGARD NEEDS TO LEAD THEM., BUT WE ARE AN OLD, WAR LOVING RACE. MUCH LIKE YOU HUMANS. NEITHER OF OUR RACES WILL FIND PEACE IN OUR LIFE TIMES.
NOW, LET US GET READY TO RETURN YOU TO EARTH.
WHA...
A GIFT FROM SOME FRIENDS IN HIGH PLACES.

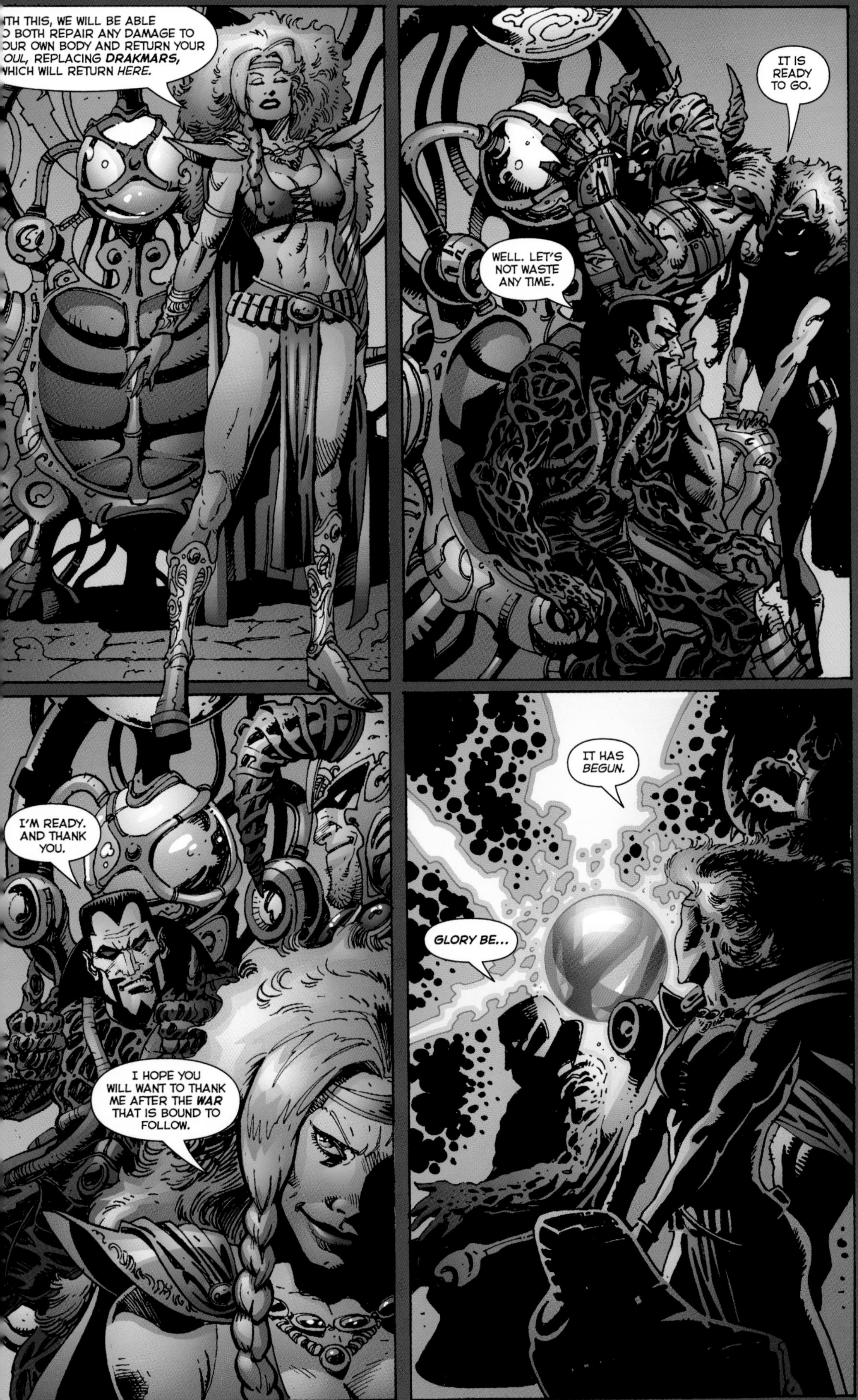
ITH THIS, WE WILL BE ABLE O BOTH REPAIR ANY DAMAGE TO OUR OWN BODY AND RETURN YOUR OUL, REPLACING DRAKMARS, WHICH WILL RETURN HERE.
IT IS READY TO GO.
WELL. LET'S NOT WASTE ANY TIME.
I'M READY. AND THANK YOU.
I HOPE YOU WILL WANT TO THANK ME AFTER THE WAR THAT IS BOUND TO FOLLOW.
IT HAS BEGUN.
GLORY BE...

OH, MAN. LOOK AT THE TIME. MY DAD'LL *SKIN* ME.

OH, *NO.* ACKROYD SET A *TEST* FOR TOMORROW. I DIDN'T GET A CHANCE TO STUDY.

I DON'T HAVE TO GO BACK TO SCHOOL UNTIL *NEXT WEEK.*

LOOK!

A *SHOOTING STAR!* UP THERE.

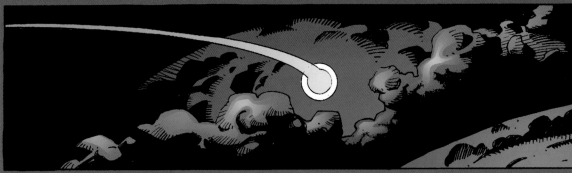

IT JUST *TURNED.*

IT'S COMING THIS WAY!

RUN!

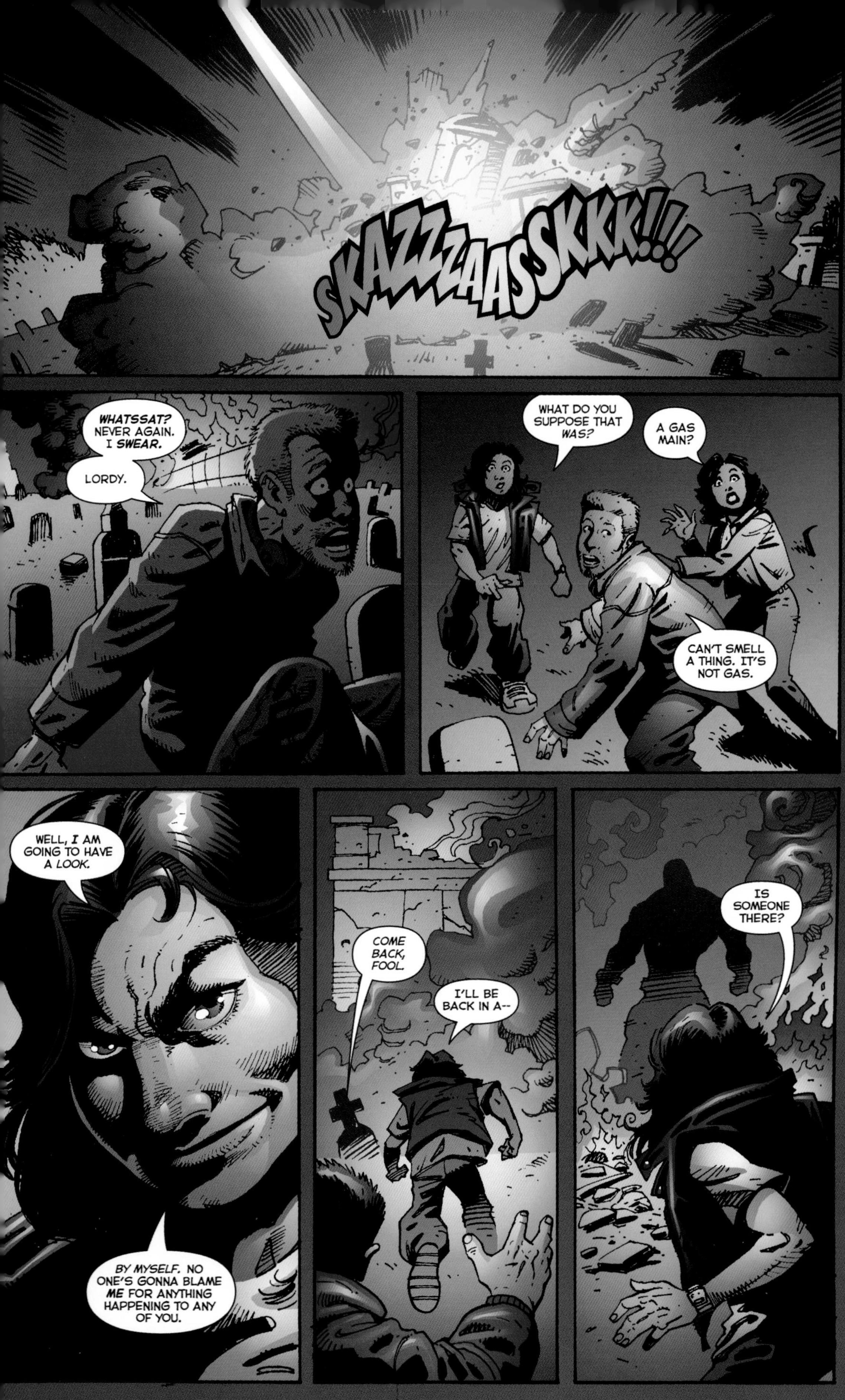
SKAZZZAASSKKK!!!!
WHATSSAT? NEVER AGAIN. I SWEAR.
LORDY.
WHAT DO YOU SUPPOSE THAT WAS?
A GAS MAIN?
CAN'T SMELL A THING. IT'S NOT GAS.
WELL, I AM GOING TO HAVE A LOOK.
BY MYSELF. NO ONE'S GONNA BLAME ME FOR ANYTHING HAPPENING TO ANY OF YOU.
COME BACK, FOOL.
I'LL BE BACK IN A--
IS SOMEONE THERE?

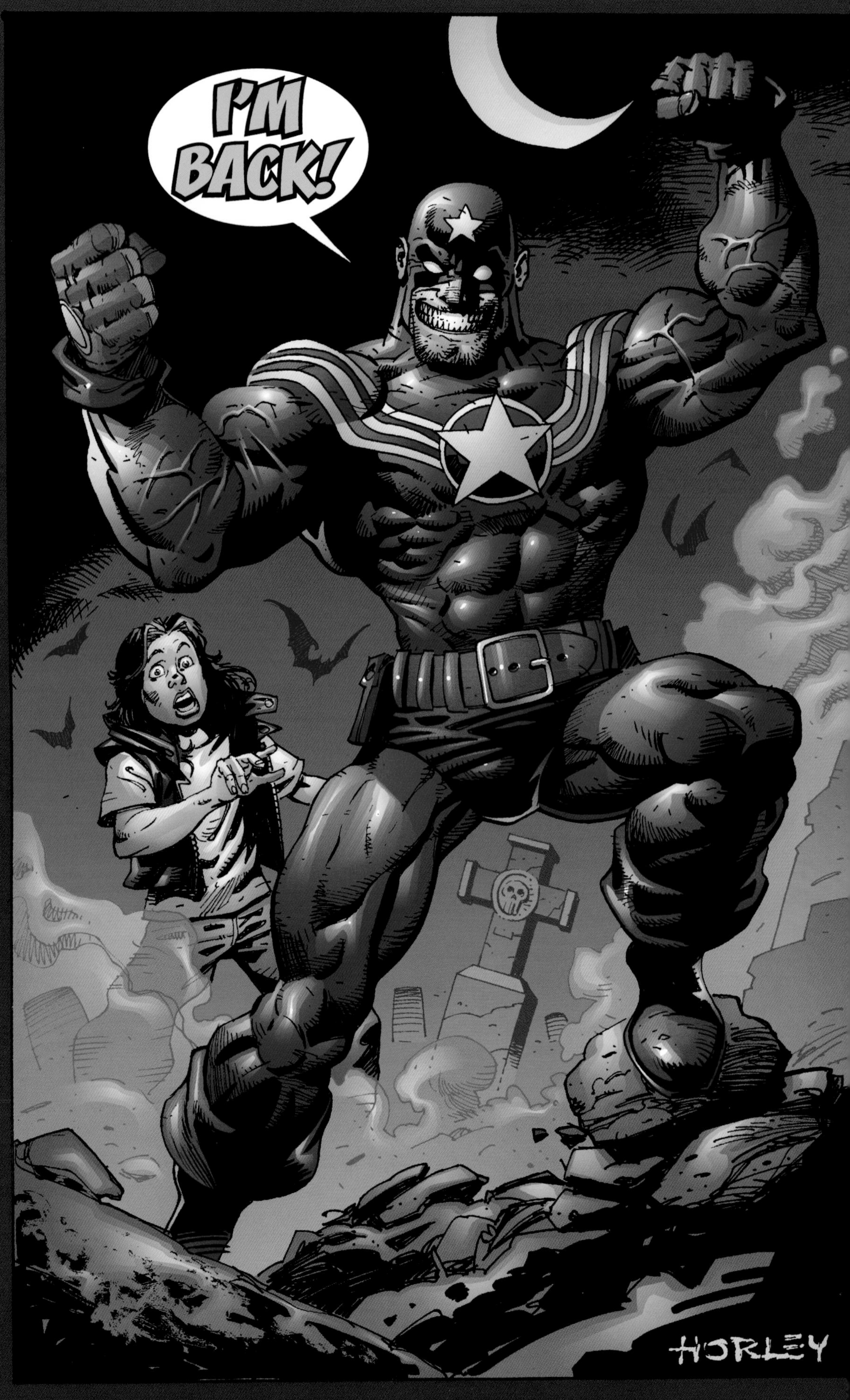
I'M BACK!
HORLEY

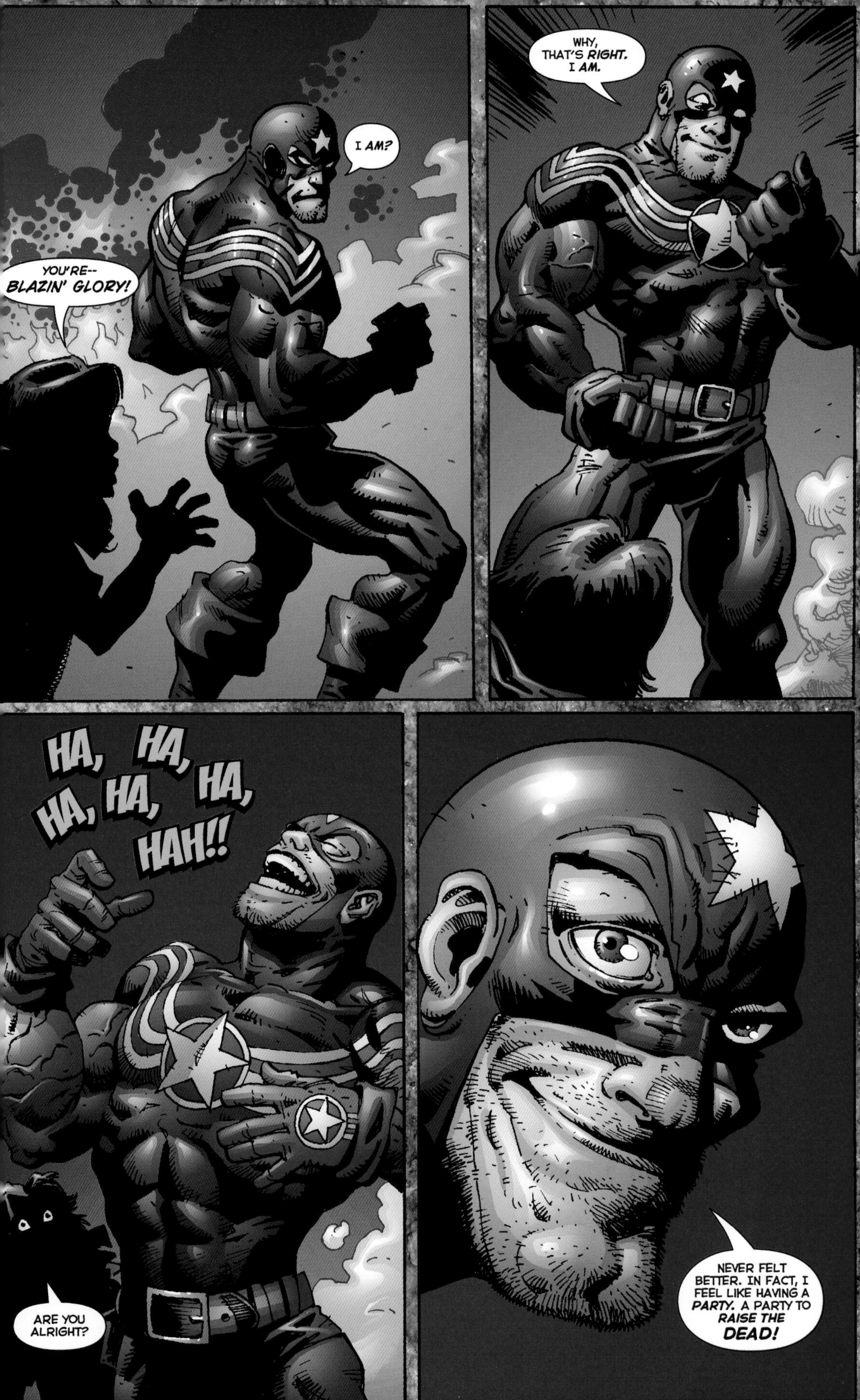
YOU'RE-- BLAZIN' GLORY!
I AM?
WHY, THAT'S RIGHT. I AM.
HA, HA, HA, HA, HA, HAH!!
ARE YOU ALRIGHT?
NEVER FELT BETTER. IN FACT, I FEEL LIKE HAVING A PARTY. A PARTY TO RAISE THE DEAD!

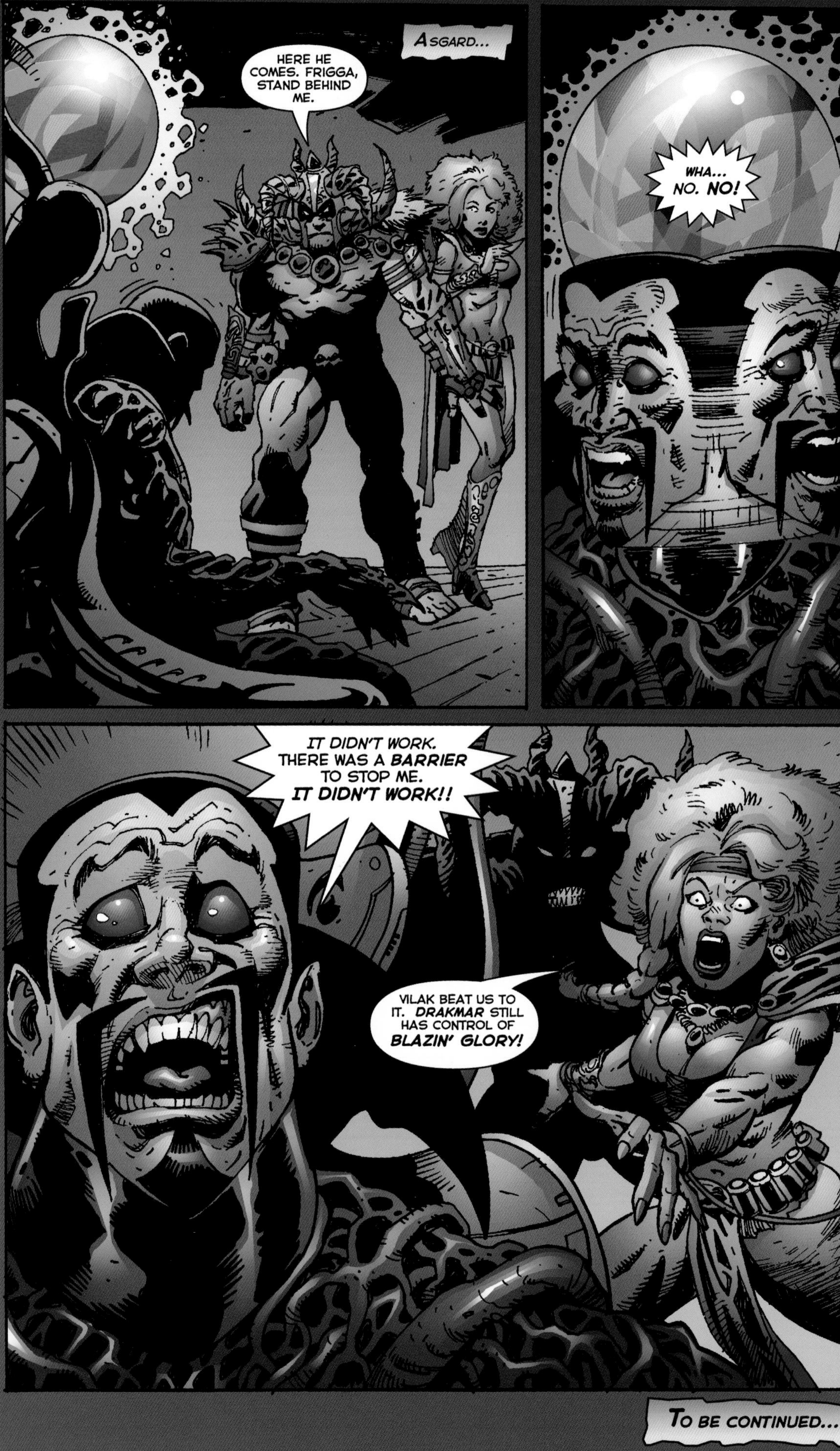

Asgard...
HERE HE COMES. FRIGGA, STAND BEHIND ME.
WHA... NO. NO!
IT DIDN'T WORK. THERE WAS A BARRIER TO STOP ME. IT DIDN'T WORK!!
VILAK BEAT US TO IT. DRAKMAR STILL HAS CONTROL OF BLAZIN' GLORY!
To be continued...

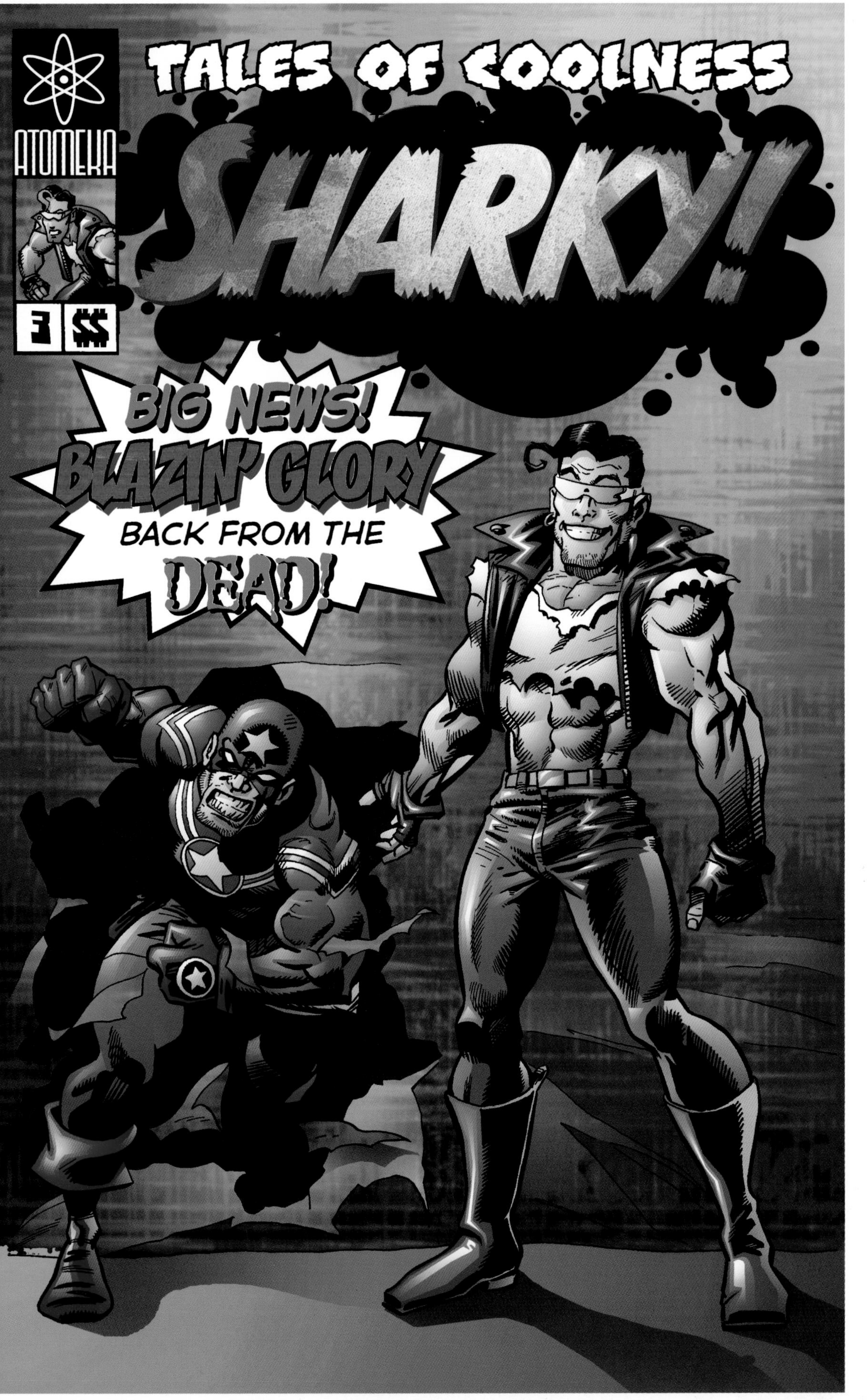
ATOMEKA
3
$$
TALES OF COOLNESS
SHARKY!
BIG NEWS!
BLAZIN' GLORY
BACK FROM THE
DEAD!

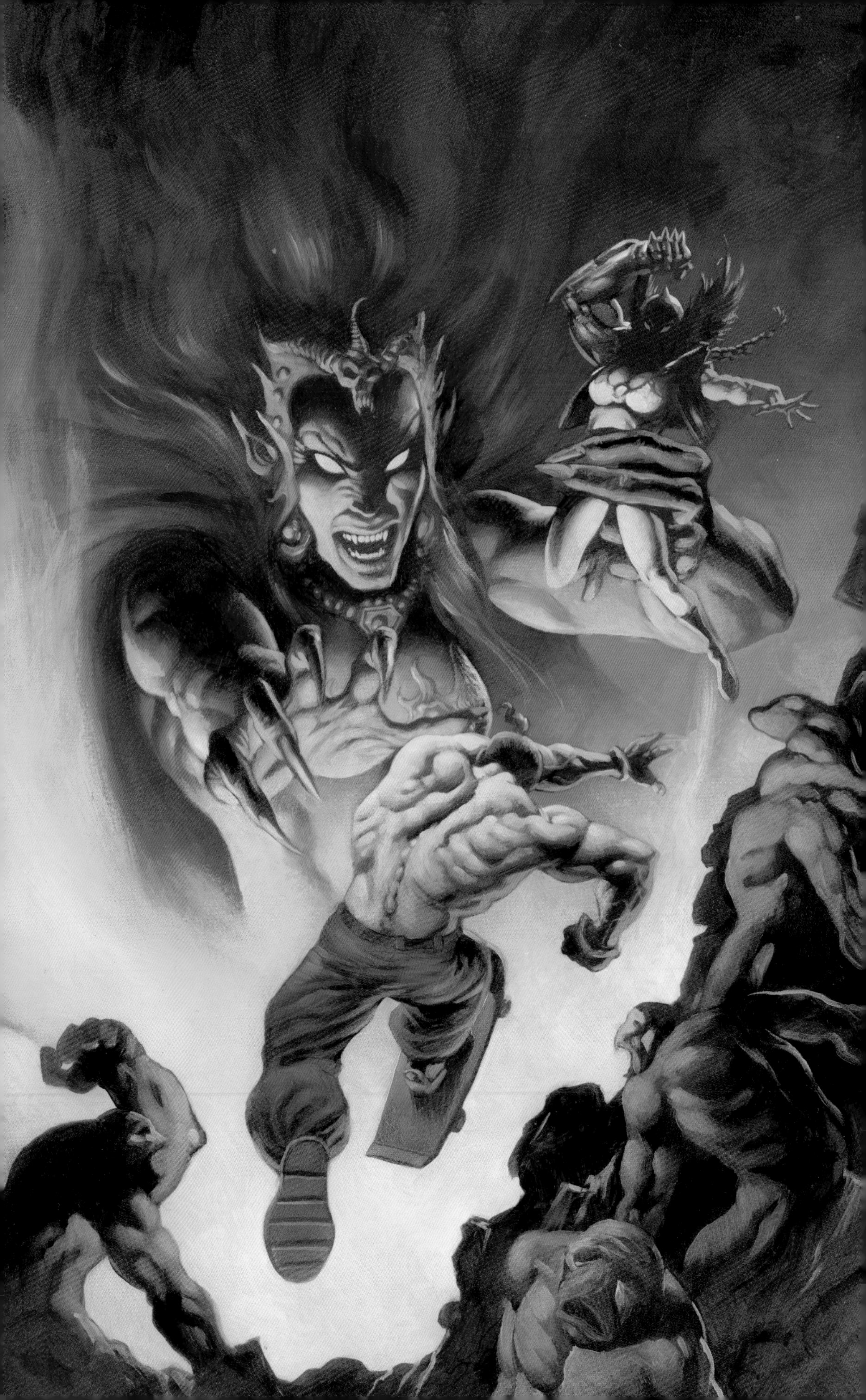

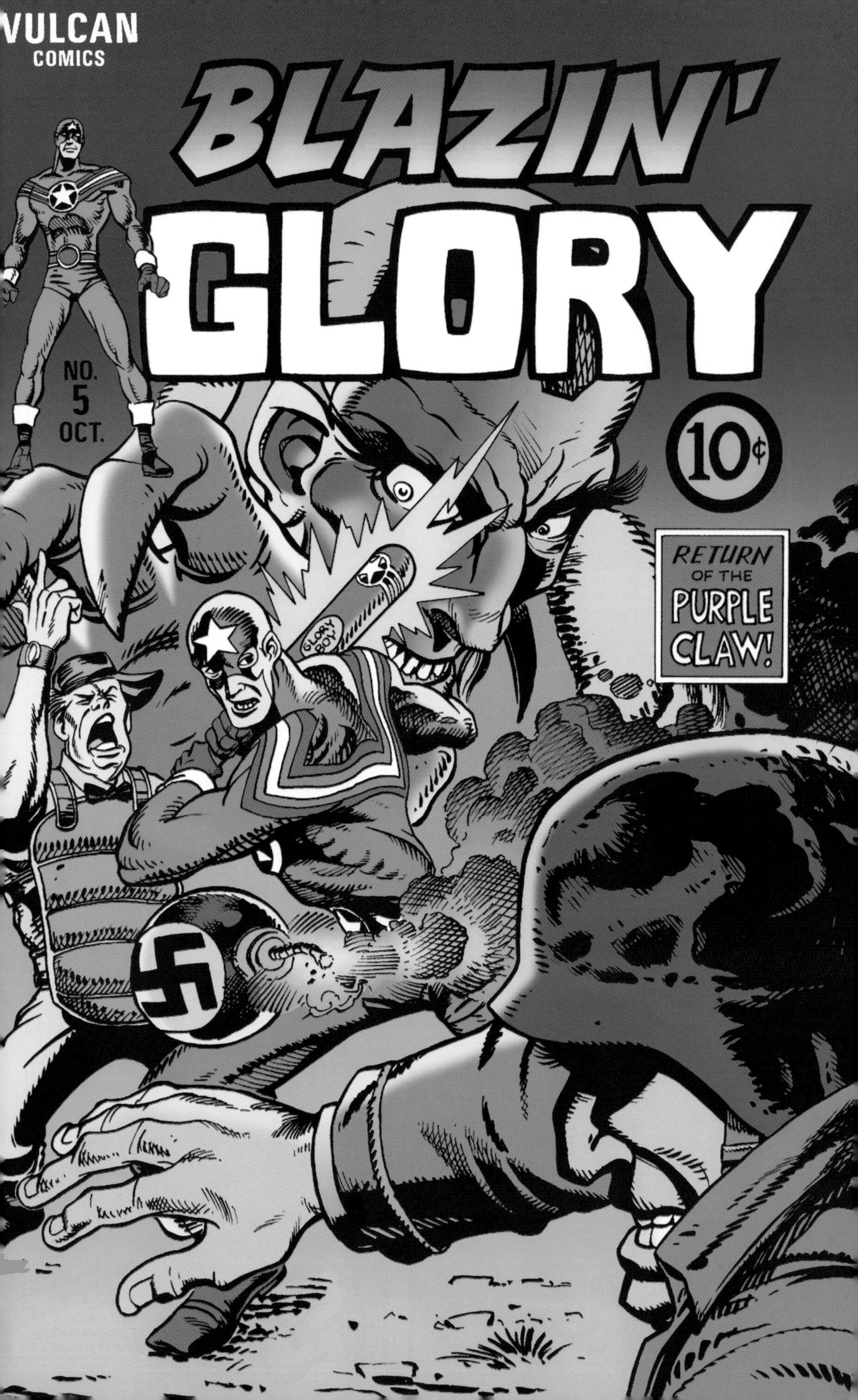
VULCAN
COMICS
BLAZIN'
GLORY
NO.
5
OCT.
10¢
GLORY BOY
RETURN
OF THE
PURPLE
CLAW!

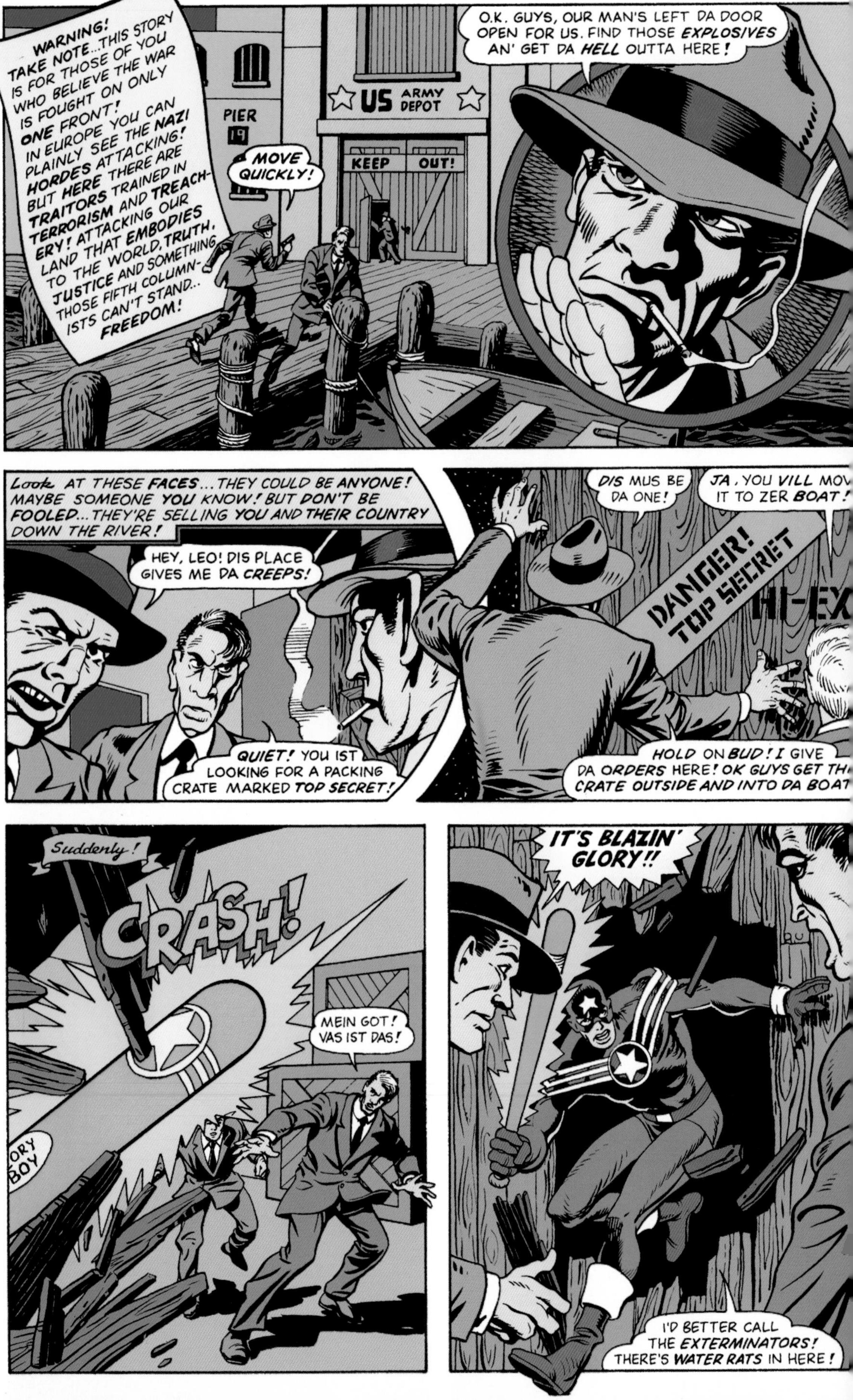

WARNING! TAKE NOTE...THIS STORY IS FOR THOSE OF YOU WHO BELIEVE THE WAR IS FOUGHT ON ONLY ONE FRONT! IN EUROPE YOU CAN PLAINLY SEE THE NAZI HORDES ATTACKING! BUT HERE THERE ARE TRAITORS TRAINED IN TERRORISM AND TREACHERY! ATTACKING OUR LAND THAT EMBODIES TO THE WORLD, TRUTH, JUSTICE AND SOMETHING THOSE FIFTH COLUMNISTS CAN'T STAND... FREEDOM!
PIER 19
US ARMY DEPOT
KEEP OUT!
MOVE QUICKLY!
O.K. GUYS, OUR MAN'S LEFT DA DOOR OPEN FOR US. FIND THOSE EXPLOSIVES AN' GET DA HELL OUTTA HERE!
Look AT THESE FACES...THEY COULD BE ANYONE! MAYBE SOMEONE YOU KNOW! BUT DON'T BE FOOLED...THEY'RE SELLING YOU AND THEIR COUNTRY DOWN THE RIVER!
HEY, LEO! DIS PLACE GIVES ME DA CREEPS!
QUIET! YOU IST LOOKING FOR A PACKING CRATE MARKED TOP SECRET!
DIS MUS BE DA ONE!
JA, YOU VILL MOV IT TO ZER BOAT!
DANGER! TOP SECRET
HI-EX
HOLD ON BUD! I GIVE DA ORDERS HERE! OK GUYS GET TH CRATE OUTSIDE AND INTO DA BOAT
Suddenly!
CRASH!
MEIN GOT! VAS IST DAS!
IT'S BLAZIN' GLORY!!
I'D BETTER CALL THE EXTERMINATORS! THERE'S WATER RATS IN HERE!

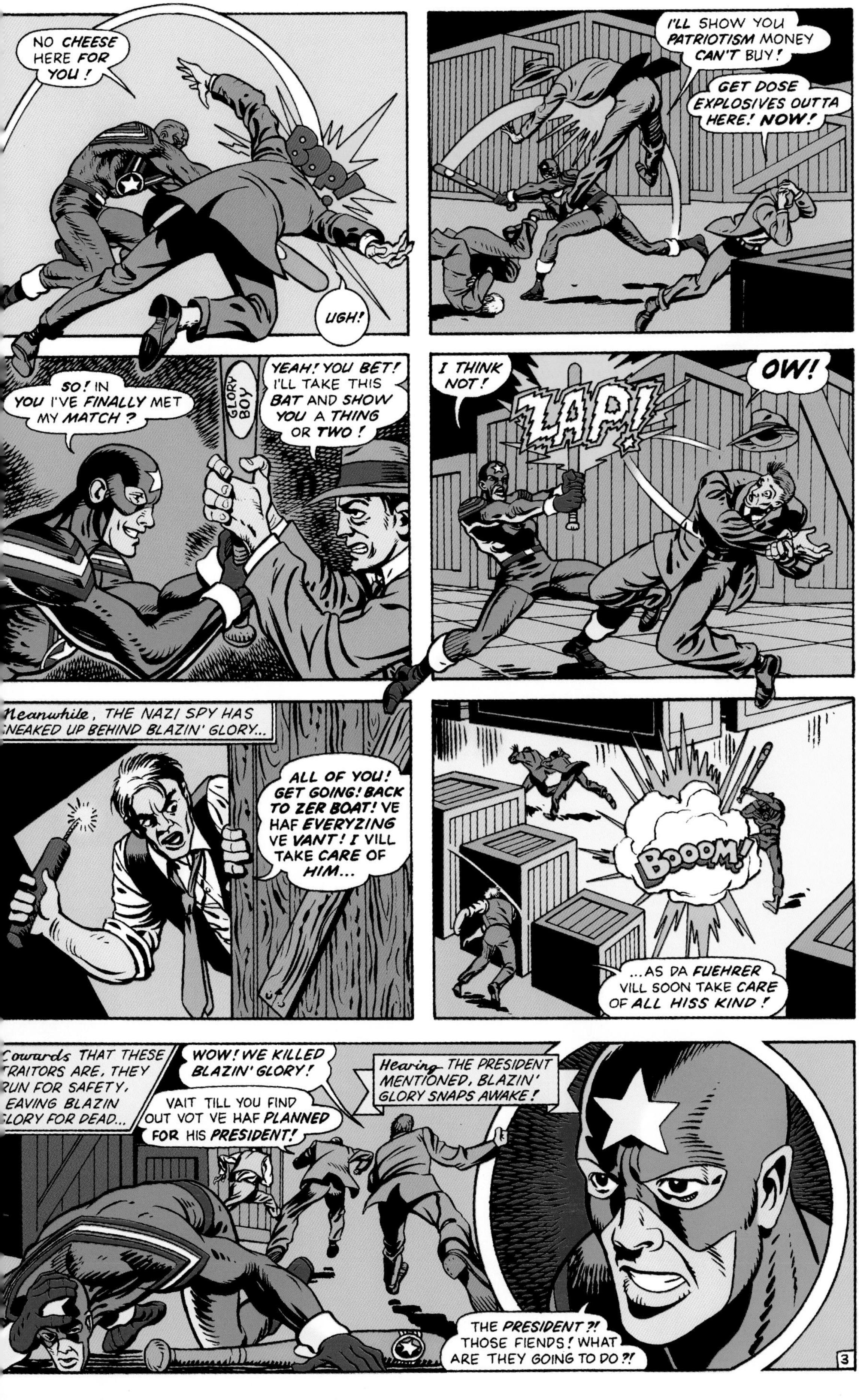
NO CHEESE HERE FOR YOU!
BOP!
UGH!
I'LL SHOW YOU PATRIOTISM MONEY CAN'T BUY!
GET DOSE EXPLOSIVES OUTTA HERE! NOW!
SO! IN YOU I'VE FINALLY MET MY MATCH?
GLORY BOY
YEAH! YOU BET! I'LL TAKE THIS BAT AND SHOW YOU A THING OR TWO!
I THINK NOT!
ZAP!
OW!
Meanwhile, THE NAZI SPY HAS SNEAKED UP BEHIND BLAZIN' GLORY...
ALL OF YOU! GET GOING! BACK TO ZER BOAT! VE HAF EVERYZING VE VANT! I VILL TAKE CARE OF HIM...
BOOOM!
...AS DA FUEHRER VILL SOON TAKE CARE OF ALL HISS KIND!
Cowards THAT THESE TRAITORS ARE, THEY RUN FOR SAFETY, LEAVING BLAZIN GLORY FOR DEAD...
WOW! WE KILLED BLAZIN' GLORY!
VAIT TILL YOU FIND OUT VOT VE HAF PLANNED FOR HIS PRESIDENT!
Hearing THE PRESIDENT MENTIONED, BLAZIN' GLORY SNAPS AWAKE!
THE PRESIDENT?! THOSE FIENDS! WHAT ARE THEY GOING TO DO?!

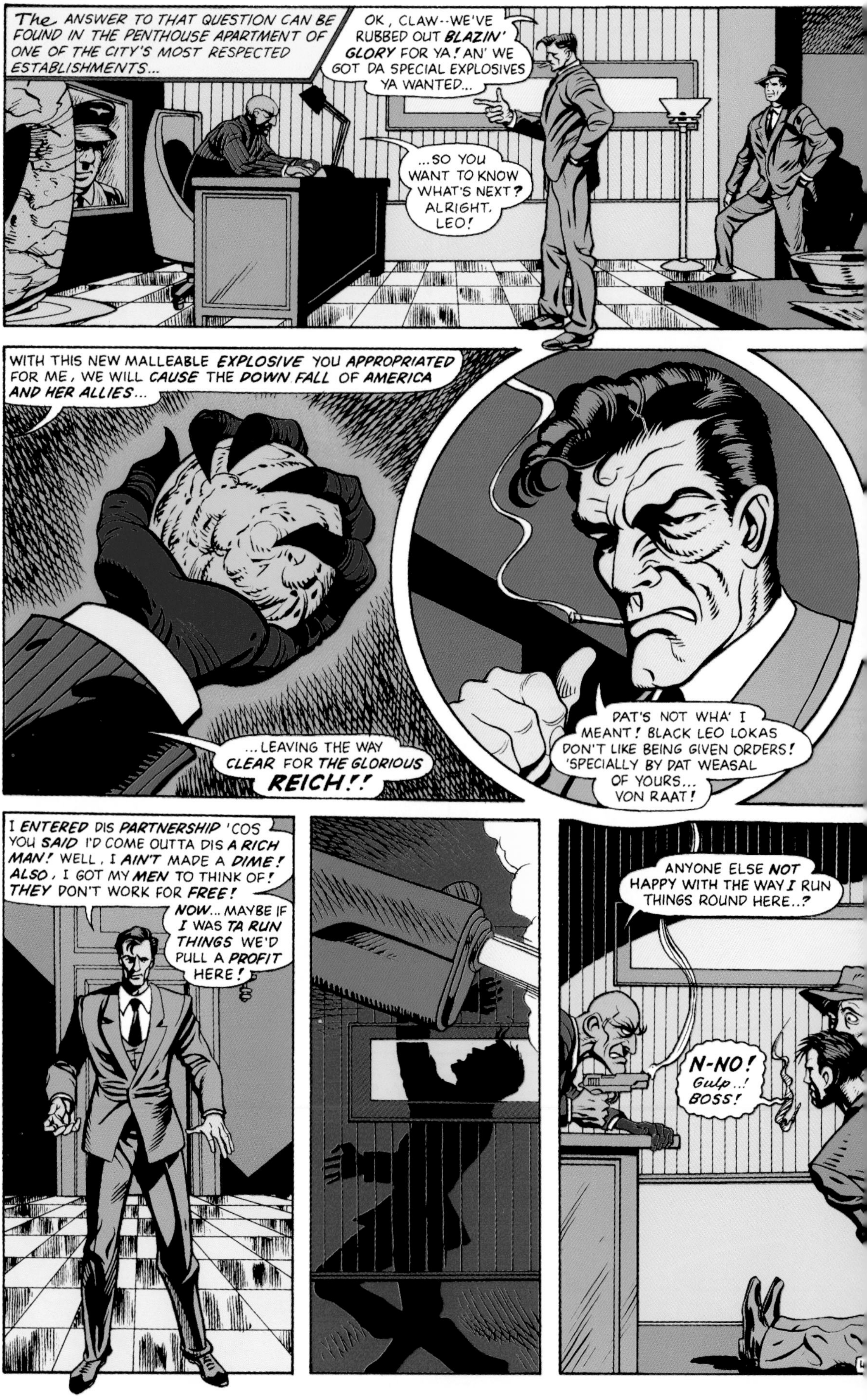
The ANSWER TO THAT QUESTION CAN BE FOUND IN THE PENTHOUSE APARTMENT OF ONE OF THE CITY'S MOST RESPECTED ESTABLISHMENTS...
OK, CLAW--WE'VE RUBBED OUT BLAZIN' GLORY FOR YA! AN' WE GOT DA SPECIAL EXPLOSIVES YA WANTED...
...SO YOU WANT TO KNOW WHAT'S NEXT? ALRIGHT, LEO!
WITH THIS NEW MALLEABLE EXPLOSIVE YOU APPROPRIATED FOR ME, WE WILL CAUSE THE DOWN FALL OF AMERICA AND HER ALLIES...
...LEAVING THE WAY CLEAR FOR THE GLORIOUS REICH!!
DAT'S NOT WHA' I MEANT! BLACK LEO LOKAS DON'T LIKE BEING GIVEN ORDERS! 'SPECIALLY BY DAT WEASAL OF YOURS... VON RAAT!
I ENTERED DIS PARTNERSHIP 'COS YOU SAID I'D COME OUTTA DIS A RICH MAN! WELL, I AIN'T MADE A DIME! ALSO, I GOT MY MEN TO THINK OF! THEY DON'T WORK FOR FREE!
NOW... MAYBE IF I WAS TA RUN THINGS WE'D PULL A PROFIT HERE!
ANYONE ELSE NOT HAPPY WITH THE WAY I RUN THINGS ROUND HERE..?
N-NO! Gulp..! BOSS!

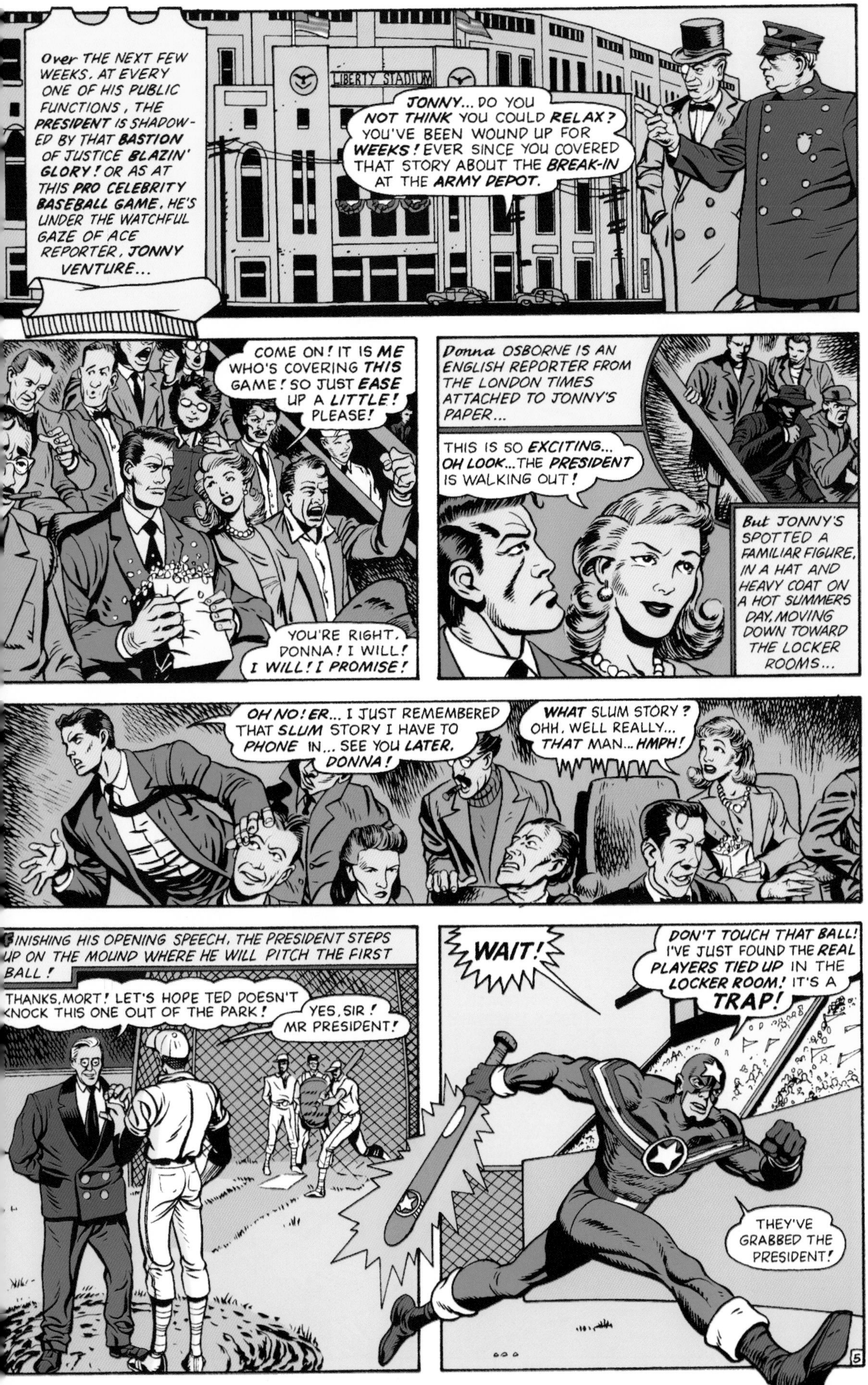
Over THE NEXT FEW WEEKS, AT EVERY ONE OF HIS PUBLIC FUNCTIONS, THE PRESIDENT IS SHADOWED BY THAT BASTION OF JUSTICE BLAZIN' GLORY! OR AS AT THIS PRO CELEBRITY BASEBALL GAME, HE'S UNDER THE WATCHFUL GAZE OF ACE REPORTER, JONNY VENTURE...
LIBERTY STADIUM
JONNY... DO YOU NOT THINK YOU COULD RELAX? YOU'VE BEEN WOUND UP FOR WEEKS! EVER SINCE YOU COVERED THAT STORY ABOUT THE BREAK-IN AT THE ARMY DEPOT.
COME ON! IT IS ME WHO'S COVERING THIS GAME! SO JUST EASE UP A LITTLE! PLEASE!
YOU'RE RIGHT, DONNA! I WILL! I WILL! I PROMISE!
Donna OSBORNE IS AN ENGLISH REPORTER FROM THE LONDON TIMES ATTACHED TO JONNY'S PAPER...
THIS IS SO EXCITING... OH LOOK... THE PRESIDENT IS WALKING OUT!
But JONNY'S SPOTTED A FAMILIAR FIGURE, IN A HAT AND HEAVY COAT ON A HOT SUMMERS DAY, MOVING DOWN TOWARD THE LOCKER ROOMS...
OH NO! ER... I JUST REMEMBERED THAT SLUM STORY I HAVE TO PHONE IN... SEE YOU LATER, DONNA!
WHAT SLUM STORY? OHH, WELL REALLY... THAT MAN... HMPH!
FINISHING HIS OPENING SPEECH, THE PRESIDENT STEPS UP ON THE MOUND WHERE HE WILL PITCH THE FIRST BALL!
THANKS, MORT! LET'S HOPE TED DOESN'T KNOCK THIS ONE OUT OF THE PARK!
YES, SIR! MR PRESIDENT!
WAIT!
DON'T TOUCH THAT BALL! I'VE JUST FOUND THE REAL PLAYERS TIED UP IN THE LOCKER ROOM! IT'S A TRAP!
THEY'VE GRABBED THE PRESIDENT!
5

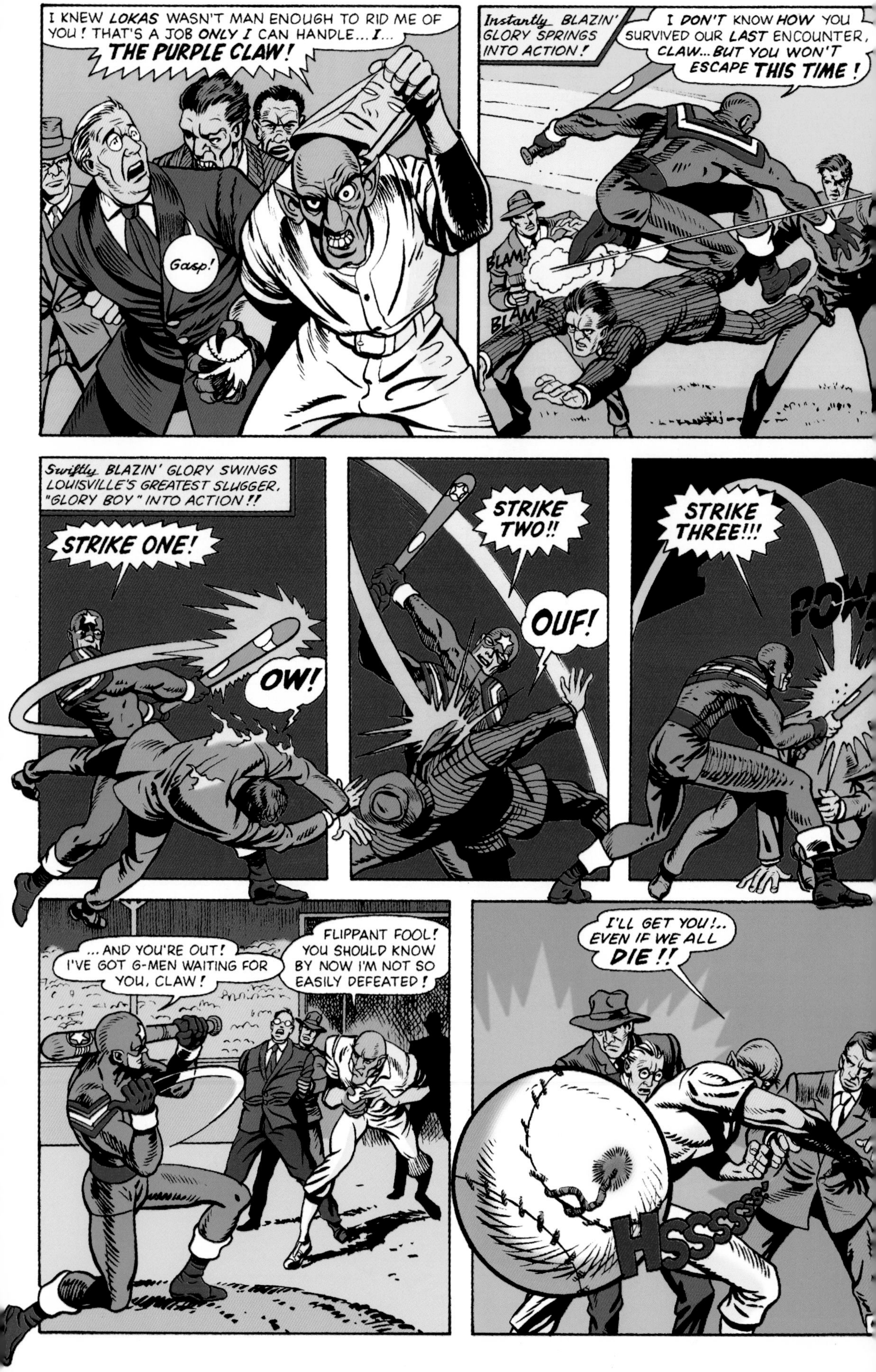
I KNEW LOKAS WASN'T MAN ENOUGH TO RID ME OF YOU! THAT'S A JOB ONLY I CAN HANDLE... I... THE PURPLE CLAW!
Gasp!
Instantly BLAZIN' GLORY SPRINGS INTO ACTION!
I DON'T KNOW HOW YOU SURVIVED OUR LAST ENCOUNTER, CLAW... BUT YOU WON'T ESCAPE THIS TIME!
BLAM!
BLAM!
Swiftly BLAZIN' GLORY SWINGS LOUISVILLE'S GREATEST SLUGGER, "GLORY BOY" INTO ACTION!!
STRIKE ONE!
OW!
STRIKE TWO!!
OUF!
STRIKE THREE!!!
... AND YOU'RE OUT! I'VE GOT G-MEN WAITING FOR YOU, CLAW!
FLIPPANT FOOL! YOU SHOULD KNOW BY NOW I'M NOT SO EASILY DEFEATED!
I'LL GET YOU!.. EVEN IF WE ALL DIE!!
HSSSSS

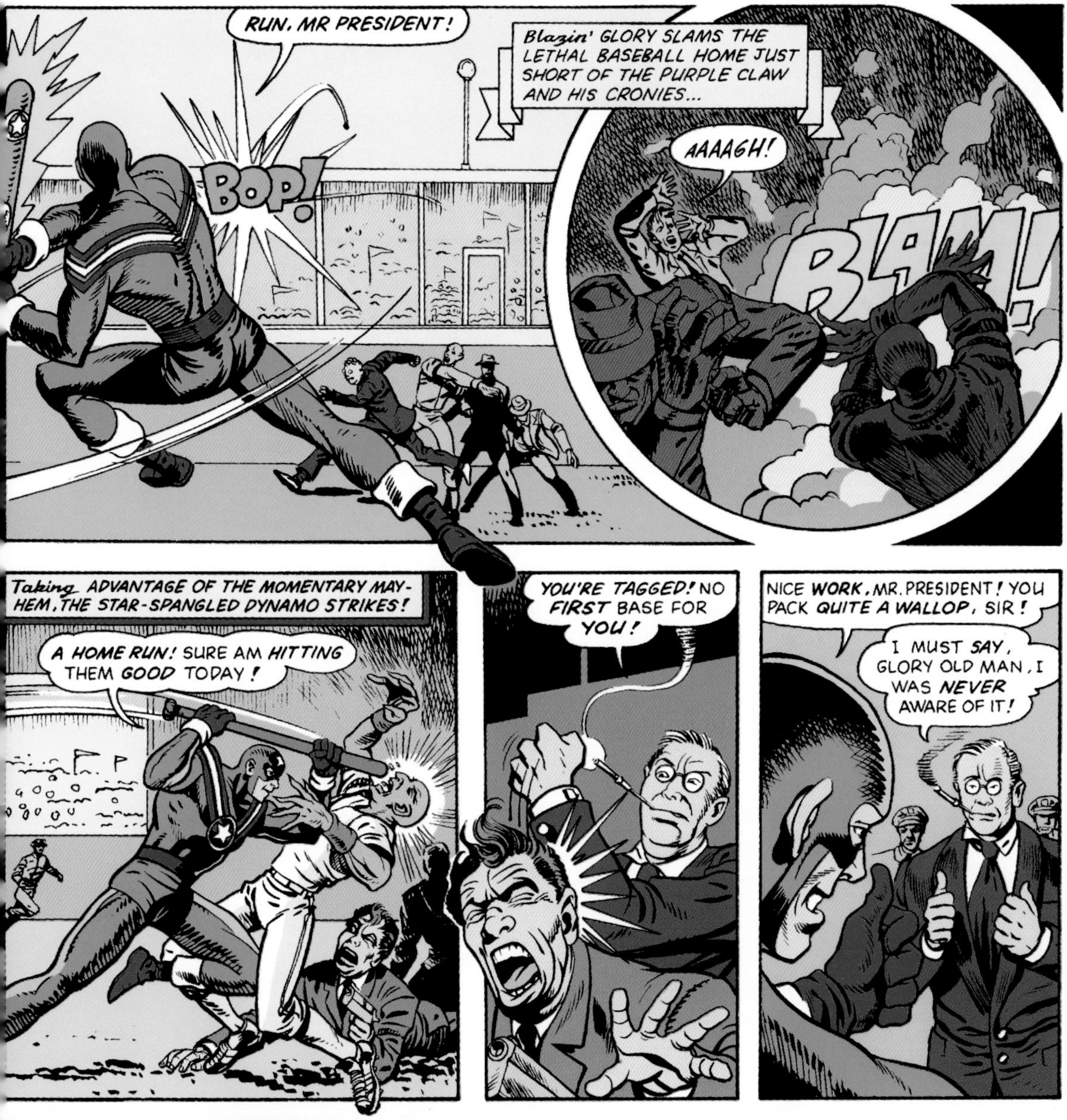
RUN, MR PRESIDENT!
Blazin' GLORY SLAMS THE LETHAL BASEBALL HOME JUST SHORT OF THE PURPLE CLAW AND HIS CRONIES...
BOP!
AAAAGH!
BLAM!
Taking ADVANTAGE OF THE MOMENTARY MAYHEM, THE STAR-SPANGLED DYNAMO STRIKES!
A HOME RUN! SURE AM HITTING THEM GOOD TODAY!
YOU'RE TAGGED! NO FIRST BASE FOR YOU!
NICE WORK, MR. PRESIDENT! YOU PACK QUITE A WALLOP, SIR!
I MUST SAY, GLORY OLD MAN, I WAS NEVER AWARE OF IT!

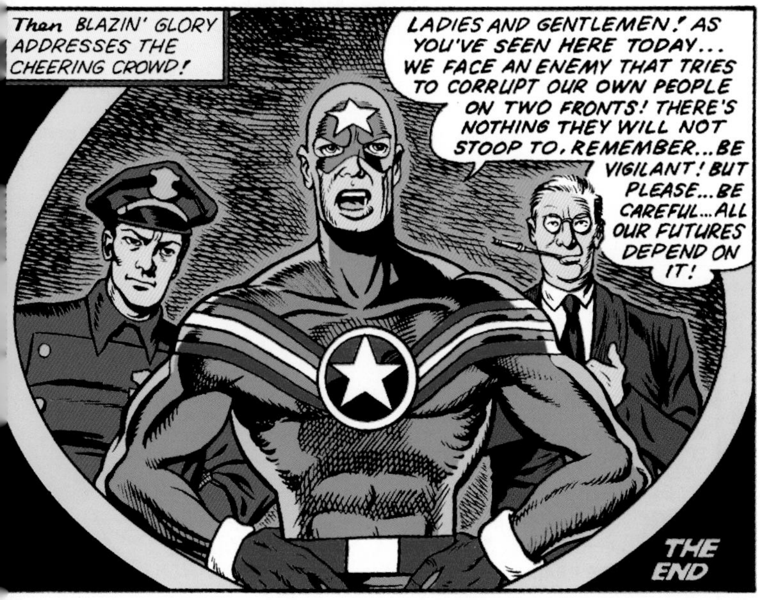
Then BLAZIN' GLORY ADDRESSES THE CHEERING CROWD!
LADIES AND GENTLEMEN! AS YOU'VE SEEN HERE TODAY... WE FACE AN ENEMY THAT TRIES TO CORRUPT OUR OWN PEOPLE ON TWO FRONTS! THERE'S NOTHING THEY WILL NOT STOOP TO, REMEMBER...BE VIGILANT! BUT PLEASE...BE CAREFUL...ALL OUR FUTURES DEPEND ON IT!
THE END

This story first appeared in **BLAZIN' GLORY No. 5 Oct. 1942.**

In various incarnations **BLAZIN'** ran more or less continually from '42, through the Gold and Silver Ages and on to '69, where he finally flickered out, unnoticed and unmourned at the height of the superhero boom.

BLAZIN' wasn't the only star in the **VULCAN COMICS** line. Older readers may also remember **BLACKDEATH, GLORY GIRL, TWO-GUN GLORY, KOGA, SPACE RACE, MONSTER HUNT, WEIRD MYSTIC, DERANGED, ZOMBA** and **LOVE ME TRUE.**

Fortunately, we've located a few file copies from this elusive line. If you'd like to see more, drop us a line and we'll check what's worthwhile in the archives.

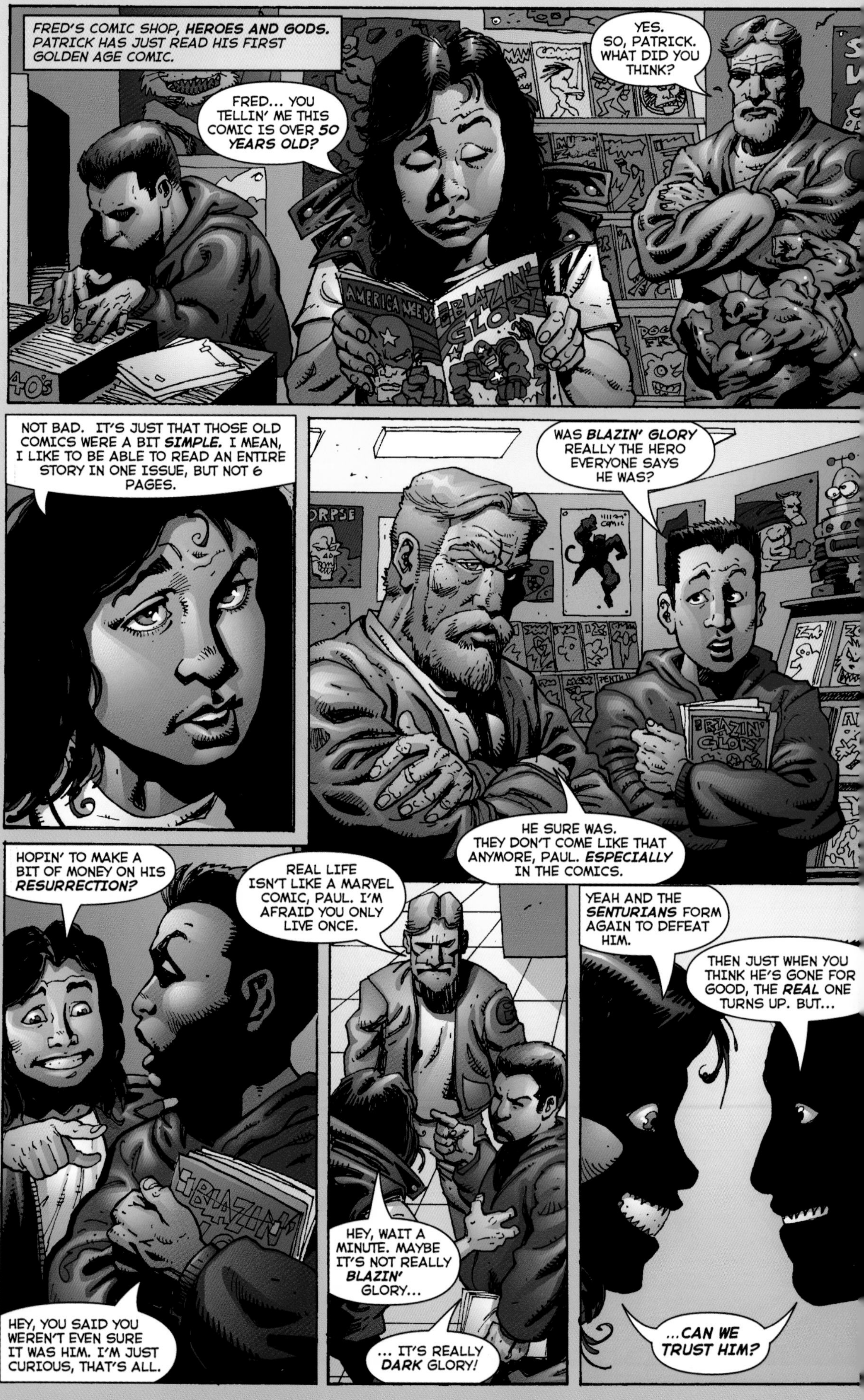
FRED'S COMIC SHOP, HEROES AND GODS. PATRICK HAS JUST READ HIS FIRST GOLDEN AGE COMIC.
FRED... YOU TELLIN' ME THIS COMIC IS OVER 50 YEARS OLD?
YES. SO, PATRICK. WHAT DID YOU THINK?
NOT BAD. IT'S JUST THAT THOSE OLD COMICS WERE A BIT SIMPLE. I MEAN, I LIKE TO BE ABLE TO READ AN ENTIRE STORY IN ONE ISSUE, BUT NOT 6 PAGES.
WAS BLAZIN' GLORY REALLY THE HERO EVERYONE SAYS HE WAS?
HE SURE WAS. THEY DON'T COME LIKE THAT ANYMORE, PAUL. ESPECIALLY IN THE COMICS.
HOPIN' TO MAKE A BIT OF MONEY ON HIS RESURRECTION?
HEY, YOU SAID YOU WEREN'T EVEN SURE IT WAS HIM. I'M JUST CURIOUS, THAT'S ALL.
REAL LIFE ISN'T LIKE A MARVEL COMIC, PAUL. I'M AFRAID YOU ONLY LIVE ONCE.
HEY, WAIT A MINUTE. MAYBE IT'S NOT REALLY BLAZIN' GLORY...
... IT'S REALLY DARK GLORY!
YEAH AND THE SENTURIANS FORM AGAIN TO DEFEAT HIM.
THEN JUST WHEN YOU THINK HE'S GONE FOR GOOD, THE REAL ONE TURNS UP. BUT...
...CAN WE TRUST HIM?

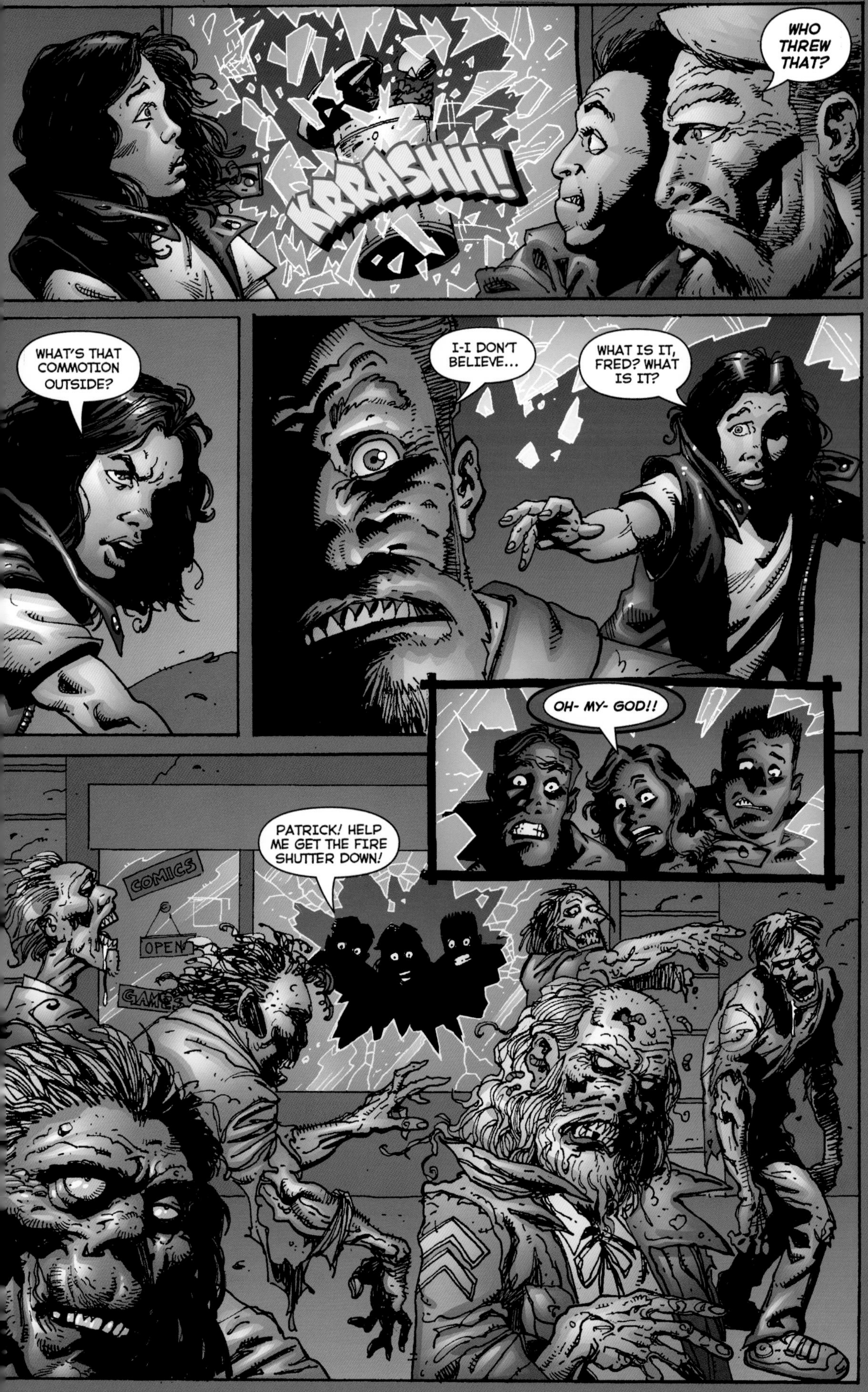
KRRASHH!
WHO THREW THAT?
WHAT'S THAT COMMOTION OUTSIDE?
I-I DON'T BELIEVE...
WHAT IS IT, FRED? WHAT IS IT?
OH- MY- GOD!!
PATRICK! HELP ME GET THE FIRE SHUTTER DOWN!
COMICS
OPEN
GAMES

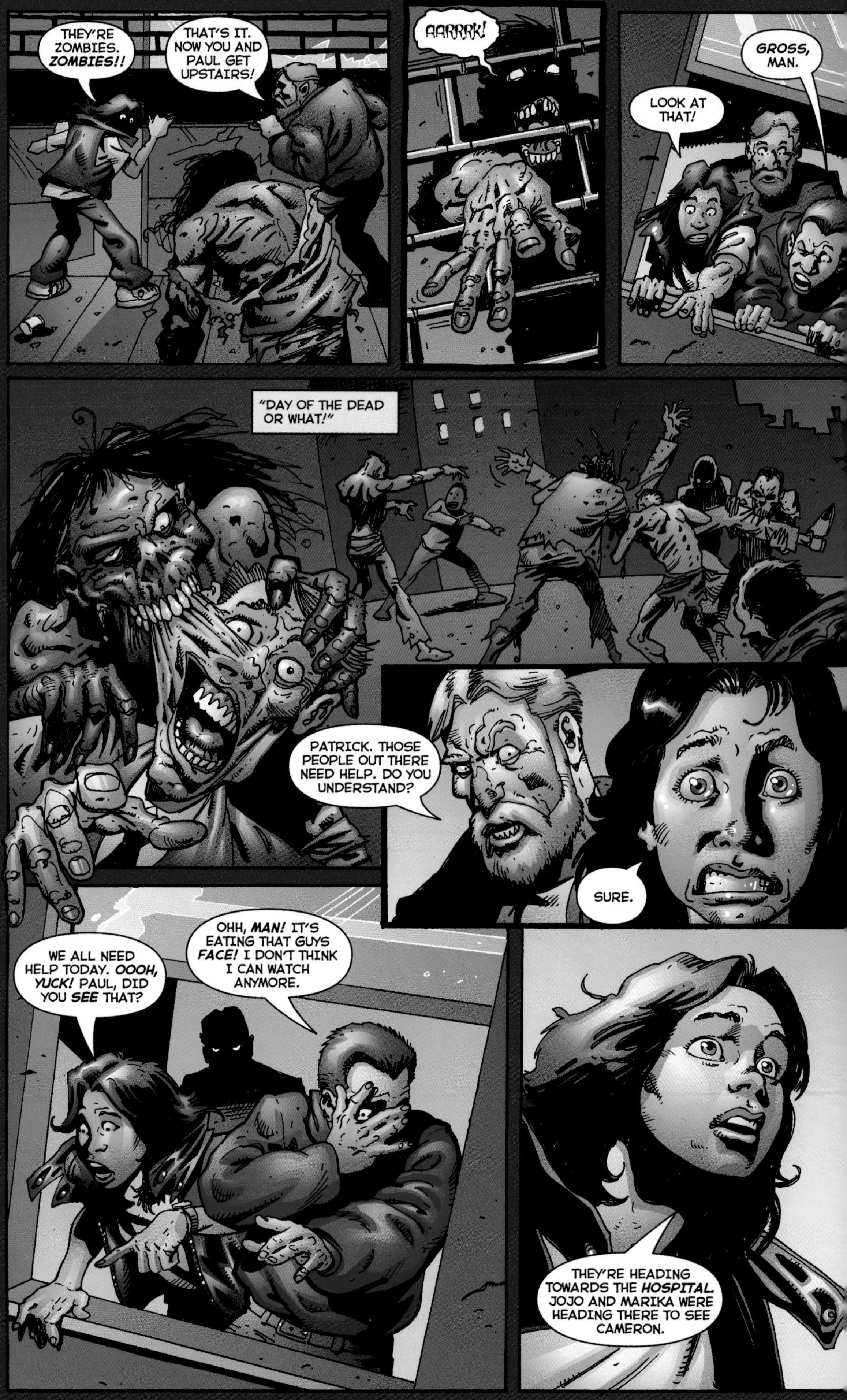
THEY'RE ZOMBIES. ZOMBIES!!
THAT'S IT. NOW YOU AND PAUL GET UPSTAIRS!
AARRRK!
LOOK AT THAT!
GROSS, MAN.
"DAY OF THE DEAD OR WHAT!"
PATRICK. THOSE PEOPLE OUT THERE NEED HELP. DO YOU UNDERSTAND?
SURE.
WE ALL NEED HELP TODAY. OOOH, YUCK! PAUL, DID YOU SEE THAT?
OHH, MAN! IT'S EATING THAT GUYS FACE! I DON'T THINK I CAN WATCH ANYMORE.
THEY'RE HEADING TOWARDS THE HOSPITAL. JOJO AND MARIKA WERE HEADING THERE TO SEE CAMERON.

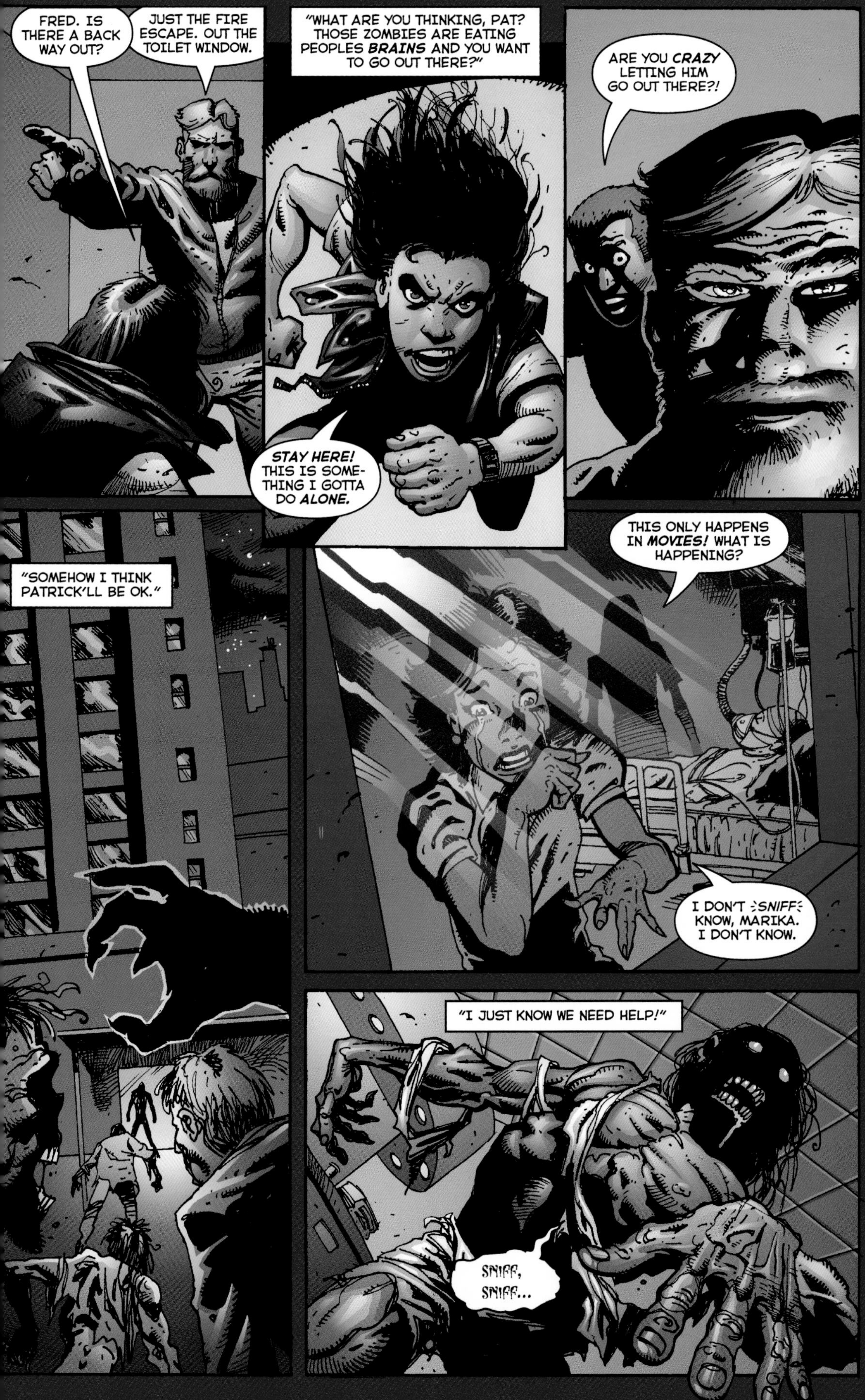

FRED. IS THERE A BACK WAY OUT?
JUST THE FIRE ESCAPE. OUT THE TOILET WINDOW.
"WHAT ARE YOU THINKING, PAT? THOSE ZOMBIES ARE EATING PEOPLES BRAINS AND YOU WANT TO GO OUT THERE?"
STAY HERE! THIS IS SOMETHING I GOTTA DO ALONE.
ARE YOU CRAZY LETTING HIM GO OUT THERE?!
"SOMEHOW I THINK PATRICK'LL BE OK."
THIS ONLY HAPPENS IN MOVIES! WHAT IS HAPPENING?
I DON'T SNIFF KNOW, MARIKA. I DON'T KNOW.
"I JUST KNOW WE NEED HELP!"
SNIFF, SNIFF...

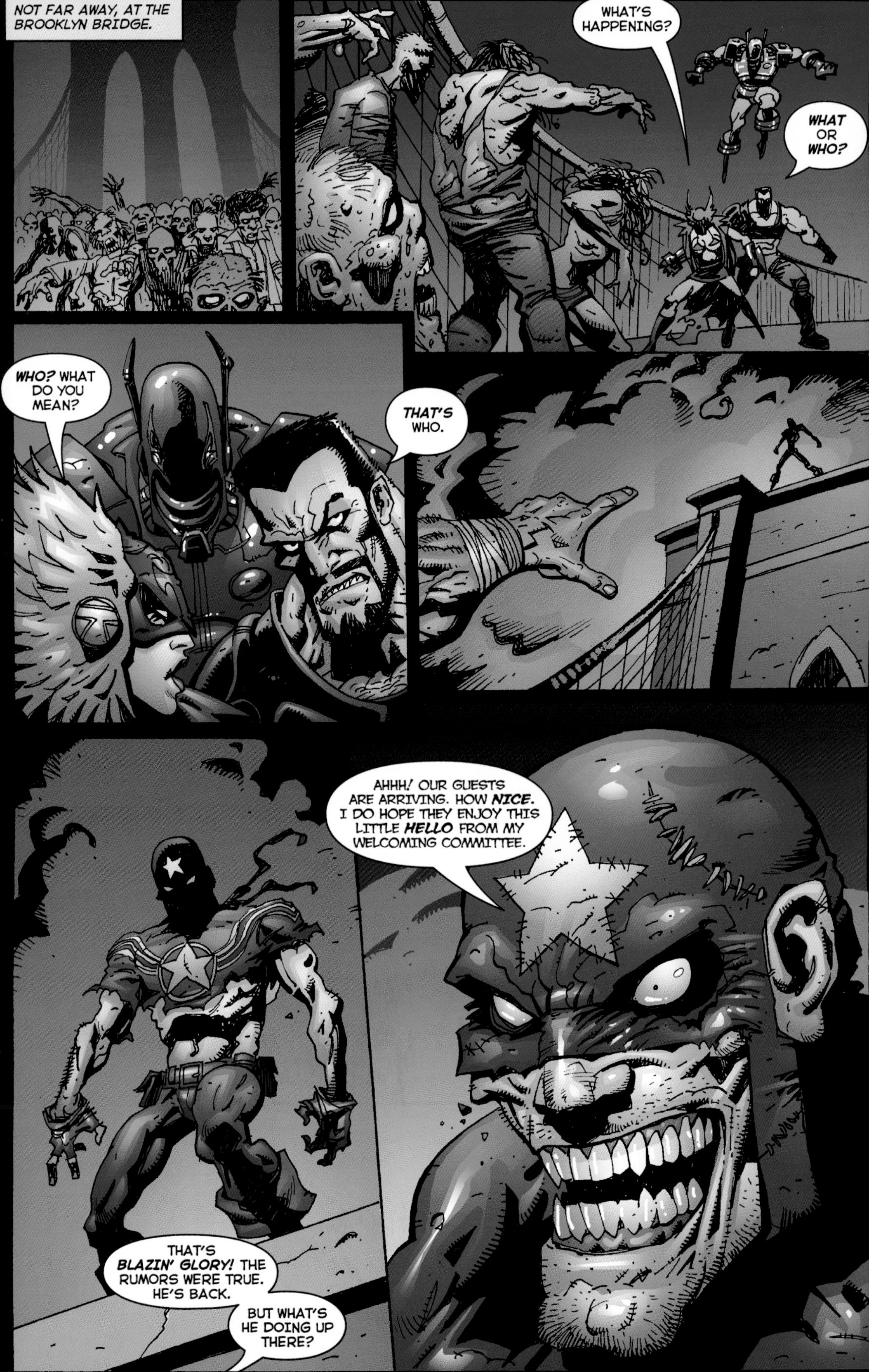
NOT FAR AWAY, AT THE BROOKLYN BRIDGE.
WHAT'S HAPPENING?
WHAT OR WHO?
WHO? WHAT DO YOU MEAN?
THAT'S WHO.
AHHH! OUR GUESTS ARE ARRIVING. HOW NICE. I DO HOPE THEY ENJOY THIS LITTLE HELLO FROM MY WELCOMING COMMITTEE.
THAT'S BLAZIN' GLORY! THE RUMORS WERE TRUE. HE'S BACK.
BUT WHAT'S HE DOING UP THERE?

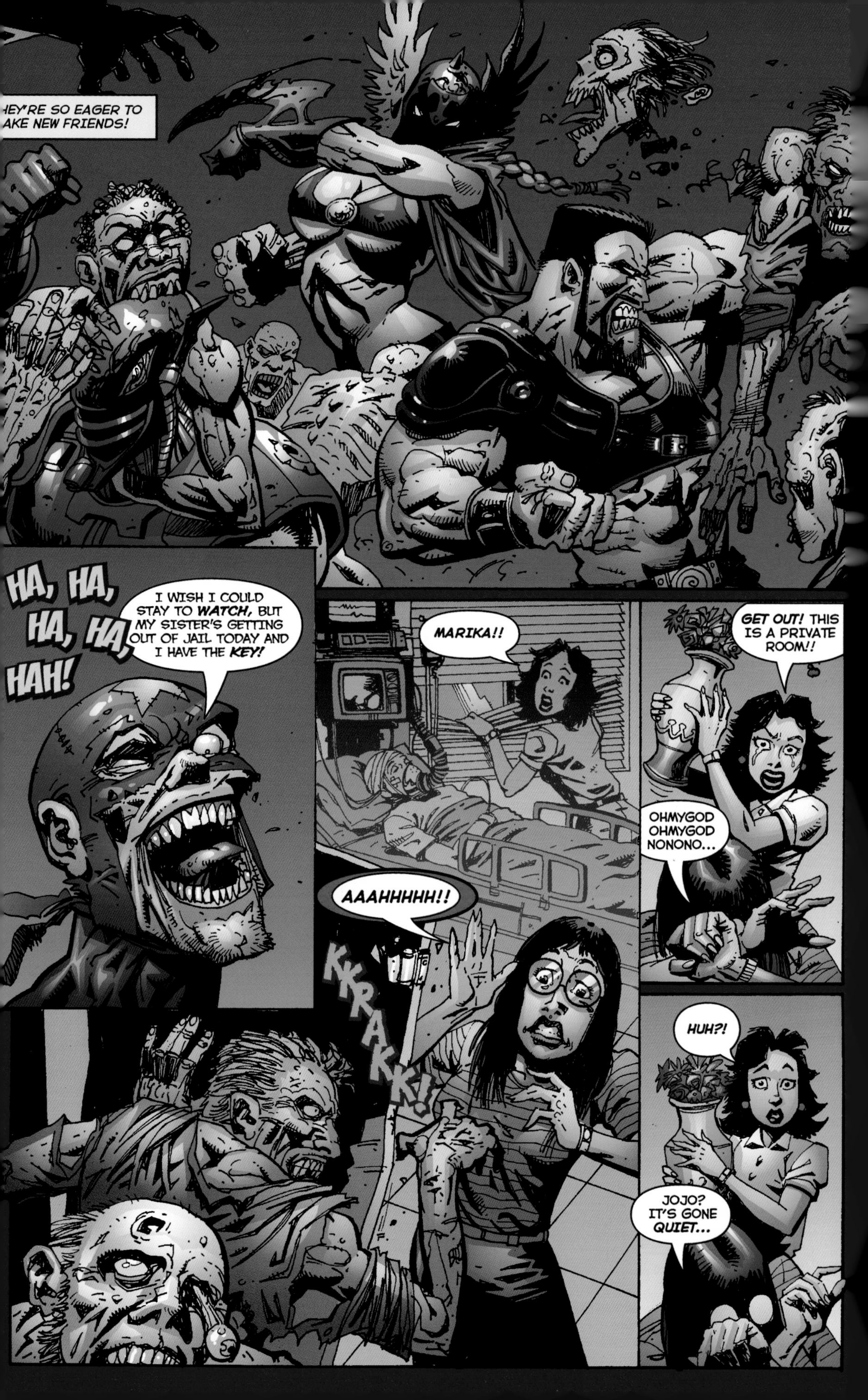
HEY'RE SO EAGER TO
AKE NEW FRIENDS!
HA, HA, HA, HA, HAH!
I WISH I COULD STAY TO WATCH, BUT MY SISTER'S GETTING OUT OF JAIL TODAY AND I HAVE THE KEY!
MARIKA!!
AAAHHHHH!!
KKRAKK!
GET OUT! THIS IS A PRIVATE ROOM!!
OHMYGOD OHMYGOD NONONO...
HUH?!
JOJO? IT'S GONE QUIET...

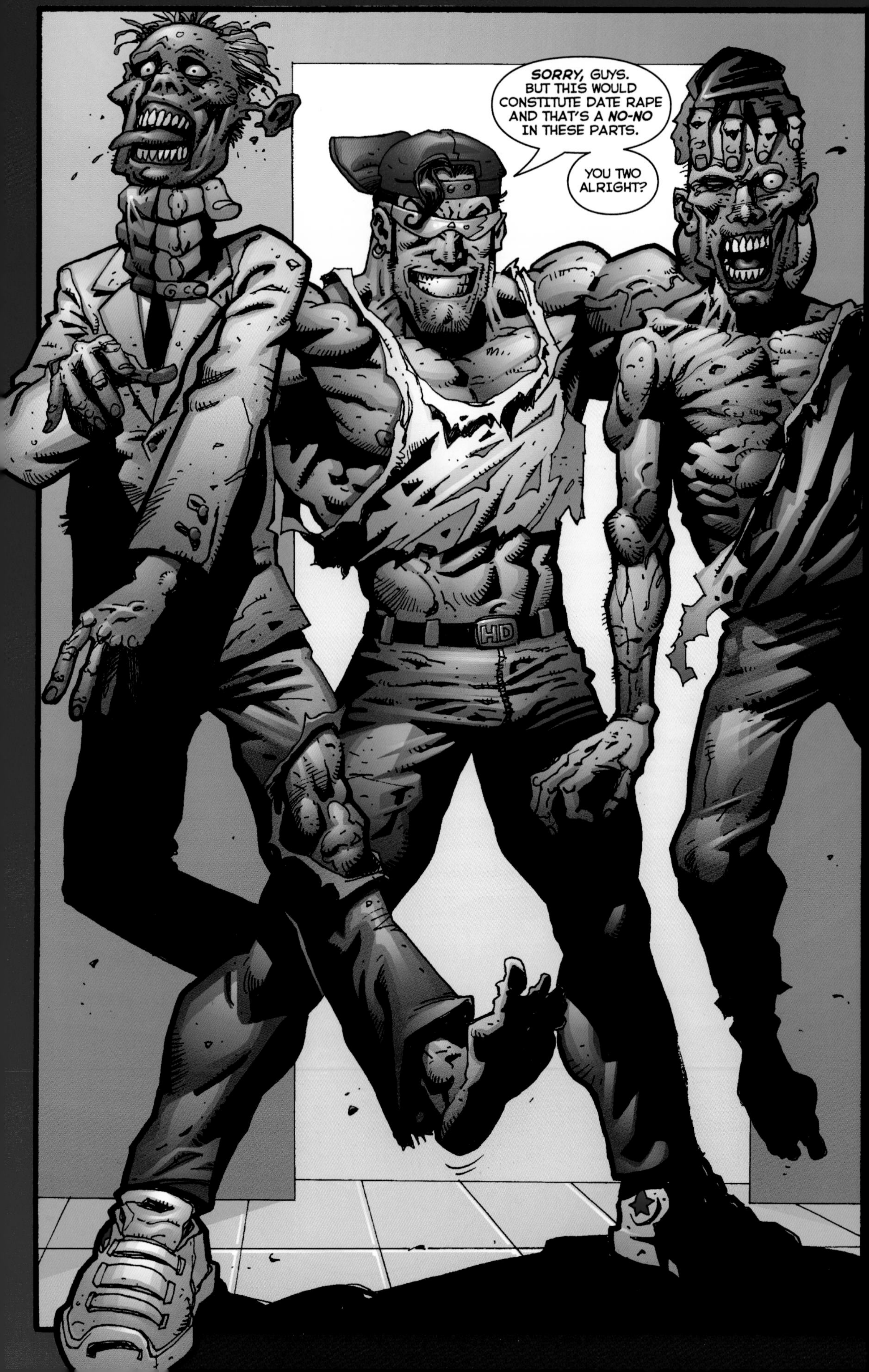
SORRY, GUYS. BUT THIS WOULD CONSTITUTE DATE RAPE AND THAT'S A NO-NO IN THESE PARTS.
YOU TWO ALRIGHT?

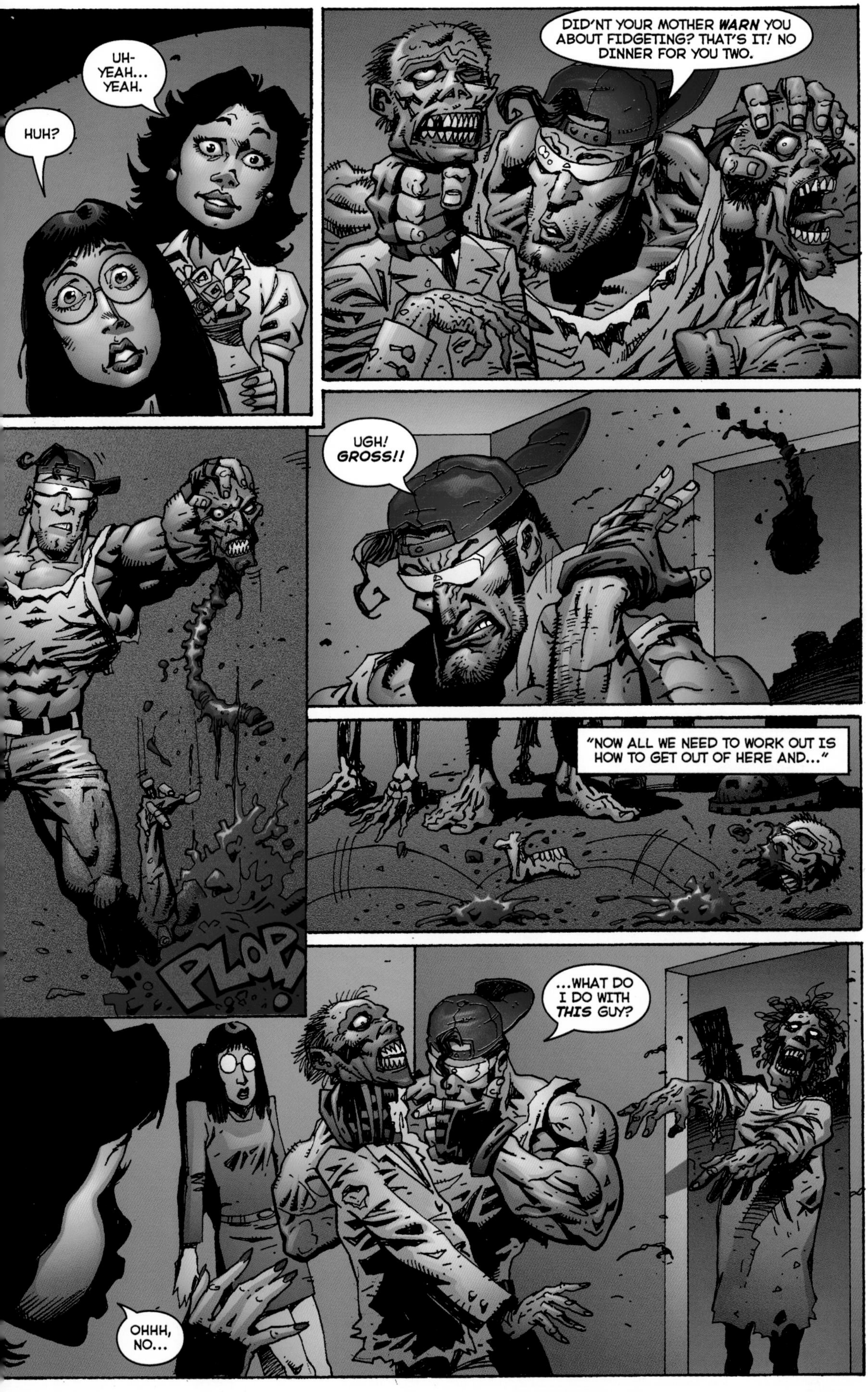
UH- YEAH... YEAH.
HUH?
DID'NT YOUR MOTHER **WARN** YOU ABOUT FIDGETING? THAT'S IT! NO DINNER FOR YOU TWO.
UGH! **GROSS!!**
PLOP
"NOW ALL WE NEED TO WORK OUT IS HOW TO GET OUT OF HERE AND..."
...WHAT DO I DO WITH **THIS** GUY?
OHHH, NO...

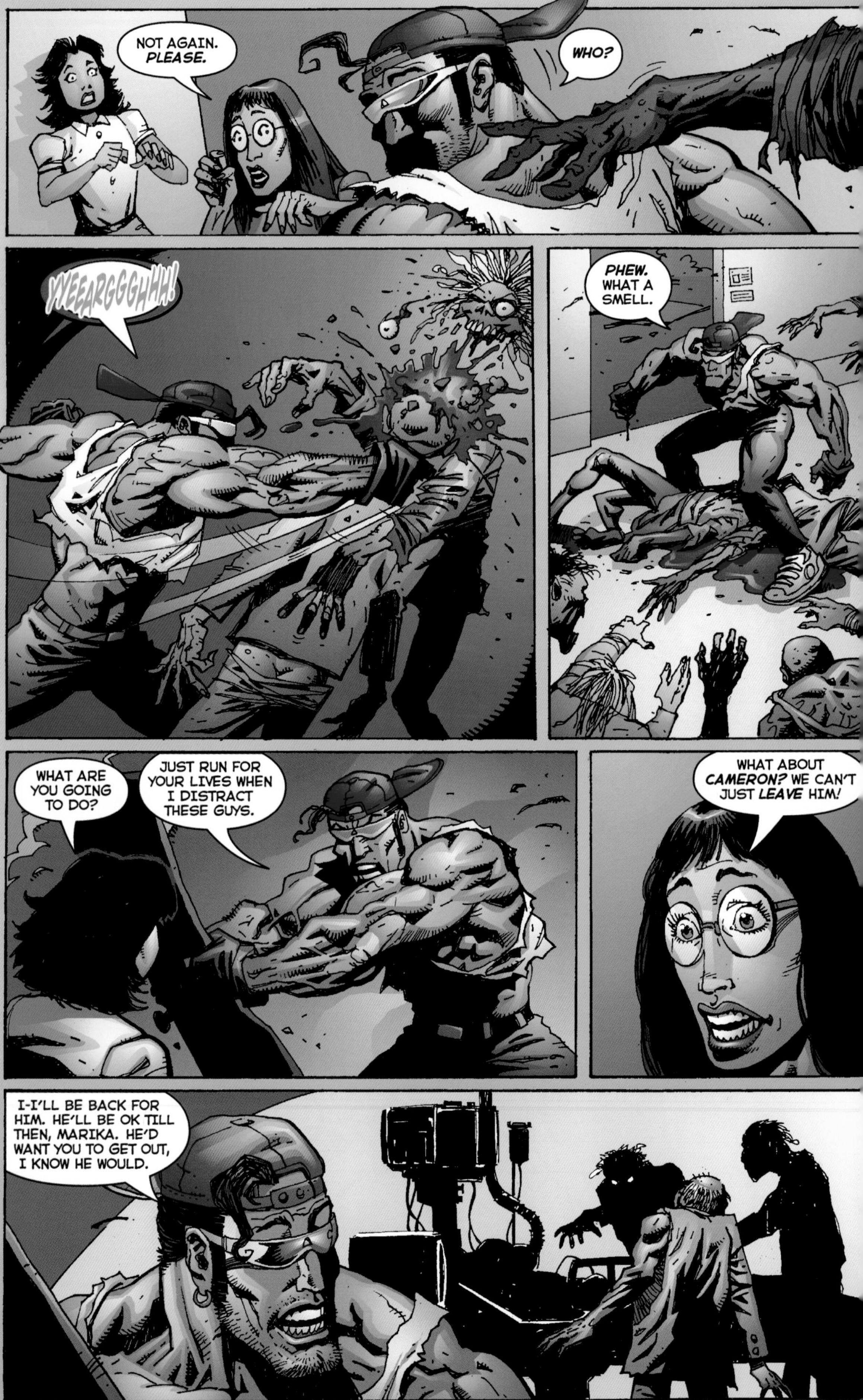
NOT AGAIN. PLEASE.
WHO?
YYEEARGGGHHH!
PHEW. WHAT A SMELL.
WHAT ARE YOU GOING TO DO?
JUST RUN FOR YOUR LIVES WHEN I DISTRACT THESE GUYS.
WHAT ABOUT CAMERON? WE CAN'T JUST LEAVE HIM!
I-I'LL BE BACK FOR HIM. HE'LL BE OK TILL THEN, MARIKA. HE'D WANT YOU TO GET OUT, I KNOW HE WOULD.

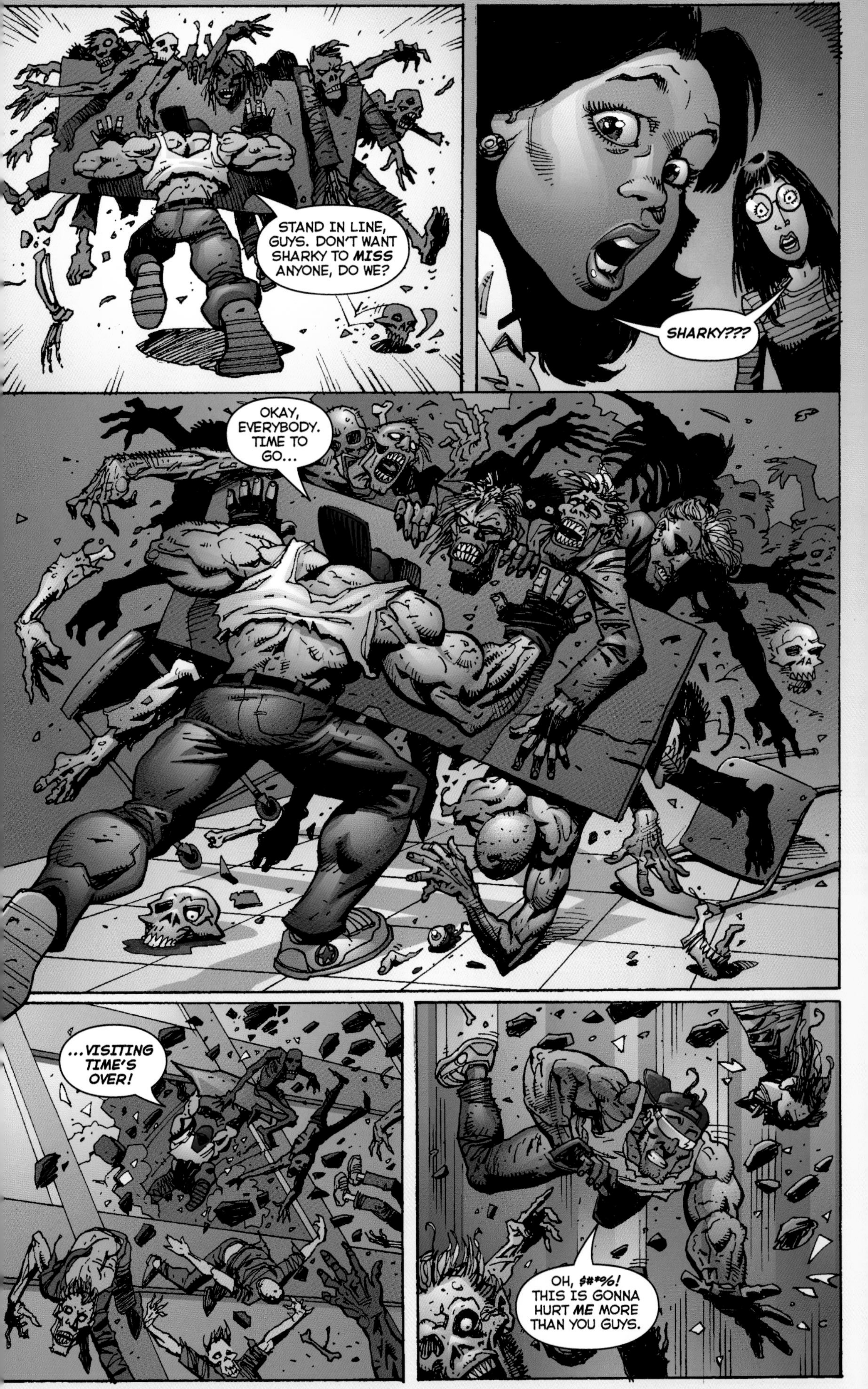
STAND IN LINE, GUYS. DON'T WANT SHARKY TO *MISS* ANYONE, DO WE?
SHARKY???
OKAY, EVERYBODY. TIME TO GO...
...VISITING TIME'S OVER!
OH, $#*%! THIS IS GONNA HURT *ME* MORE THAN YOU GUYS.

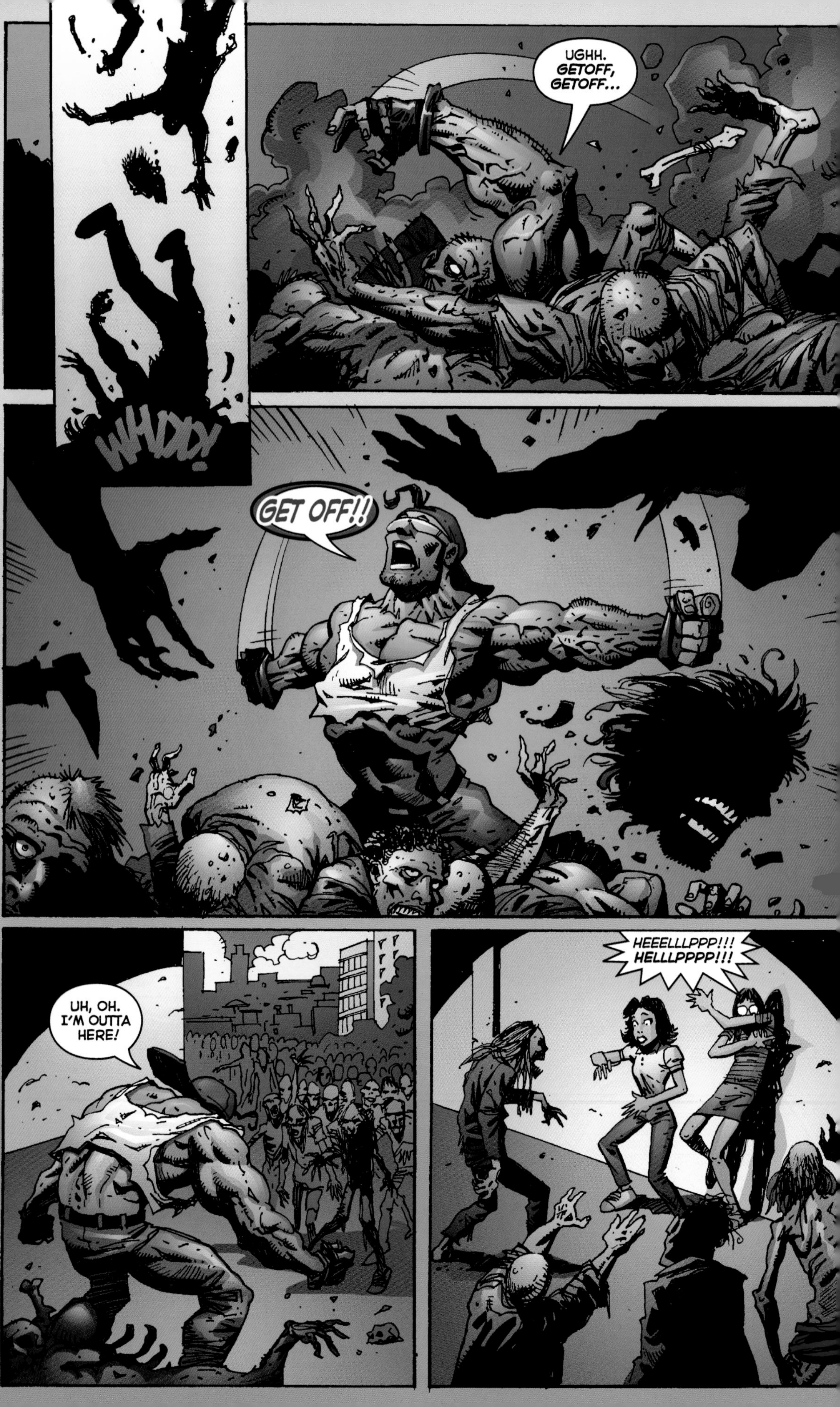
UGHH. GETOFF, GETOFF...
WHDD!
GET OFF!!
UH, OH. I'M OUTTA HERE!
HEEELLLPPP!!! HELLLPPPP!!!

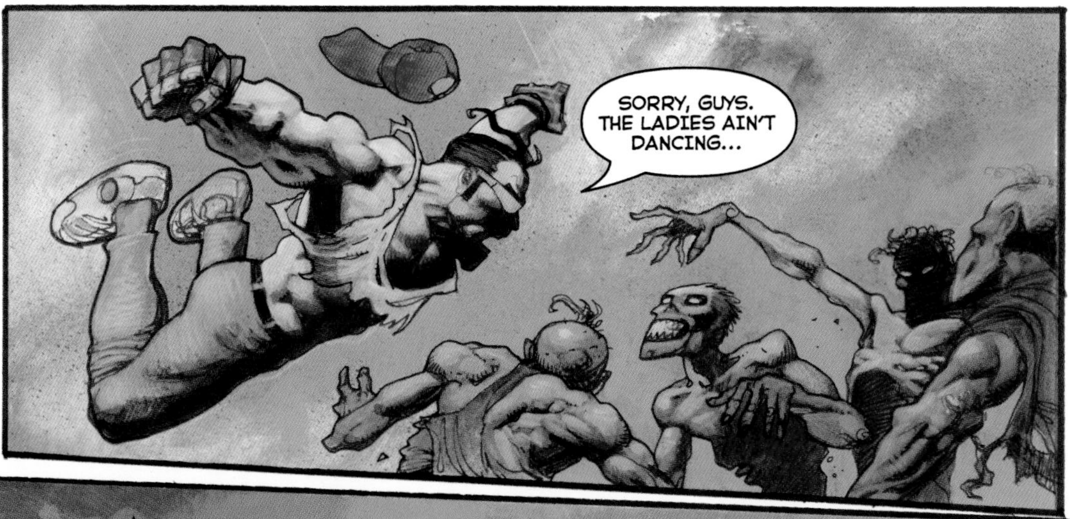
SORRY, GUYS. THE LADIES AIN'T DANCING...

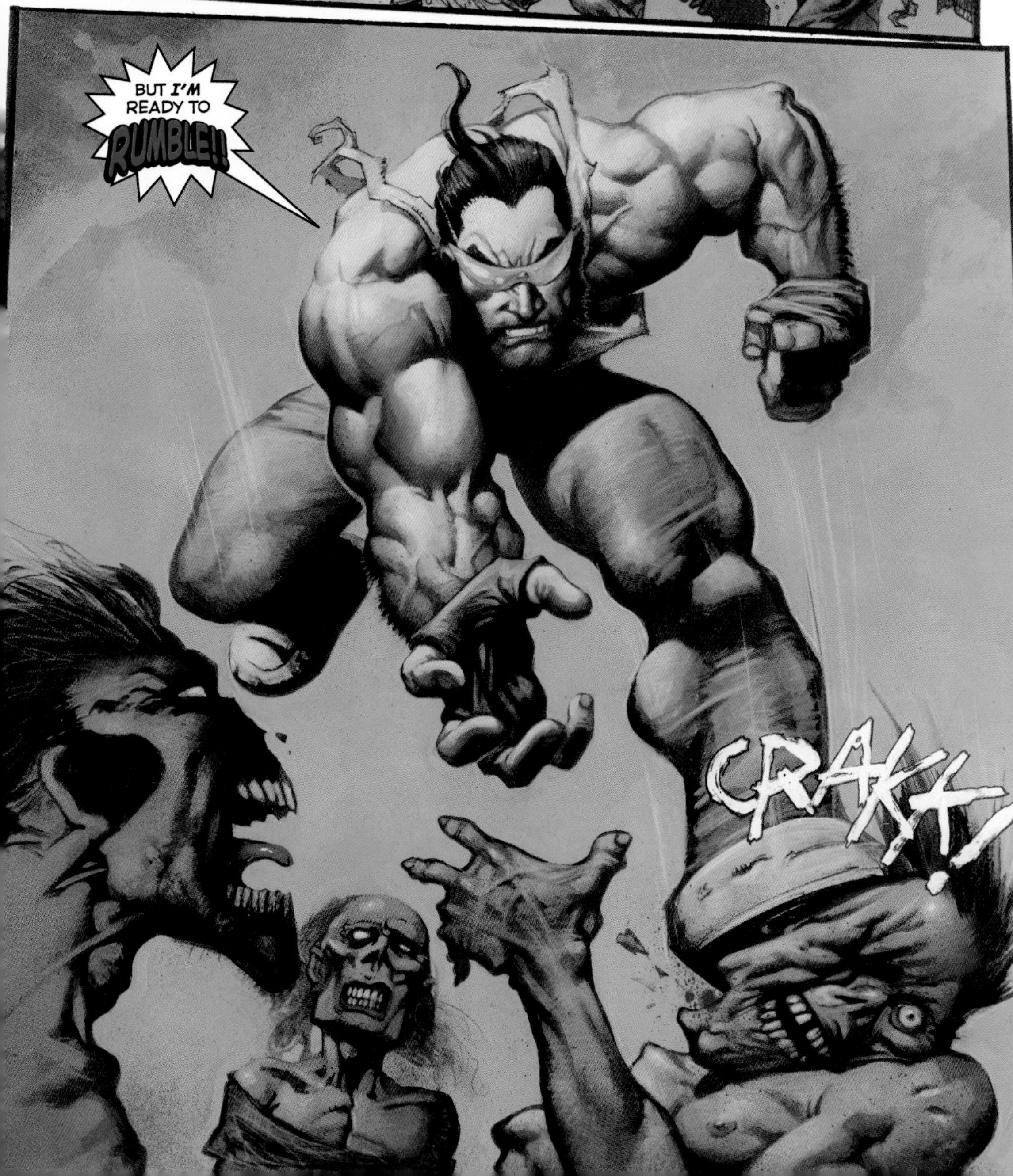
BUT I'M READY TO RUMBLE!!
CRAKK!

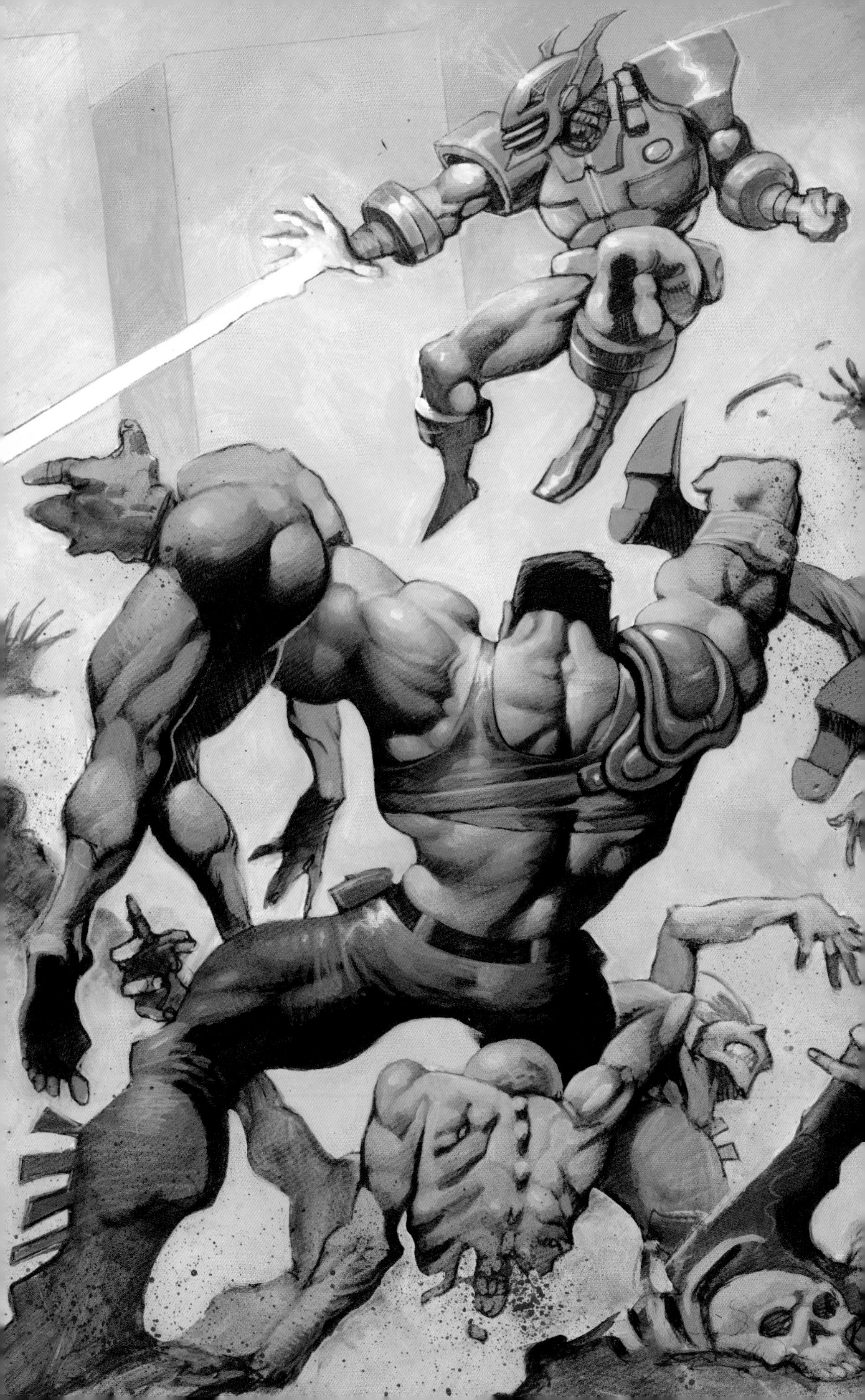

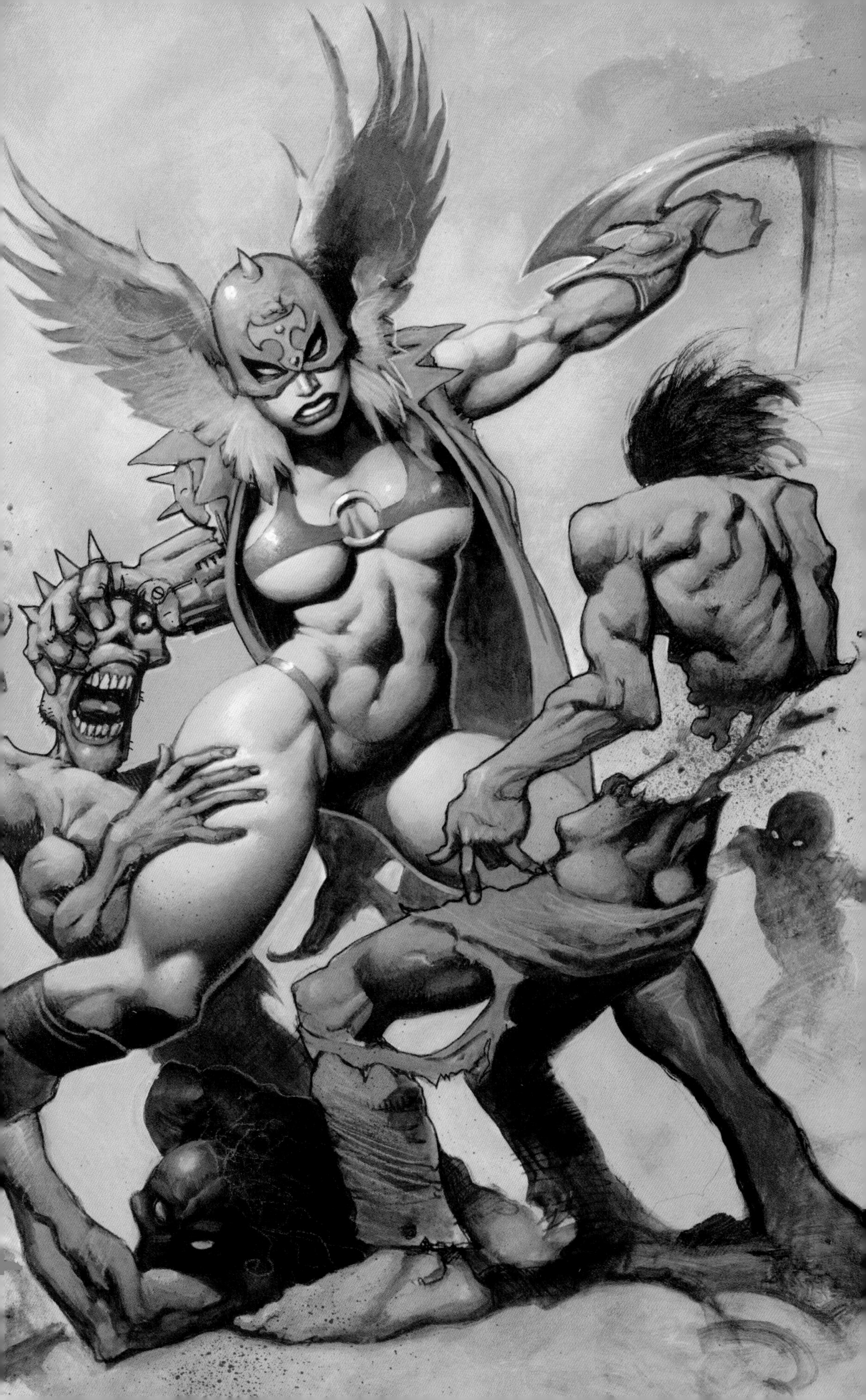

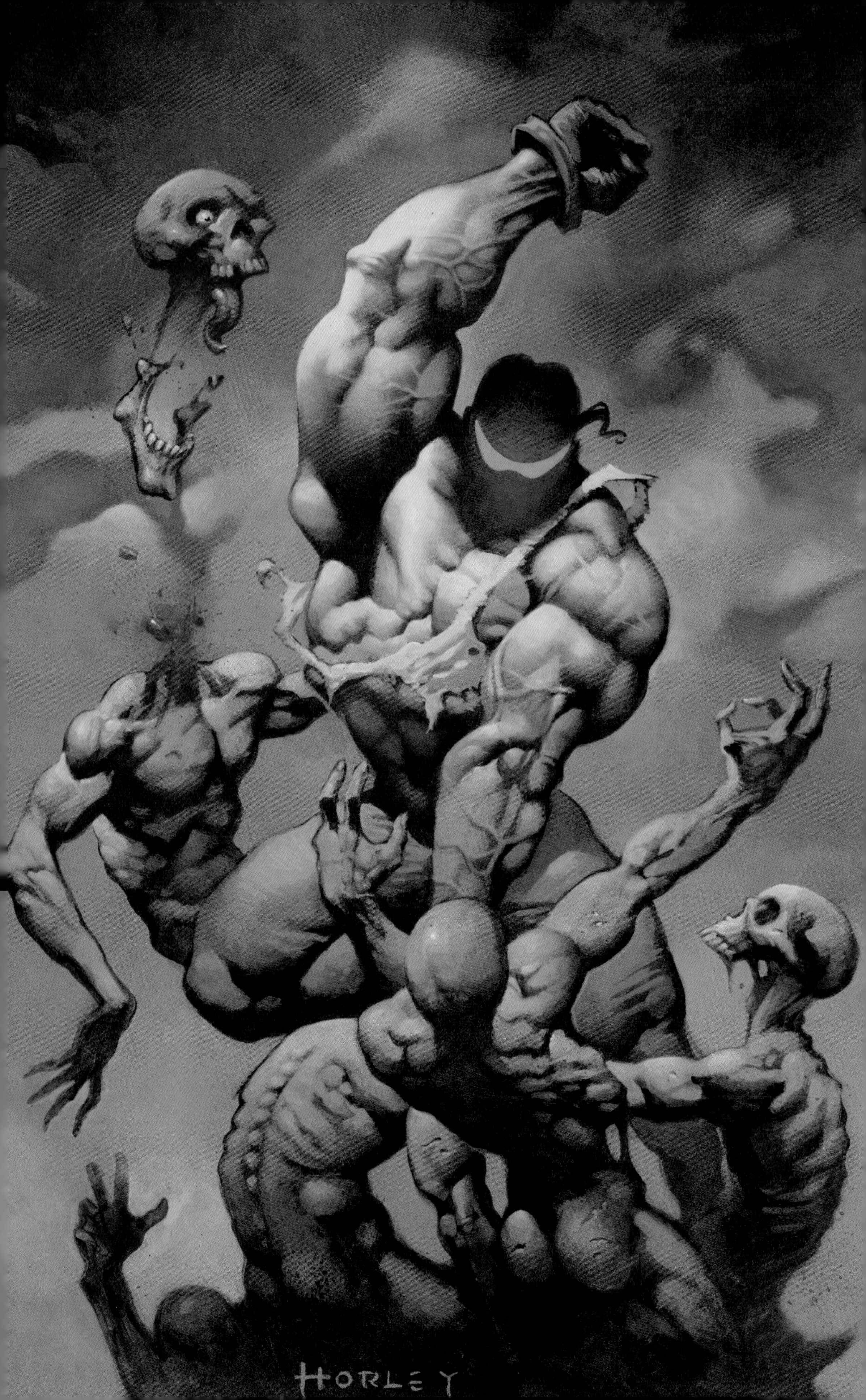
HORLEY

STERN INDUSTRIES, THE BIGGEST PRIVATE COMPANY IN THE WORLD.

IT WORKS HAND IN HAND WITH ALMOST EVERY MAJOR GOVERNMENT.

I SHOULD *LEAVE* YOU HERE AFTER WHAT YOU *DID* TO ME...

BUT THAT DOES NOT MEAN IT CAN'T KEEP ITS OWN SECRETS.

...BUT BLOOD IS SUPPOSED TO BE THICKER THAN WATER. SHALL WE FIND OUT?

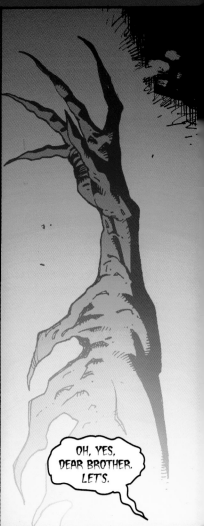

OH, YES, DEAR BROTHER. LET'S.

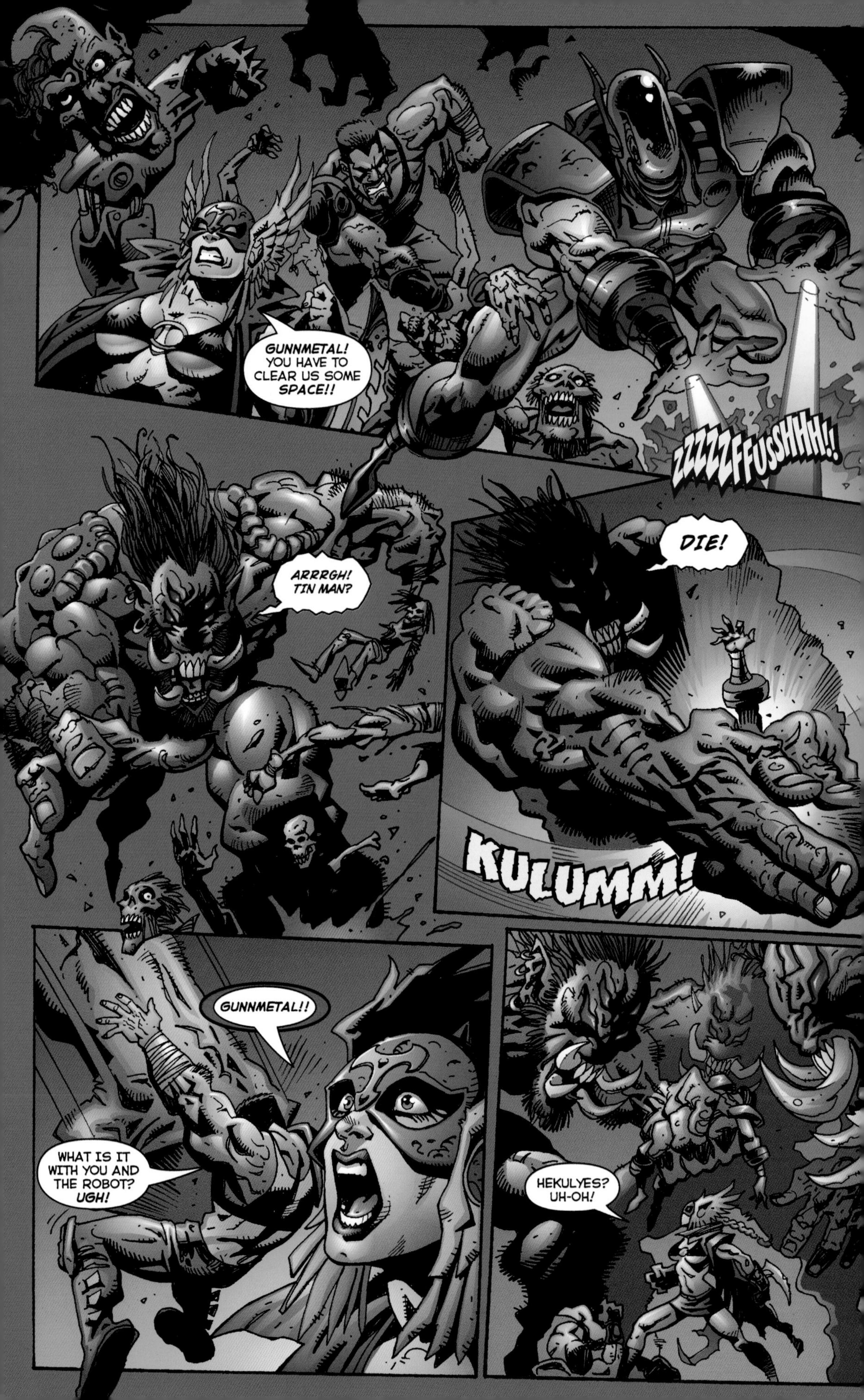
GUNNMETAL! YOU HAVE TO CLEAR US SOME SPACE!!
ZZZZZFFUSSHHH!!
ARRRGH! TIN MAN?
DIE!
KULUMM!
GUNNMETAL!!
WHAT IS IT WITH YOU AND THE ROBOT? UGH!
HEKULYES? UH-OH!

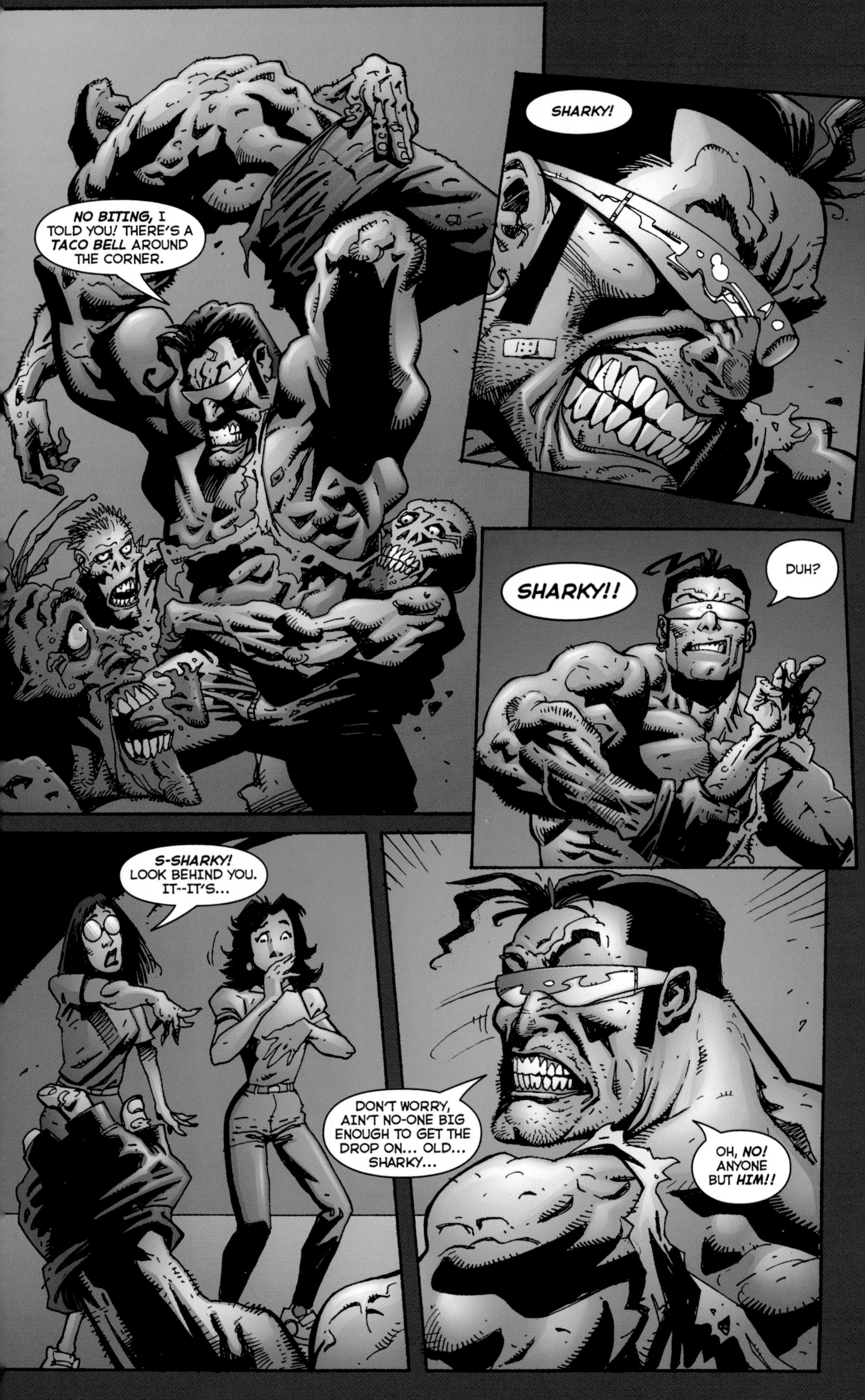

NO BITING, I TOLD YOU! THERE'S A TACO BELL AROUND THE CORNER.
SHARKY!
SHARKY!!
DUH?
S-SHARKY! LOOK BEHIND YOU. IT--IT'S...
DON'T WORRY, AIN'T NO-ONE BIG ENOUGH TO GET THE DROP ON... OLD... SHARKY...
OH, NO! ANYONE BUT HIM!!

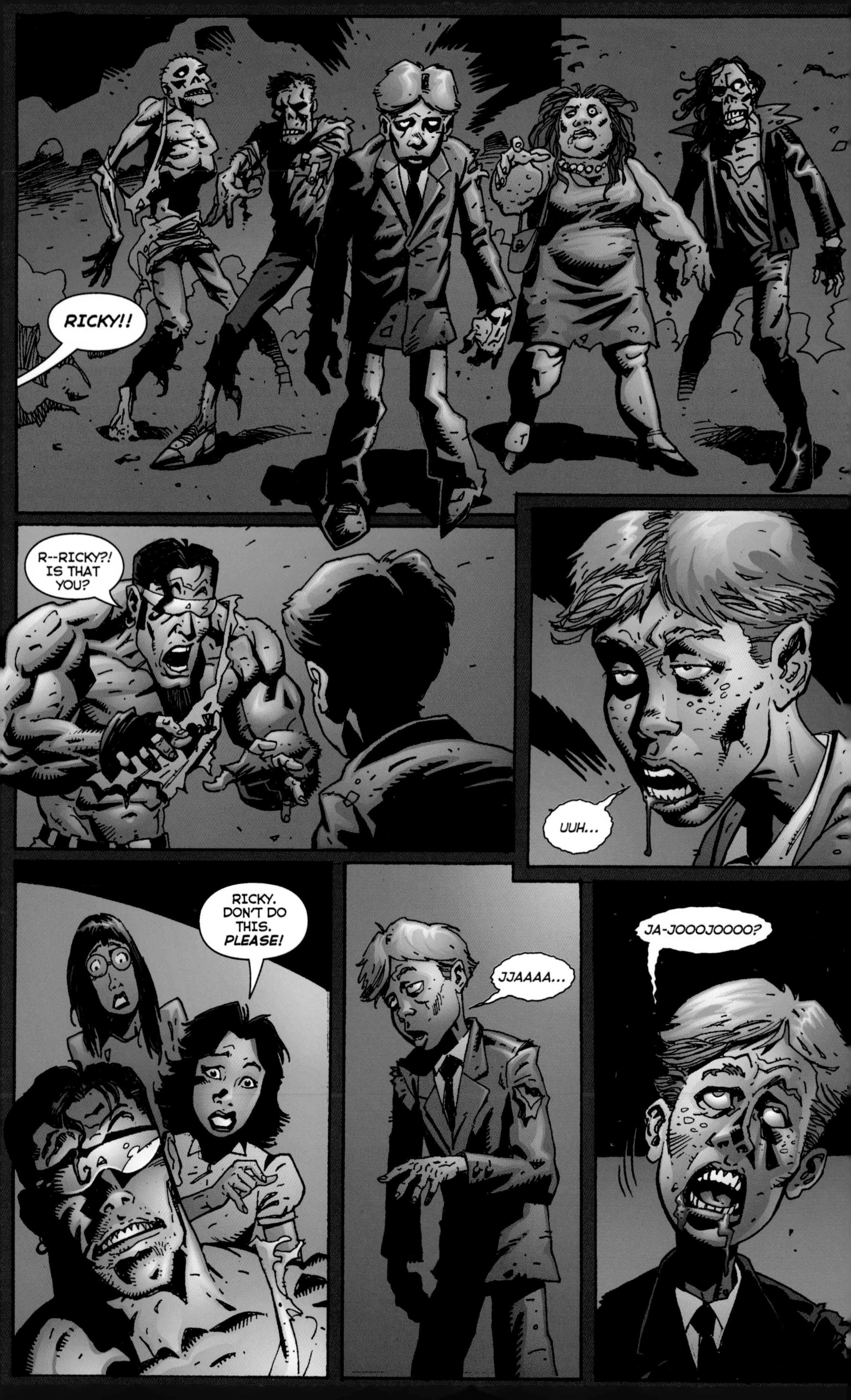
RICKY!!
R--RICKY?! IS THAT YOU?
UUH...
RICKY. DON'T DO THIS. PLEASE!
JJAAAA...
JA-JOOOJOOOO?

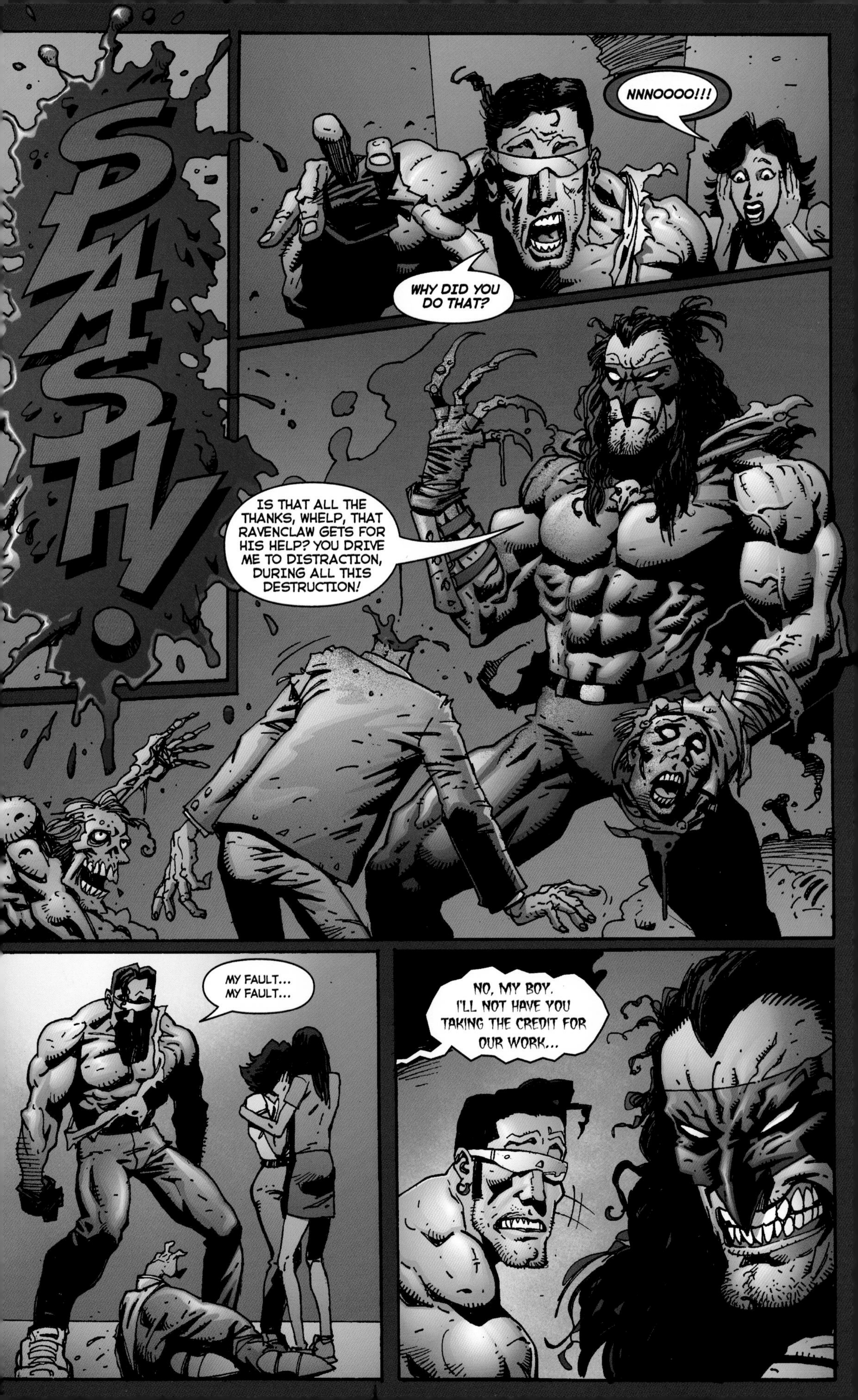
SPLASH!
NNNOOOO!!!
WHY DID YOU DO THAT?
IS THAT ALL THE THANKS, WHELP, THAT RAVENCLAW GETS FOR HIS HELP? YOU DRIVE ME TO DISTRACTION, DURING ALL THIS DESTRUCTION!
MY FAULT... MY FAULT...
NO, MY BOY. I'LL NOT HAVE YOU TAKING THE CREDIT FOR OUR WORK...

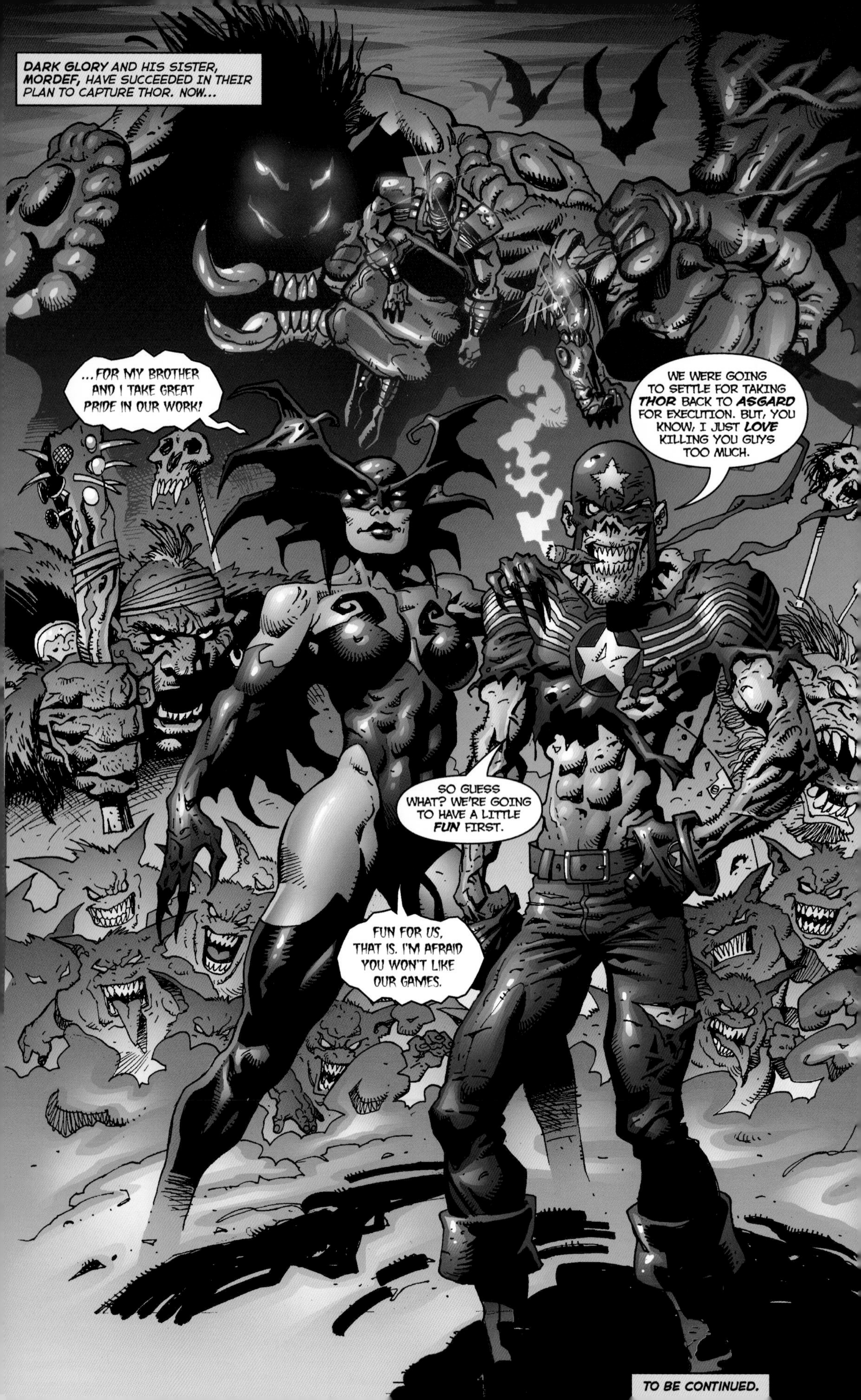
DARK GLORY AND HIS SISTER, MORDEF, HAVE SUCCEEDED IN THEIR PLAN TO CAPTURE THOR. NOW...
...FOR MY BROTHER AND I TAKE GREAT PRIDE IN OUR WORK!
WE WERE GOING TO SETTLE FOR TAKING THOR BACK TO ASGARD FOR EXECUTION. BUT, YOU KNOW, I JUST LOVE KILLING YOU GUYS TOO MUCH.
SO GUESS WHAT? WE'RE GOING TO HAVE A LITTLE FUN FIRST.
FUN FOR US, THAT IS. I'M AFRAID YOU WON'T LIKE OUR GAMES.
TO BE CONTINUED.

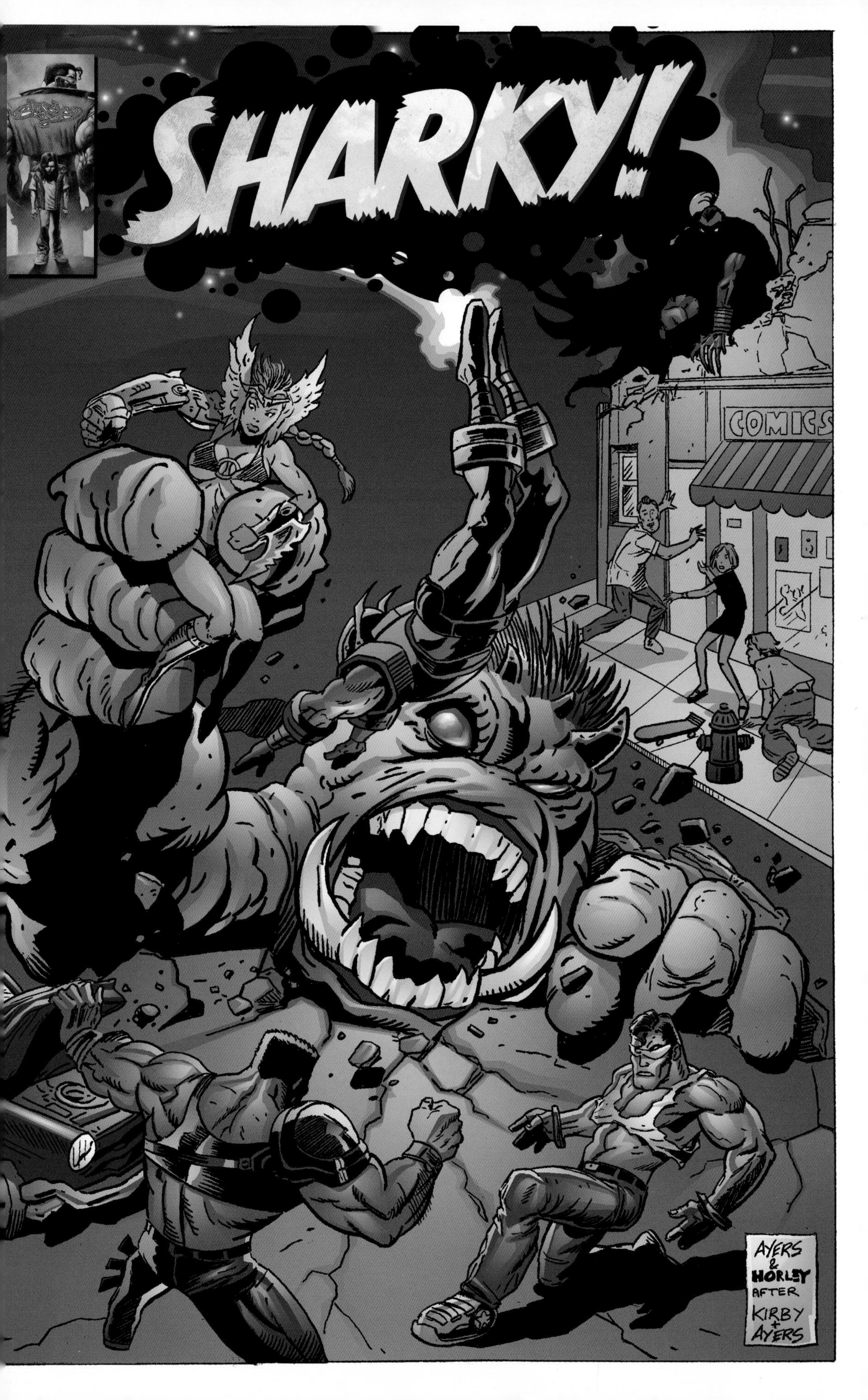
SHARKY!
COMICS
AYERS & HORLEY AFTER KIRBY + AYERS

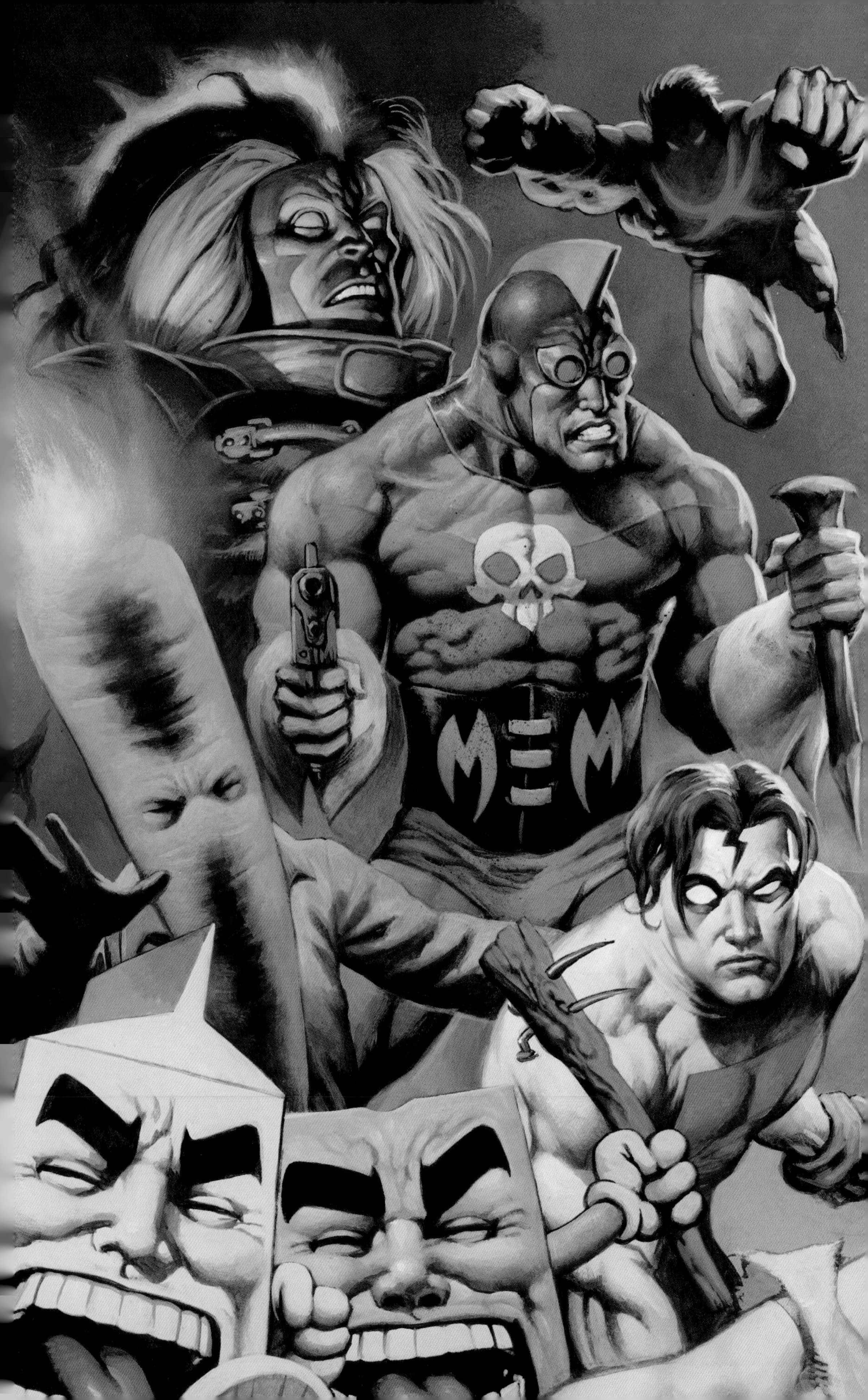

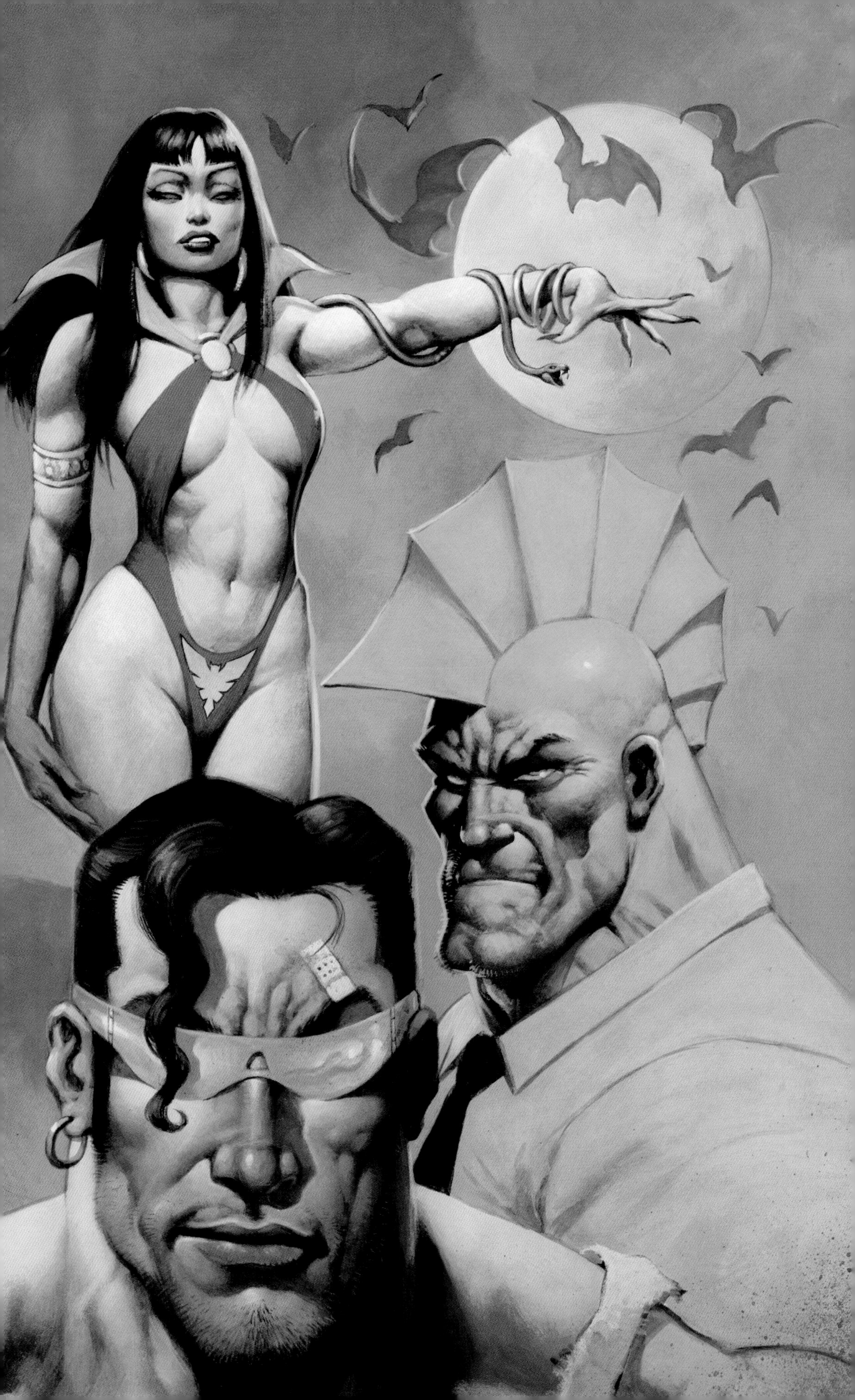

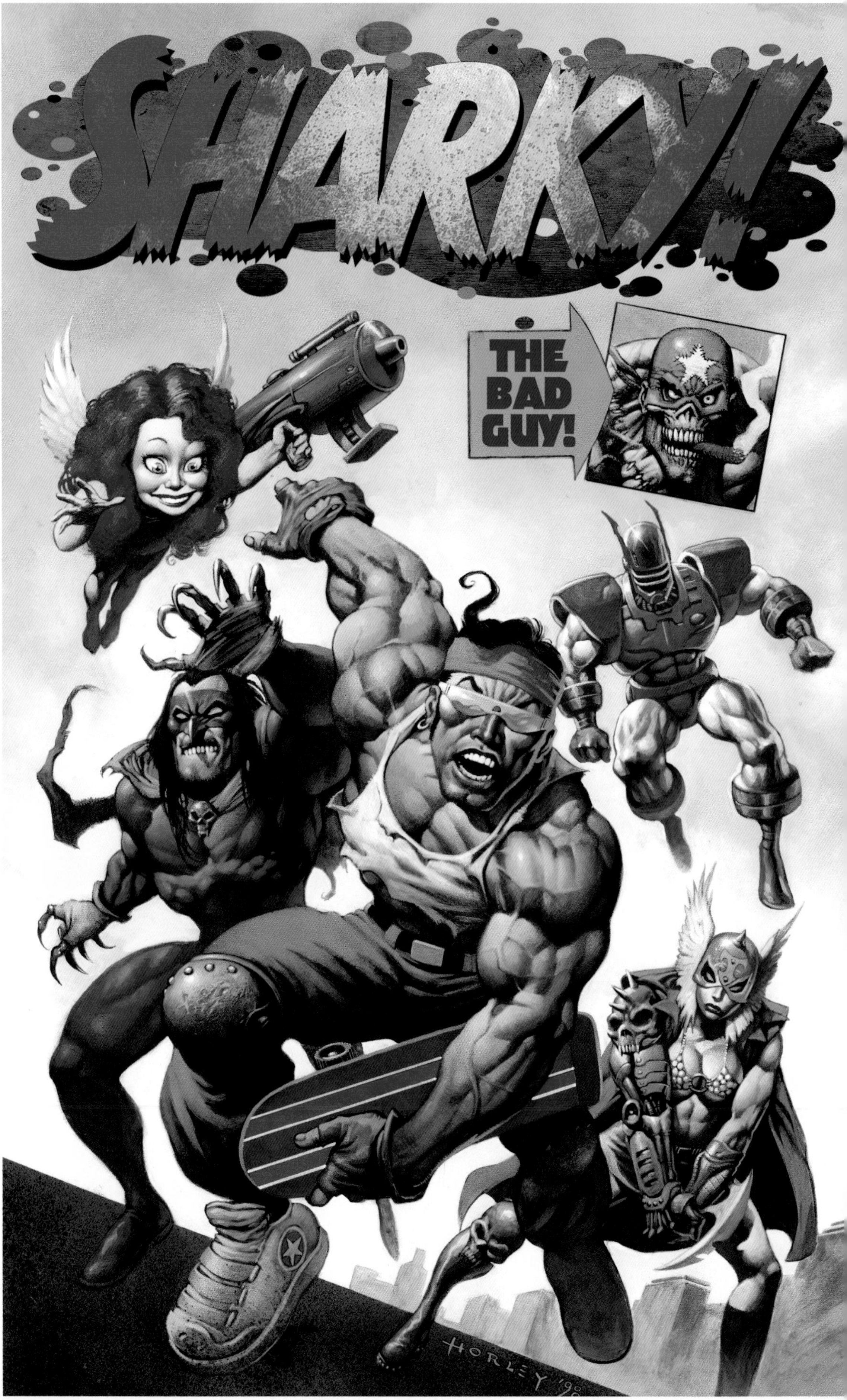
SHARKY!
THE BAD GUY!
HORLEY '98

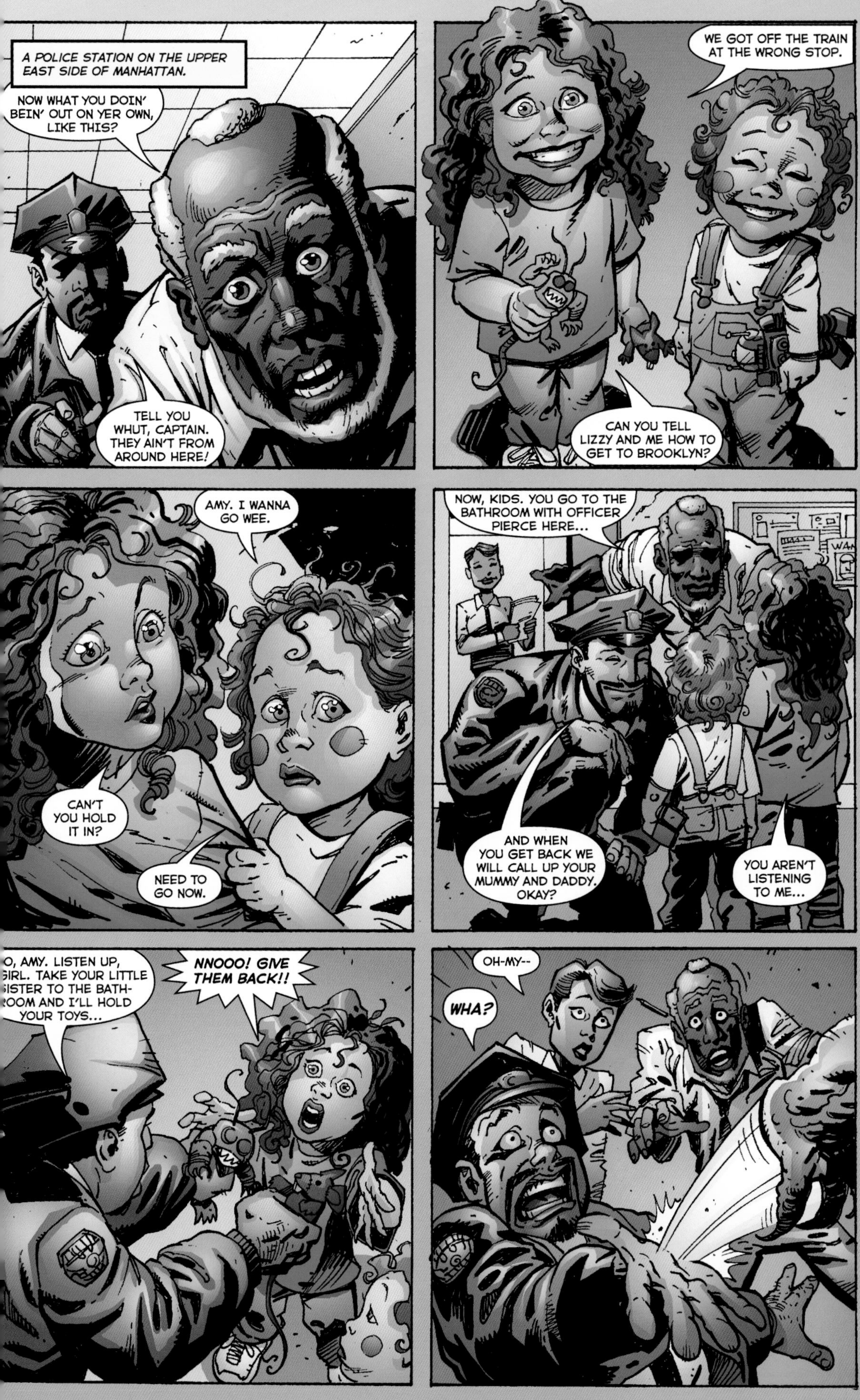

A POLICE STATION ON THE UPPER EAST SIDE OF MANHATTAN.
NOW WHAT YOU DOIN' BEIN' OUT ON YER OWN, LIKE THIS?
TELL YOU WHUT, CAPTAIN. THEY AIN'T FROM AROUND HERE!
WE GOT OFF THE TRAIN AT THE WRONG STOP.
CAN YOU TELL LIZZY AND ME HOW TO GET TO BROOKLYN?
AMY. I WANNA GO WEE.
CAN'T YOU HOLD IT IN?
NEED TO GO NOW.
NOW, KIDS. YOU GO TO THE BATHROOM WITH OFFICER PIERCE HERE...
AND WHEN YOU GET BACK WE WILL CALL UP YOUR MUMMY AND DADDY. OKAY?
YOU AREN'T LISTENING TO ME...
O, AMY. LISTEN UP, GIRL. TAKE YOUR LITTLE SISTER TO THE BATH-ROOM AND I'LL HOLD YOUR TOYS...
NNOOO! GIVE THEM BACK!!
OH-MY--
WHA?

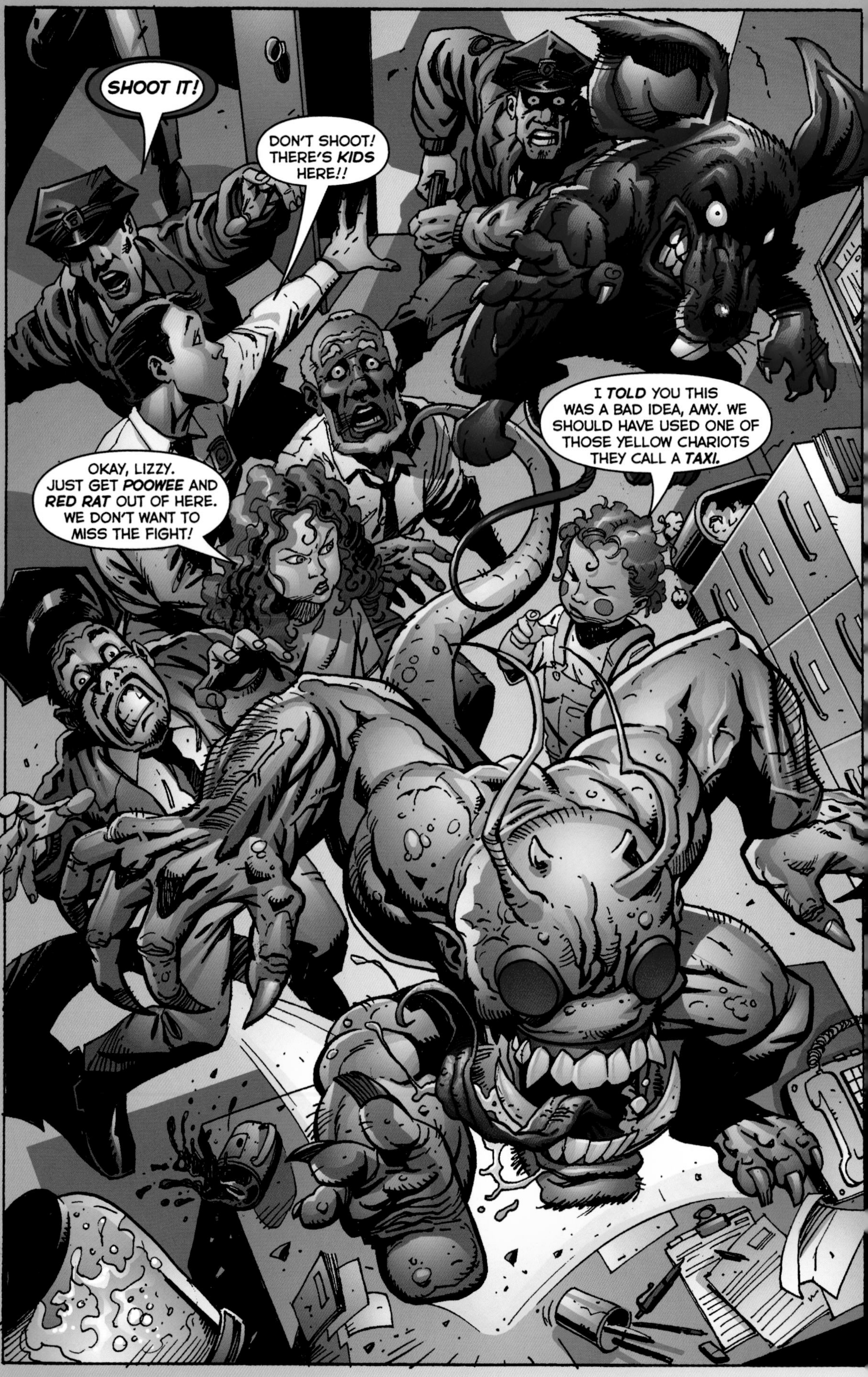
SHOOT IT!
DON'T SHOOT! THERE'S KIDS HERE!!
I TOLD YOU THIS WAS A BAD IDEA, AMY. WE SHOULD HAVE USED ONE OF THOSE YELLOW CHARIOTS THEY CALL A TAXI.
OKAY, LIZZY. JUST GET POOWEE AND RED RAT OUT OF HERE. WE DON'T WANT TO MISS THE FIGHT!

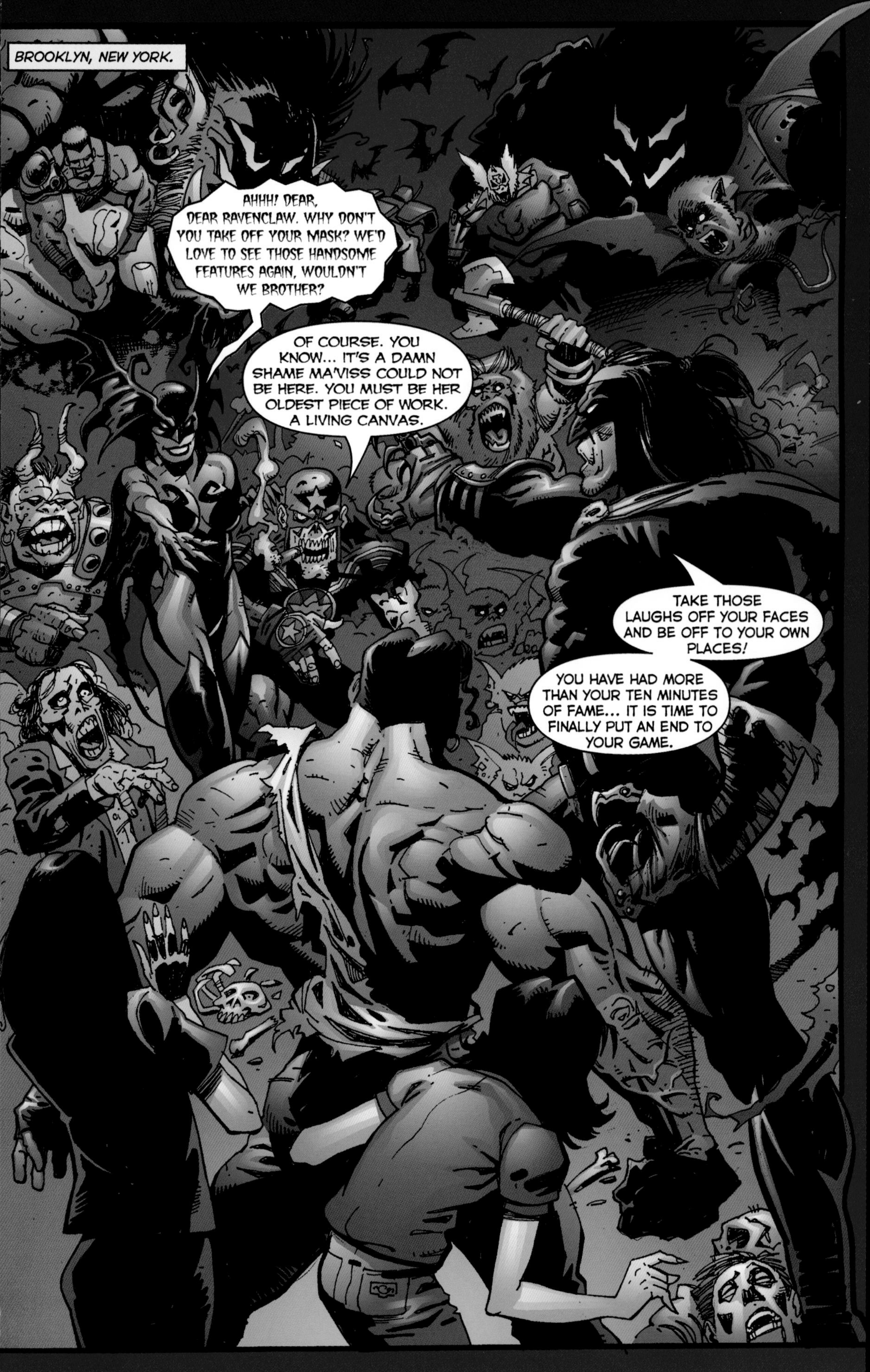
BROOKLYN, NEW YORK.
AHHH! DEAR, DEAR RAVENCLAW. WHY DON'T YOU TAKE OFF YOUR MASK? WE'D LOVE TO SEE THOSE HANDSOME FEATURES AGAIN, WOULDN'T WE BROTHER?
OF COURSE. YOU KNOW... IT'S A DAMN SHAME MA'VISS COULD NOT BE HERE. YOU MUST BE HER OLDEST PIECE OF WORK. A LIVING CANVAS.
TAKE THOSE LAUGHS OFF YOUR FACES AND BE OFF TO YOUR OWN PLACES!
YOU HAVE HAD MORE THAN YOUR TEN MINUTES OF FAME... IT IS TIME TO FINALLY PUT AN END TO YOUR GAME.

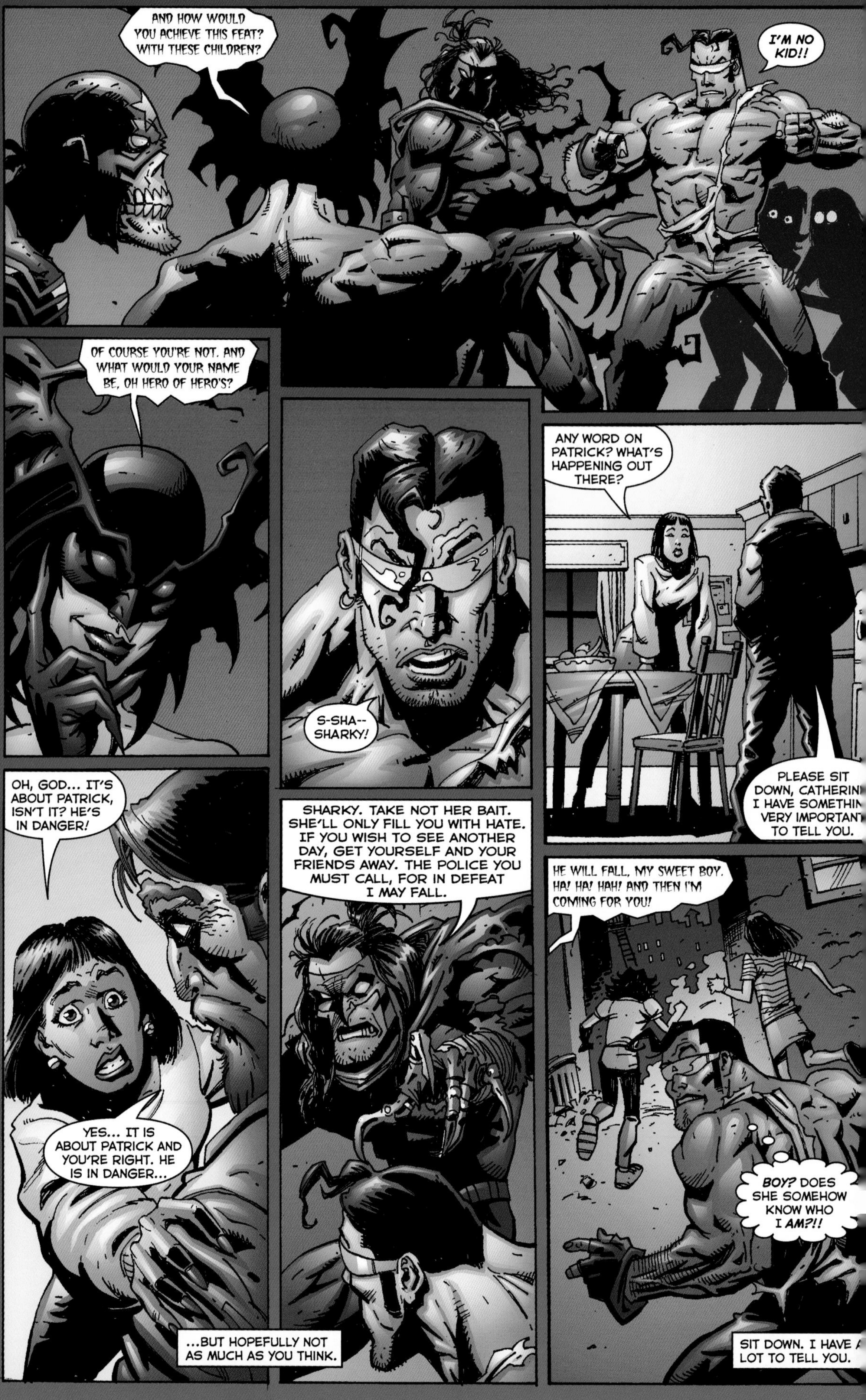
AND HOW WOULD YOU ACHIEVE THIS FEAT? WITH THESE CHILDREN?
I'M NO KID!!
OF COURSE YOU'RE NOT. AND WHAT WOULD YOUR NAME BE, OH HERO OF HERO'S?
S-SHA-- SHARKY!
ANY WORD ON PATRICK? WHAT'S HAPPENING OUT THERE?
PLEASE SIT DOWN, CATHERIN I HAVE SOMETHIN VERY IMPORTAN TO TELL YOU.
OH, GOD... IT'S ABOUT PATRICK, ISN'T IT? HE'S IN DANGER!
YES... IT IS ABOUT PATRICK AND YOU'RE RIGHT. HE IS IN DANGER...
...BUT HOPEFULLY NOT AS MUCH AS YOU THINK.
SHARKY. TAKE NOT HER BAIT. SHE'LL ONLY FILL YOU WITH HATE. IF YOU WISH TO SEE ANOTHER DAY, GET YOURSELF AND YOUR FRIENDS AWAY. THE POLICE YOU MUST CALL, FOR IN DEFEAT I MAY FALL.
HE WILL FALL, MY SWEET BOY. HA! HA! HAH! AND THEN I'M COMING FOR YOU!
BOY? DOES SHE SOMEHOW KNOW WHO I AM?!!
SIT DOWN. I HAVE A LOT TO TELL YOU.

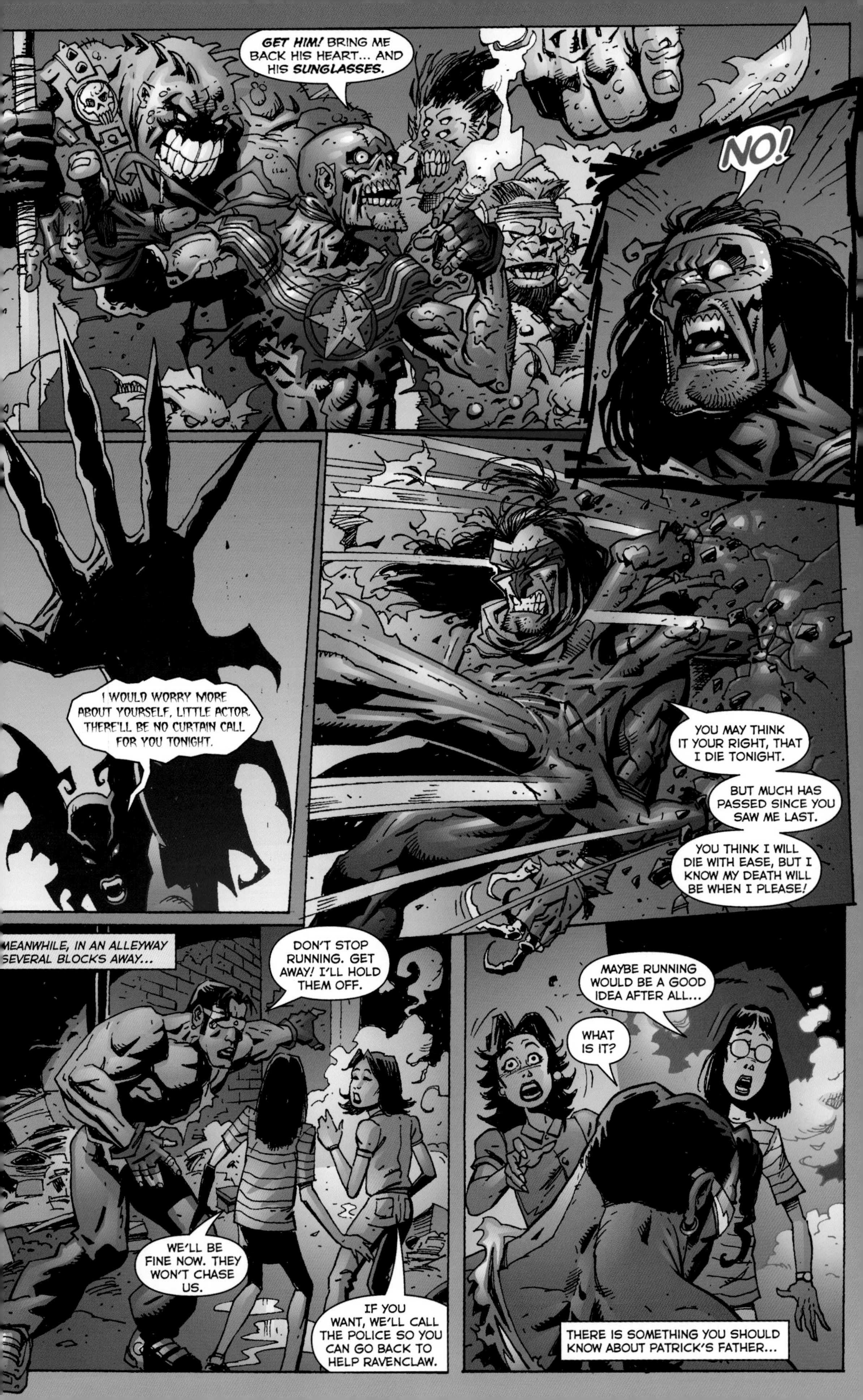
GET HIM! BRING ME BACK HIS HEART... AND HIS SUNGLASSES.
NO!
I WOULD WORRY MORE ABOUT YOURSELF, LITTLE ACTOR. THERE'LL BE NO CURTAIN CALL FOR YOU TONIGHT.
YOU MAY THINK IT YOUR RIGHT, THAT I DIE TONIGHT.
BUT MUCH HAS PASSED SINCE YOU SAW ME LAST.
YOU THINK I WILL DIE WITH EASE, BUT I KNOW MY DEATH WILL BE WHEN I PLEASE!
MEANWHILE, IN AN ALLEYWAY SEVERAL BLOCKS AWAY...
DON'T STOP RUNNING. GET AWAY! I'LL HOLD THEM OFF.
WE'LL BE FINE NOW. THEY WON'T CHASE US.
IF YOU WANT, WE'LL CALL THE POLICE SO YOU CAN GO BACK TO HELP RAVENCLAW.
MAYBE RUNNING WOULD BE A GOOD IDEA AFTER ALL...
WHAT IS IT?
THERE IS SOMETHING YOU SHOULD KNOW ABOUT PATRICK'S FATHER...

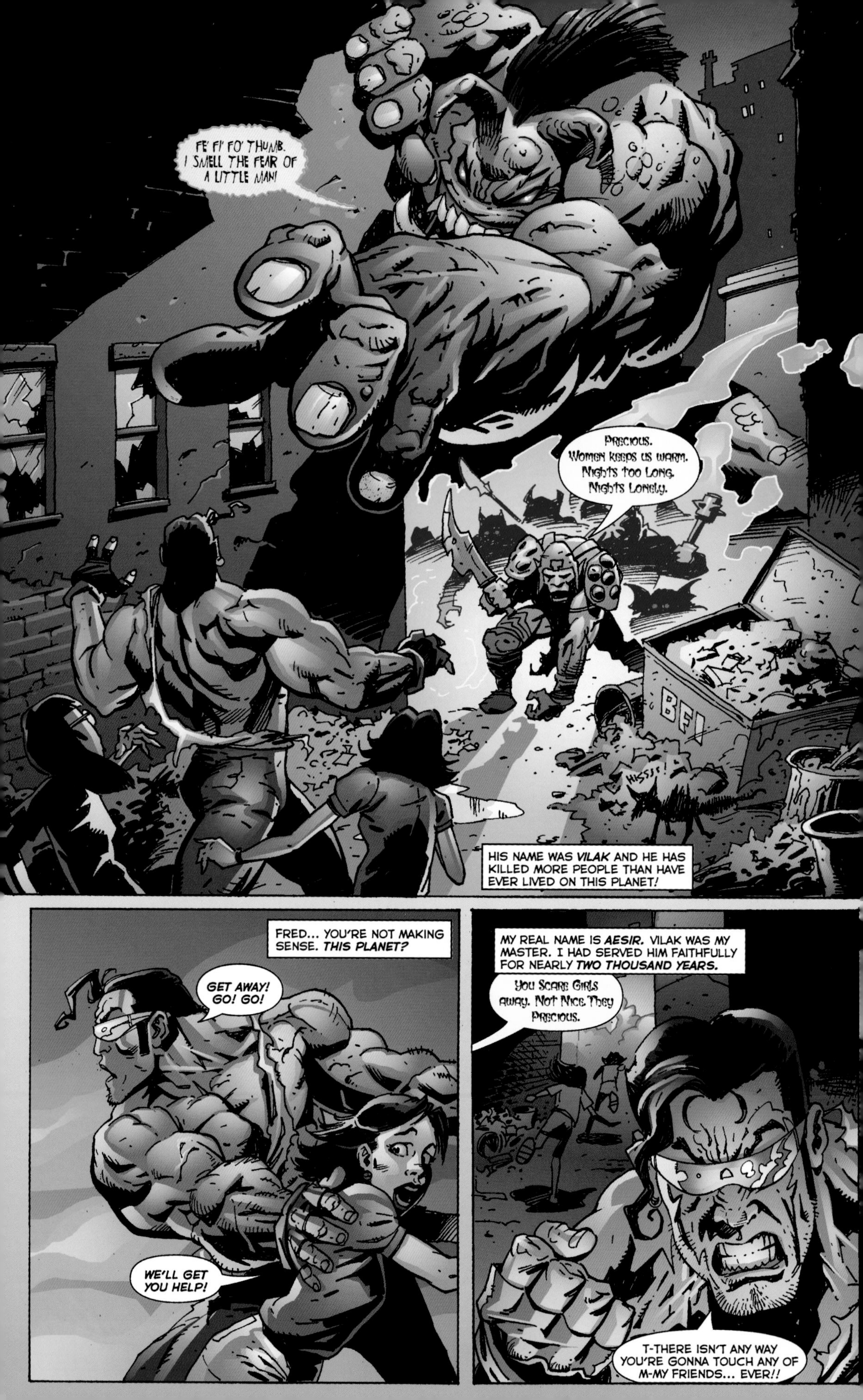
FE' FI' FO' THUMB. I SMELL THE FEAR OF A LITTLE MAN!
Precious. Women keeps us warm. Nights too Long. Nights Lonely.
HISSS!
BFI
HIS NAME WAS VILAK AND HE HAS KILLED MORE PEOPLE THAN HAVE EVER LIVED ON THIS PLANET!
FRED... YOU'RE NOT MAKING SENSE. THIS PLANET?
GET AWAY! GO! GO!
WE'LL GET YOU HELP!
MY REAL NAME IS AESIR. VILAK WAS MY MASTER. I HAD SERVED HIM FAITHFULLY FOR NEARLY TWO THOUSAND YEARS.
You Scare Girls away. Not Nice. They Precious.
T-THERE ISN'T ANY WAY YOU'RE GONNA TOUCH ANY OF M-MY FRIENDS... EVER!!

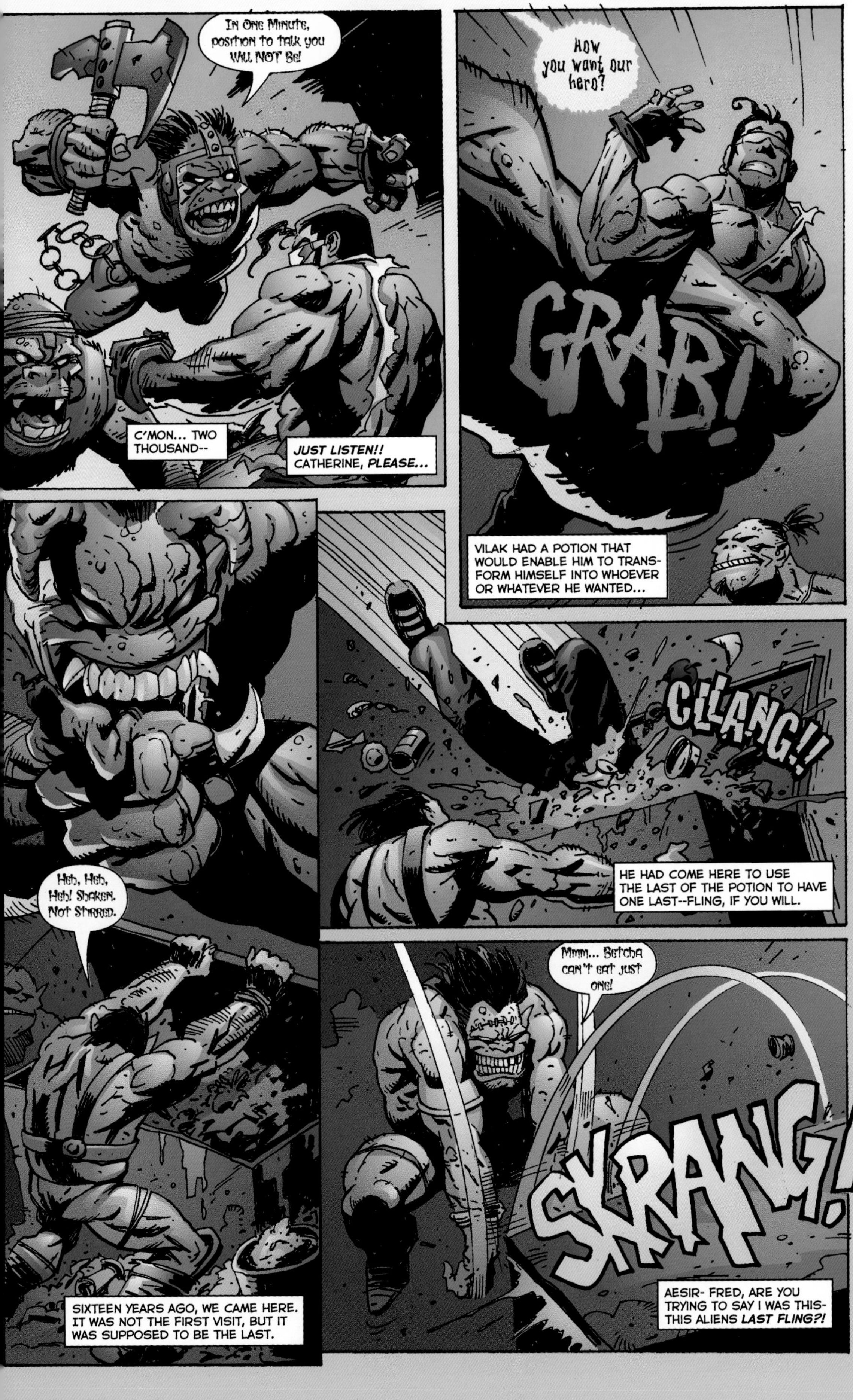
In One Minute, position to talk you will NOT Be!
C'MON... TWO THOUSAND--
JUST LISTEN!! CATHERINE, PLEASE...
How you want our hero?
GRAB!
VILAK HAD A POTION THAT WOULD ENABLE HIM TO TRANS-FORM HIMSELF INTO WHOEVER OR WHATEVER HE WANTED...
Heh, Heh, Heh! Shaken. Not Stirred.
CLLANG!!
HE HAD COME HERE TO USE THE LAST OF THE POTION TO HAVE ONE LAST--FLING, IF YOU WILL.
SIXTEEN YEARS AGO, WE CAME HERE. IT WAS NOT THE FIRST VISIT, BUT IT WAS SUPPOSED TO BE THE LAST.
Mmm... Betcha can't eat just one!
SKRANG!
AESIR- FRED, ARE YOU TRYING TO SAY I WAS THIS- THIS ALIENS LAST FLING?!

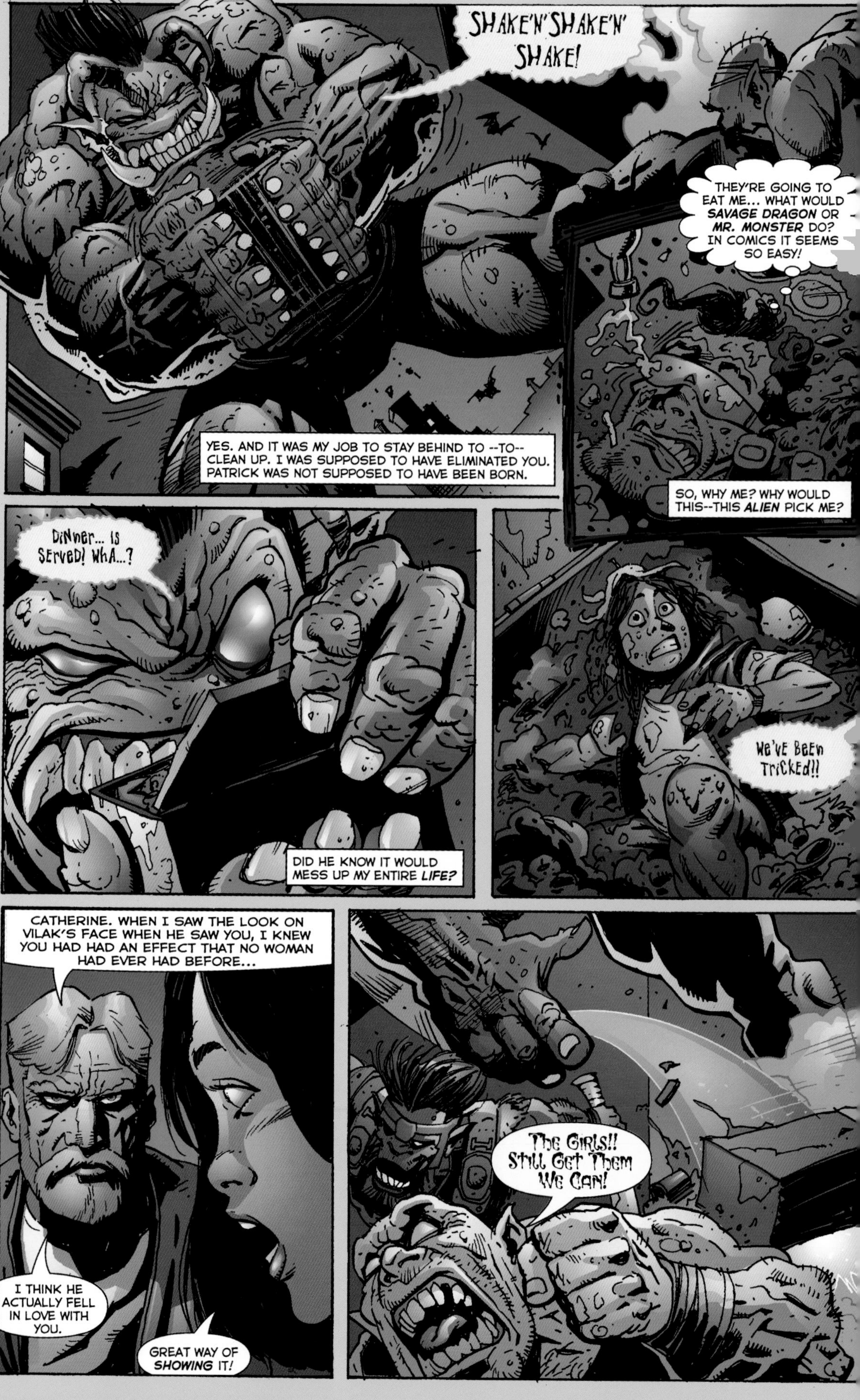
SHAKE'N' SHAKE'N' SHAKE!
THEY'RE GOING TO EAT ME... WHAT WOULD SAVAGE DRAGON OR MR. MONSTER DO? IN COMICS IT SEEMS SO EASY!
YES. AND IT WAS MY JOB TO STAY BEHIND TO --TO-- CLEAN UP. I WAS SUPPOSED TO HAVE ELIMINATED YOU. PATRICK WAS NOT SUPPOSED TO HAVE BEEN BORN.
SO, WHY ME? WHY WOULD THIS--THIS ALIEN PICK ME?
DINNER... IS SERVED! WHA...?
DID HE KNOW IT WOULD MESS UP MY ENTIRE LIFE?
WE'VE BEEN TRICKED!!
CATHERINE. WHEN I SAW THE LOOK ON VILAK'S FACE WHEN HE SAW YOU, I KNEW YOU HAD HAD AN EFFECT THAT NO WOMAN HAD EVER HAD BEFORE...
I THINK HE ACTUALLY FELL IN LOVE WITH YOU.
GREAT WAY OF SHOWING IT!
THE GIRLS!! STILL GET THEM WE CAN!

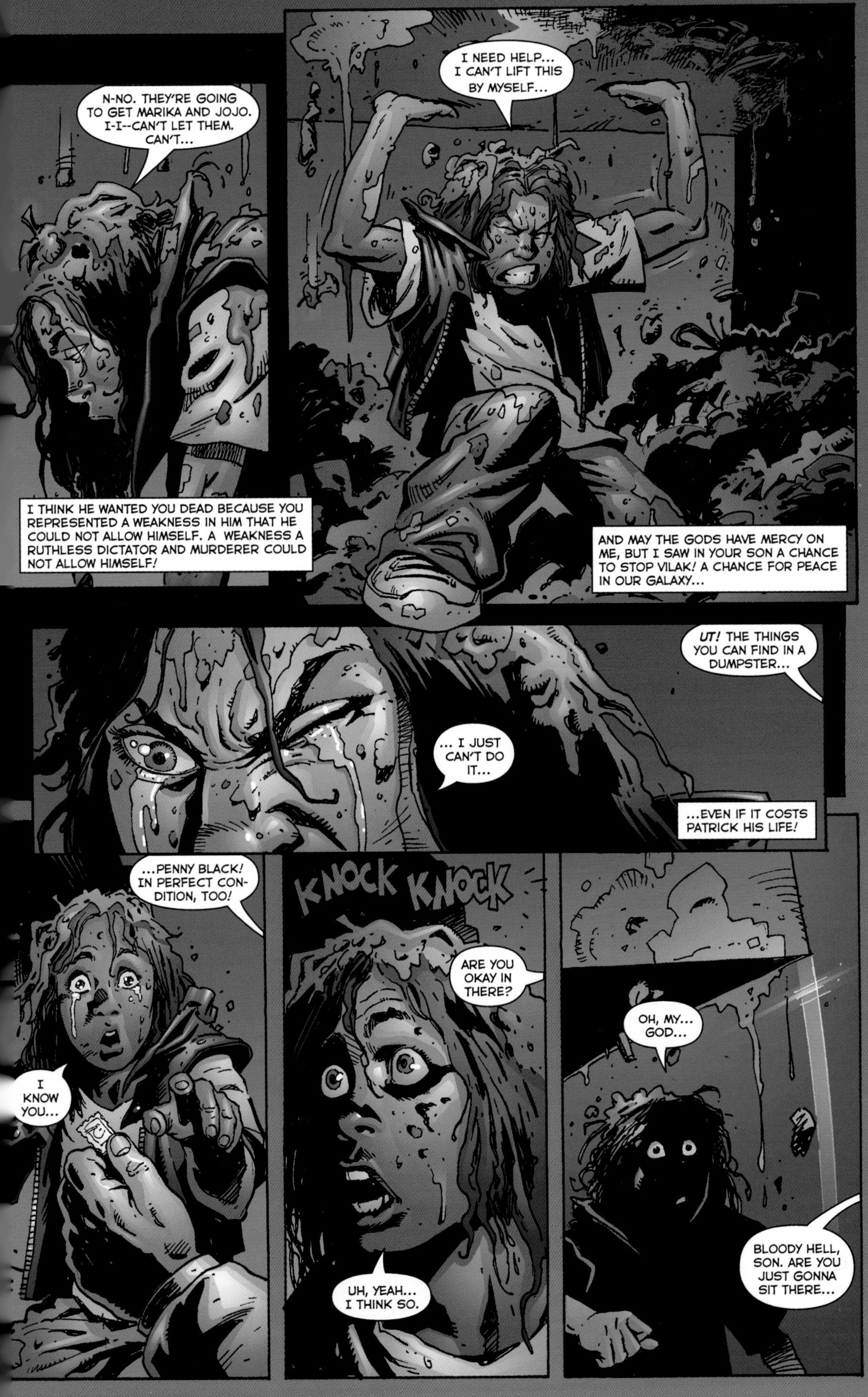
N-NO. THEY'RE GOING TO GET MARIKA AND JOJO. I-I--CAN'T LET THEM. CAN'T...
I THINK HE WANTED YOU DEAD BECAUSE YOU REPRESENTED A WEAKNESS IN HIM THAT HE COULD NOT ALLOW HIMSELF. A WEAKNESS A RUTHLESS DICTATOR AND MURDERER COULD NOT ALLOW HIMSELF!
I NEED HELP... I CAN'T LIFT THIS BY MYSELF...
AND MAY THE GODS HAVE MERCY ON ME, BUT I SAW IN YOUR SON A CHANCE TO STOP VILAK! A CHANCE FOR PEACE IN OUR GALAXY...
UT! THE THINGS YOU CAN FIND IN A DUMPSTER...
... I JUST CAN'T DO IT...
...EVEN IF IT COSTS PATRICK HIS LIFE!
...PENNY BLACK! IN PERFECT CONDITION, TOO!
I KNOW YOU...
KNOCK KNOCK
ARE YOU OKAY IN THERE?
UH, YEAH... I THINK SO.
OH, MY... GOD...
BLOODY HELL, SON. ARE YOU JUST GONNA SIT THERE...

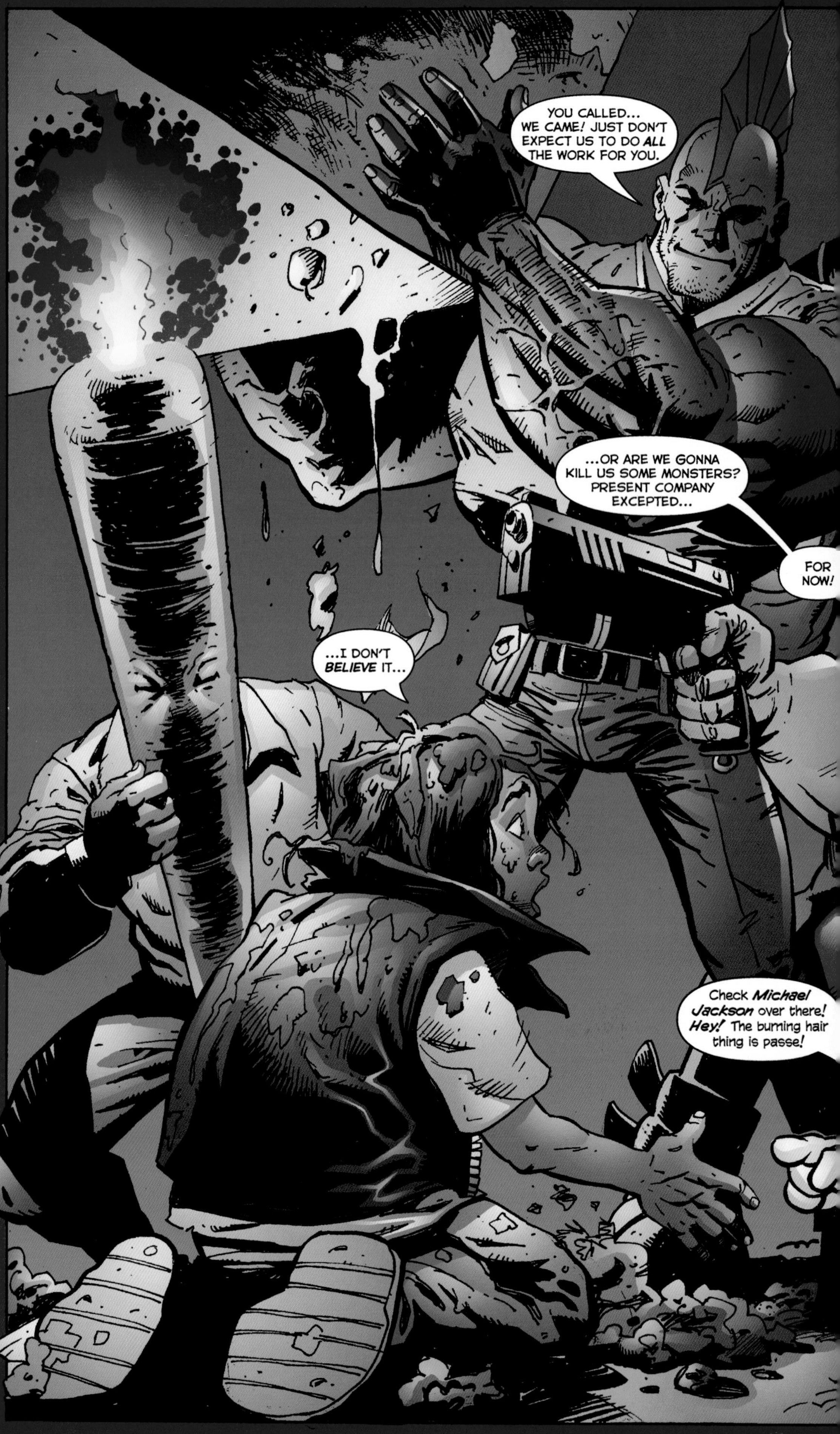
YOU CALLED... WE CAME! JUST DON'T EXPECT US TO DO ALL THE WORK FOR YOU.
...OR ARE WE GONNA KILL US SOME MONSTERS? PRESENT COMPANY EXCEPTED...
FOR NOW!
...I DON'T BELIEVE IT...
Check Michael Jackson over there! Hey! The burning hair thing is passe!

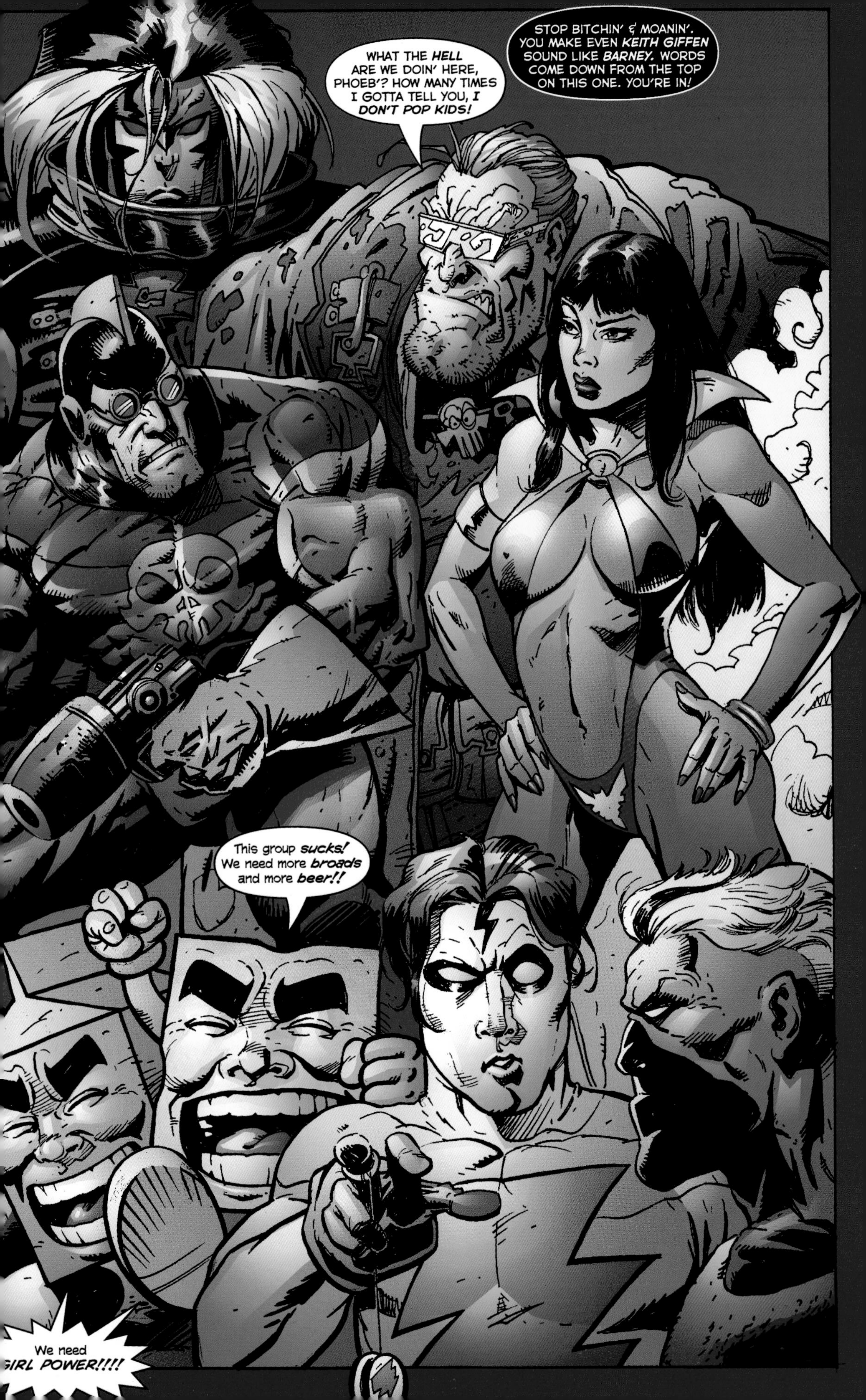
WHAT THE HELL ARE WE DOIN' HERE, PHOEB'? HOW MANY TIMES I GOTTA TELL YOU, I DON'T POP KIDS!
STOP BITCHIN' & MOANIN'. YOU MAKE EVEN KEITH GIFFEN SOUND LIKE BARNEY. WORDS COME DOWN FROM THE TOP ON THIS ONE. YOU'RE IN!
This group sucks! We need more broads and more beer!!
We need GIRL POWER!!!!!

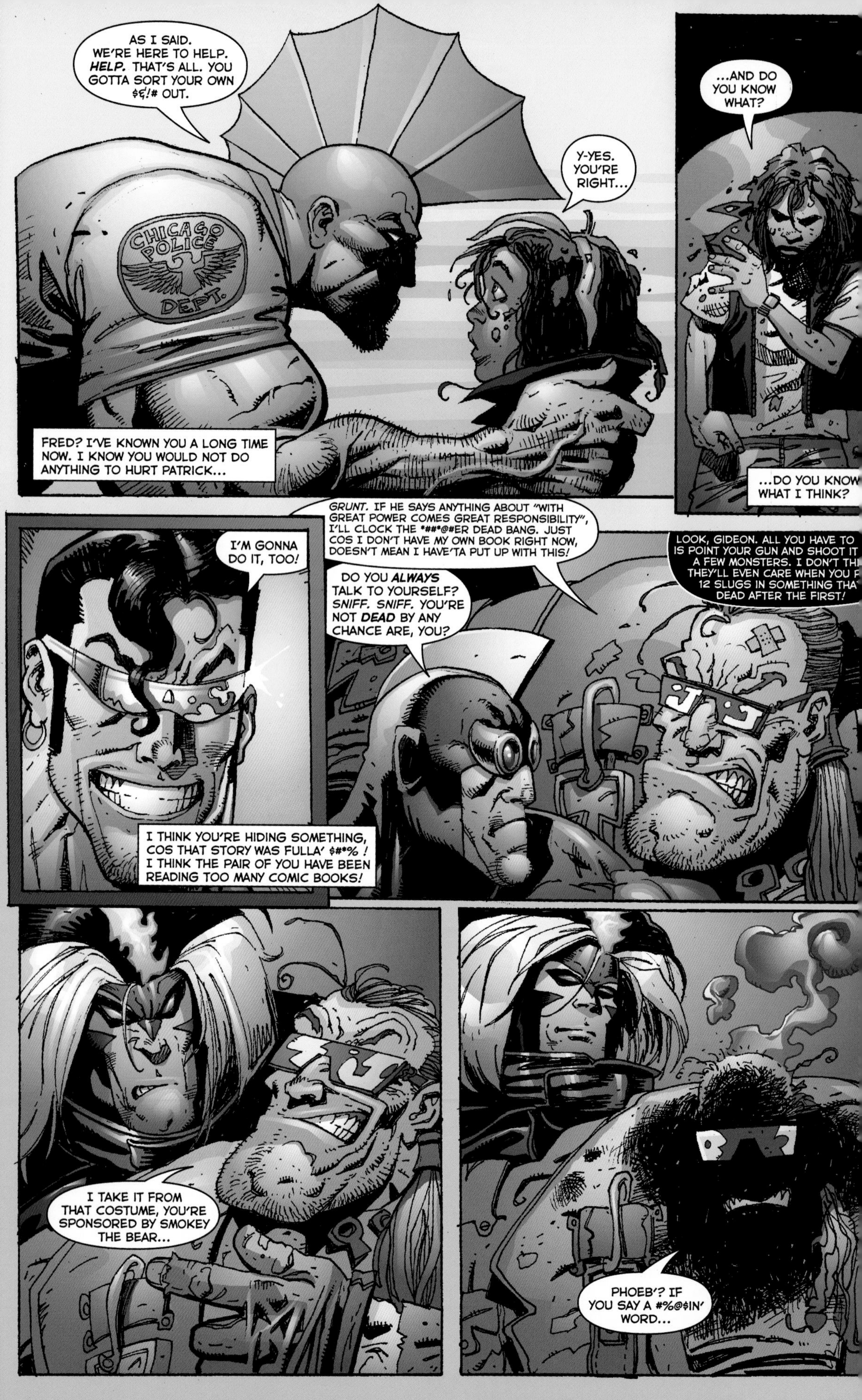
AS I SAID. WE'RE HERE TO HELP. *HELP.* THAT'S ALL. YOU GOTTA SORT YOUR OWN $€!# OUT.
Y-YES. YOU'RE RIGHT...
FRED? I'VE KNOWN YOU A LONG TIME NOW. I KNOW YOU WOULD NOT DO ANYTHING TO HURT PATRICK...
CHICAGO POLICE DEPT.
...AND DO YOU KNOW WHAT?
...DO YOU KNOW WHAT I THINK?
I'M GONNA DO IT, TOO!
I THINK YOU'RE HIDING SOMETHING, COS THAT STORY WAS FULLA' $#*% ! I THINK THE PAIR OF YOU HAVE BEEN READING TOO MANY COMIC BOOKS!
GRUNT. IF HE SAYS ANYTHING ABOUT "WITH GREAT POWER COMES GREAT RESPONSIBILITY", I'LL CLOCK THE *##*@#ER DEAD BANG. JUST COS I DON'T HAVE MY OWN BOOK RIGHT NOW, DOESN'T MEAN I HAVE'TA PUT UP WITH THIS!
DO YOU *ALWAYS* TALK TO YOURSELF? *SNIFF. SNIFF.* YOU'RE NOT *DEAD* BY ANY CHANCE ARE, YOU?
LOOK, GIDEON. ALL YOU HAVE TO IS POINT YOUR GUN AND SHOOT IT A FEW MONSTERS. I DON'T THI THEY'LL EVEN CARE WHEN YOU P 12 SLUGS IN SOMETHING THA DEAD AFTER THE FIRST!
I TAKE IT FROM THAT COSTUME, YOU'RE SPONSORED BY SMOKEY THE BEAR...
PHOEB'? IF YOU SAY A #%@$IN' WORD...

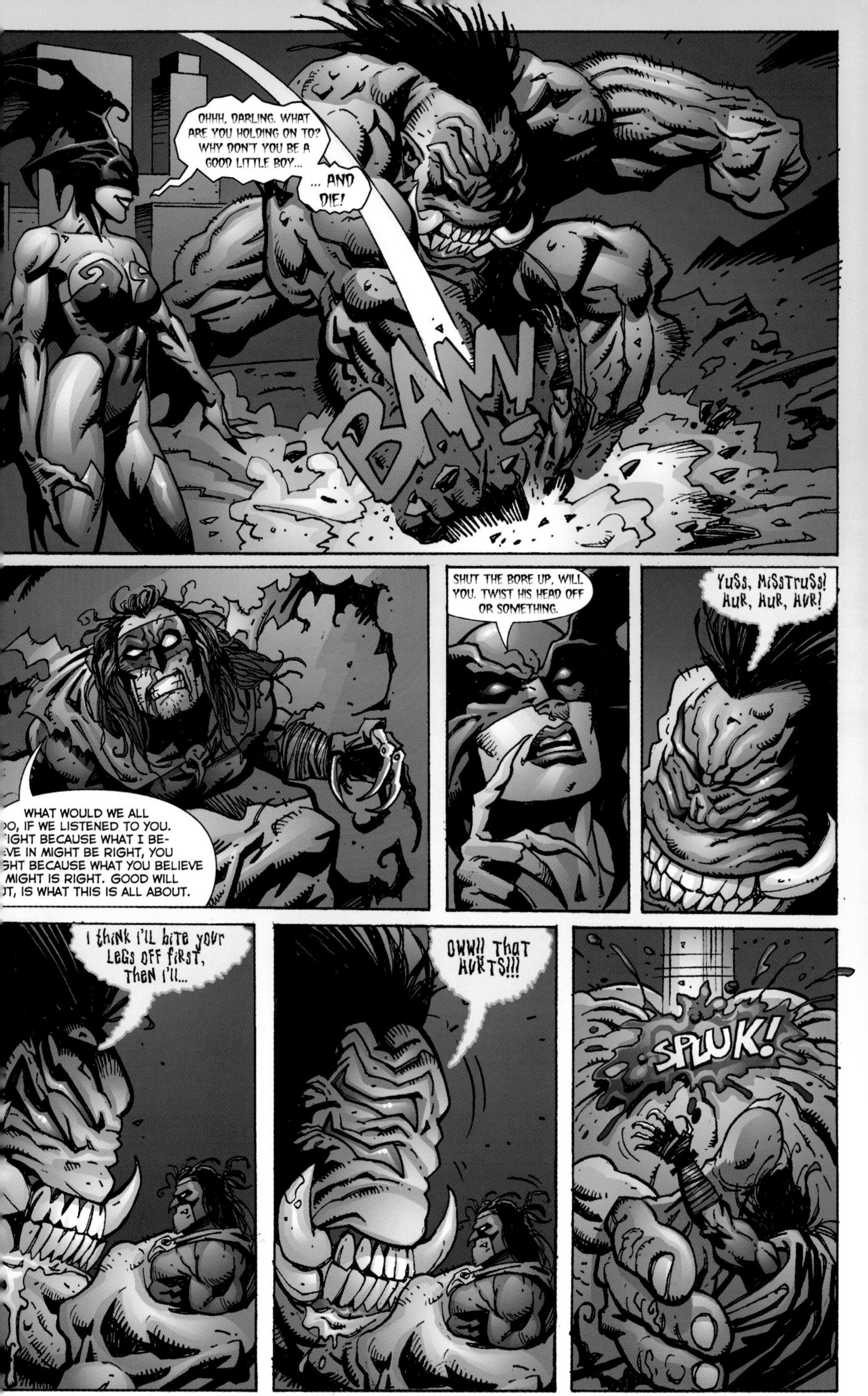
OHHH, DARLING. WHAT ARE YOU HOLDING ON TO? WHY DON'T YOU BE A GOOD LITTLE BOY...
... AND DIE!
BAM
WHAT WOULD WE ALL
O, IF WE LISTENED TO YOU.
IGHT BECAUSE WHAT I BE-
VE IN MIGHT BE RIGHT, YOU
GHT BECAUSE WHAT YOU BELIEVE
MIGHT IS RIGHT. GOOD WILL
T, IS WHAT THIS IS ALL ABOUT.
SHUT THE BORE UP, WILL YOU. TWIST HIS HEAD OFF OR SOMETHING.
YUSS, MISSTRUSS! HUR, HUR, HUR!
I think I'll bite your legs off first, then I'll...
OWW!! That HURTS!!!
SPLUK!

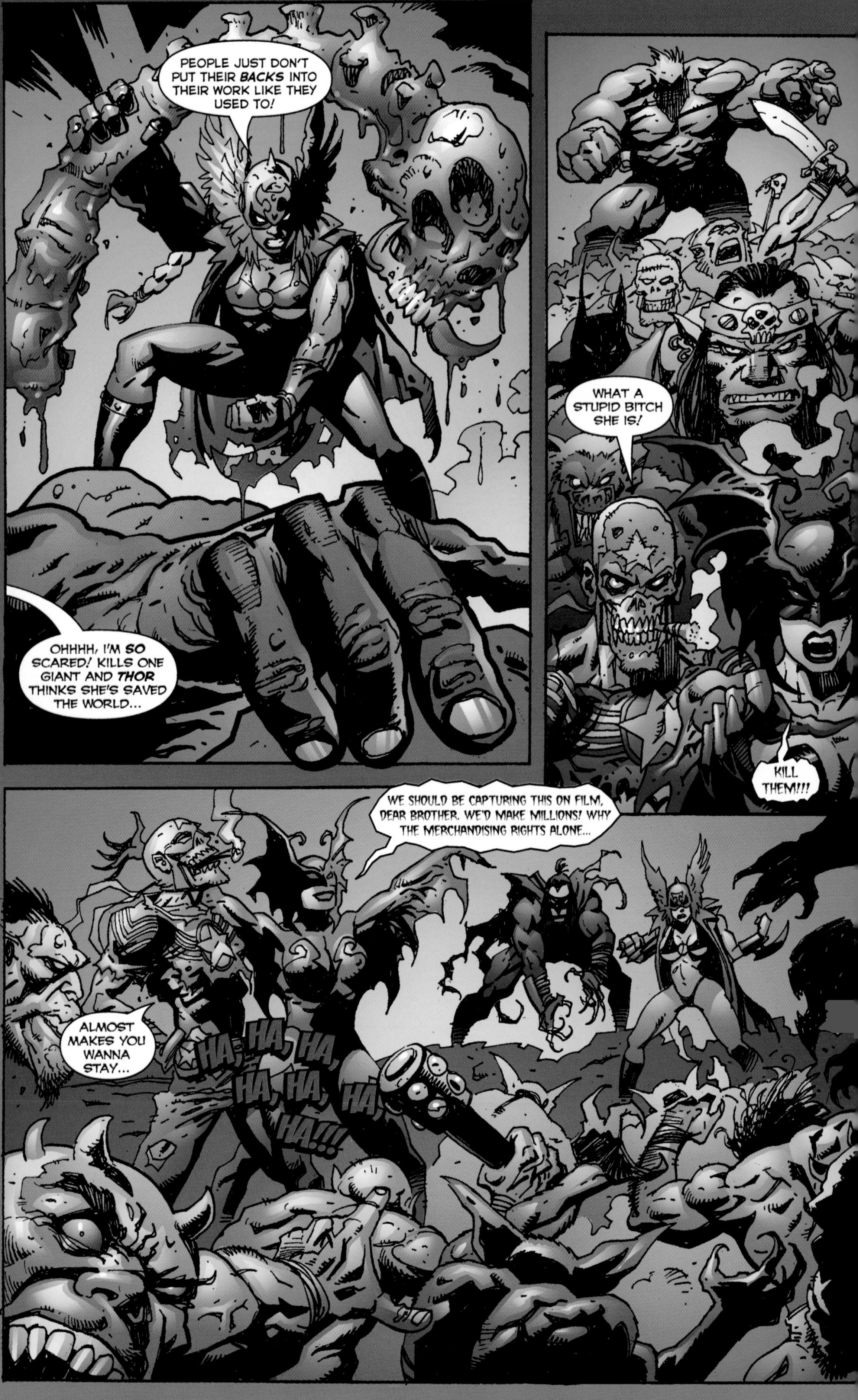
PEOPLE JUST DON'T PUT THEIR BACKS INTO THEIR WORK LIKE THEY USED TO!
OHHHH, I'M SO SCARED! KILLS ONE GIANT AND THOR THINKS SHE'S SAVED THE WORLD...
WHAT A STUPID BITCH SHE IS!
KILL THEM!!!
WE SHOULD BE CAPTURING THIS ON FILM, DEAR BROTHER. WE'D MAKE MILLIONS! WHY THE MERCHANDISING RIGHTS ALONE...
ALMOST MAKES YOU WANNA STAY...
HA, HA, HA, HA, HA, HA, HA!!!

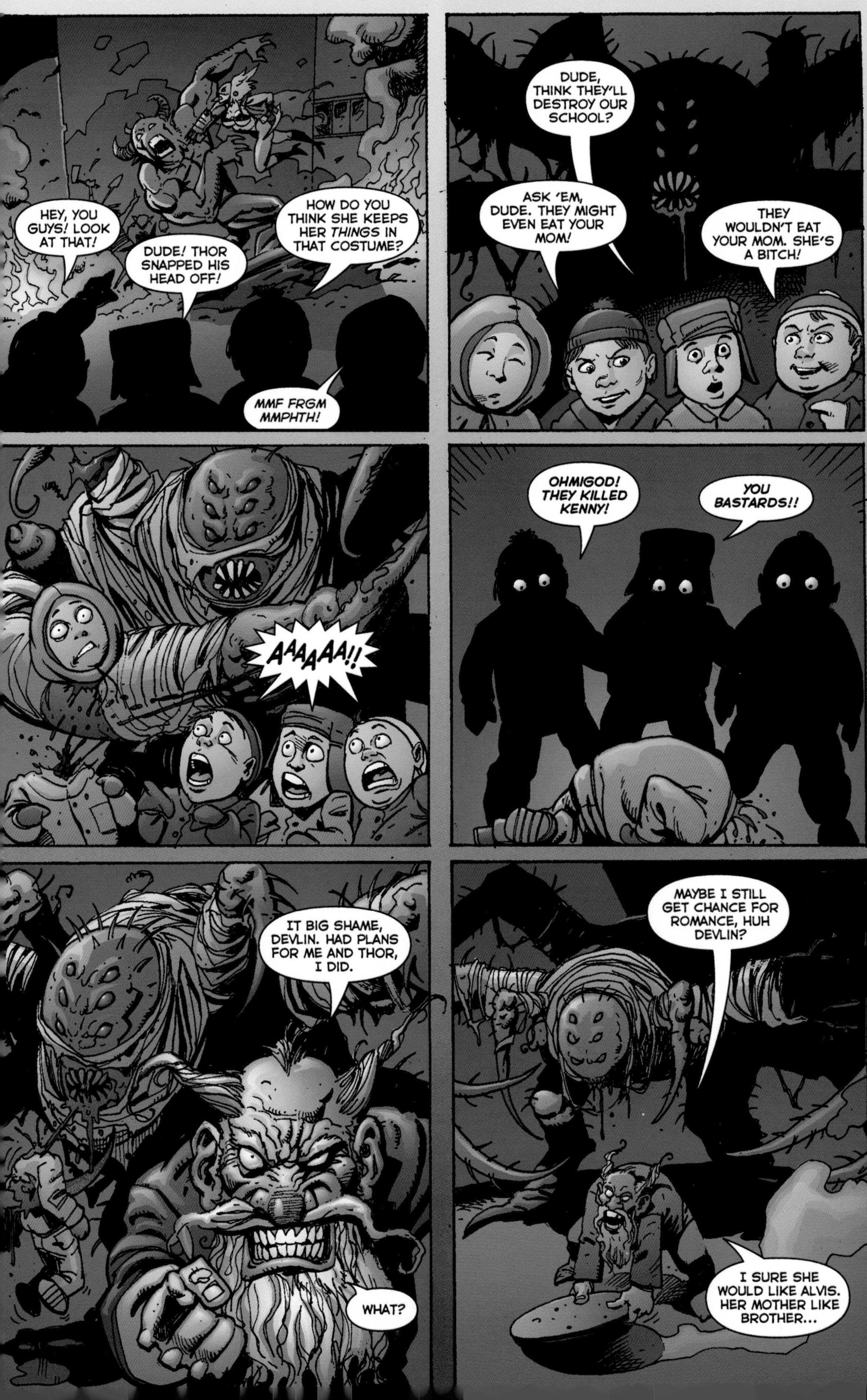
HEY, YOU GUYS! LOOK AT THAT!
DUDE! THOR SNAPPED HIS HEAD OFF!
HOW DO YOU THINK SHE KEEPS HER *THINGS* IN THAT COSTUME?
MMF FRGM MMPHTH!
DUDE, THINK THEY'LL DESTROY OUR SCHOOL?
ASK 'EM, DUDE. THEY MIGHT EVEN EAT YOUR MOM!
THEY WOULDN'T EAT YOUR MOM. SHE'S A BITCH!
AAAAAA!!
OHMIGOD! THEY KILLED KENNY!
YOU BASTARDS!!
IT BIG SHAME, DEVLIN. HAD PLANS FOR ME AND THOR, I DID.
WHAT?
MAYBE I STILL GET CHANCE FOR ROMANCE, HUH DEVLIN?
I SURE SHE WOULD LIKE ALVIS. HER MOTHER LIKE BROTHER...

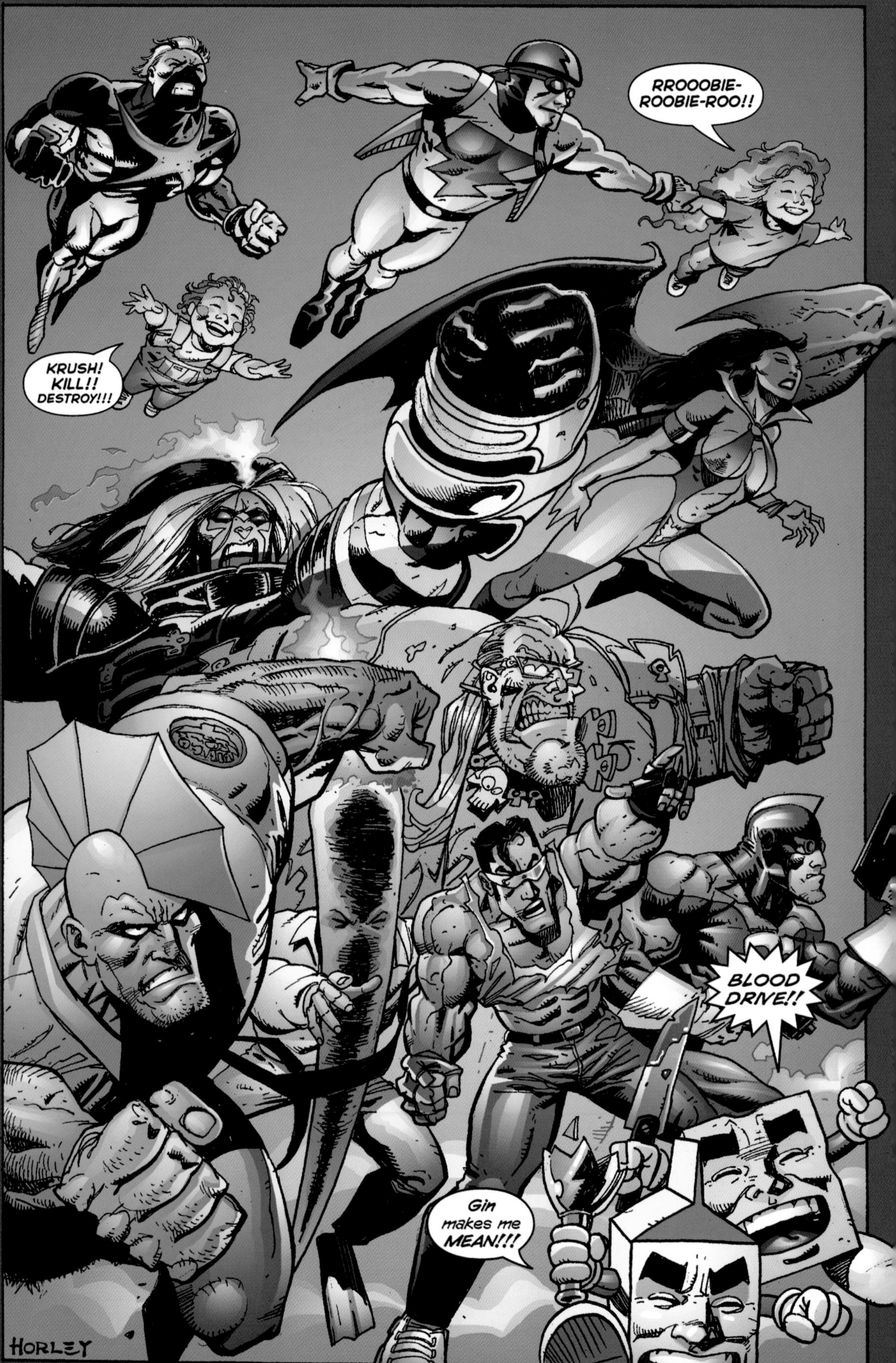
RROOOBIE-ROOBIE-ROO!!
KRUSH! KILL!! DESTROY!!!
BLOOD DRIVE!!
Gin makes me MEAN!!!
HORLEY

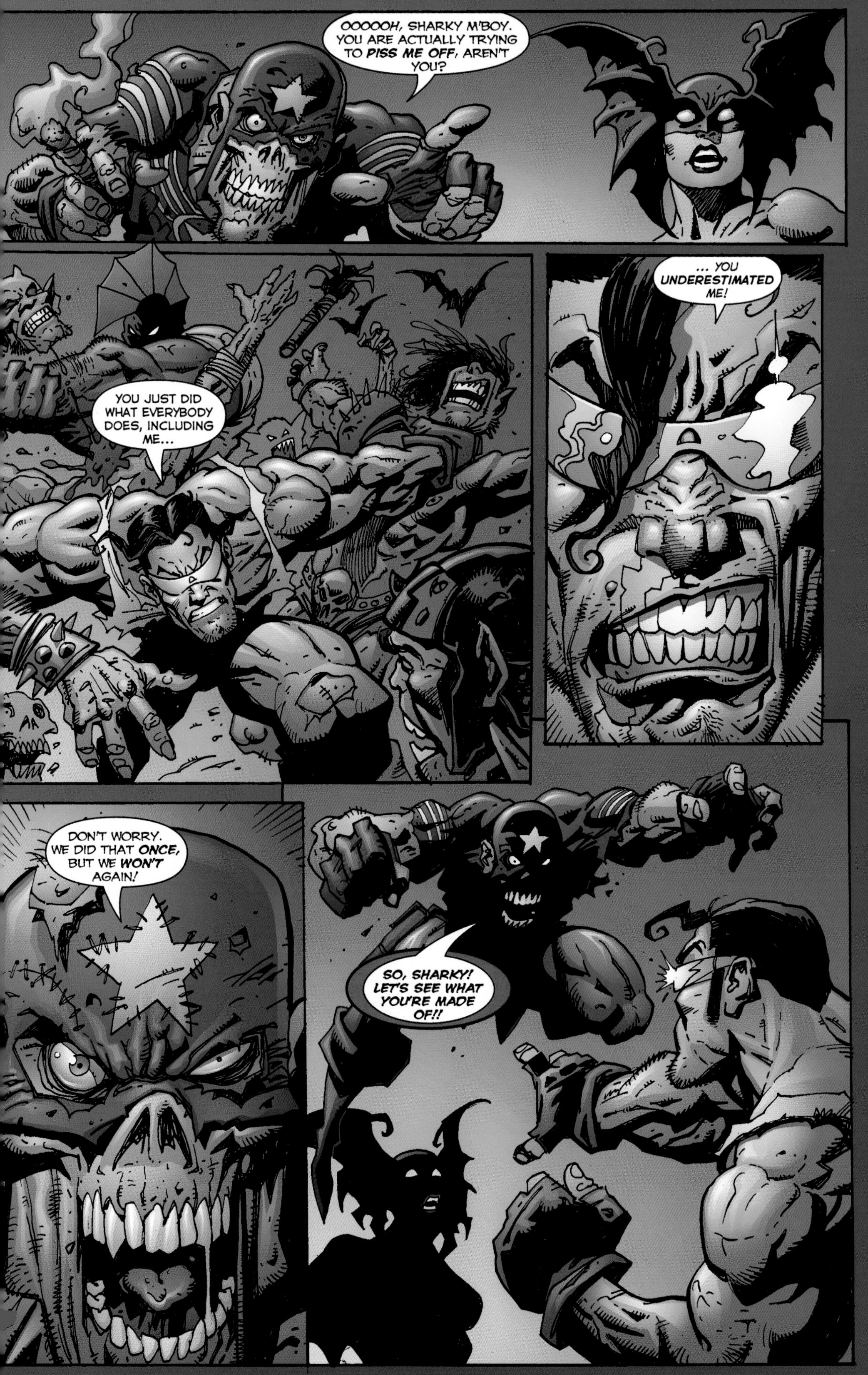
OOOOOH, SHARKY M'BOY. YOU ARE ACTUALLY TRYING TO PISS ME OFF, AREN'T YOU?
YOU JUST DID WHAT EVERYBODY DOES, INCLUDING ME...
... YOU UNDERESTIMATED ME!
DON'T WORRY. WE DID THAT ONCE, BUT WE WON'T AGAIN!
SO, SHARKY! LET'S SEE WHAT YOU'RE MADE OF!!

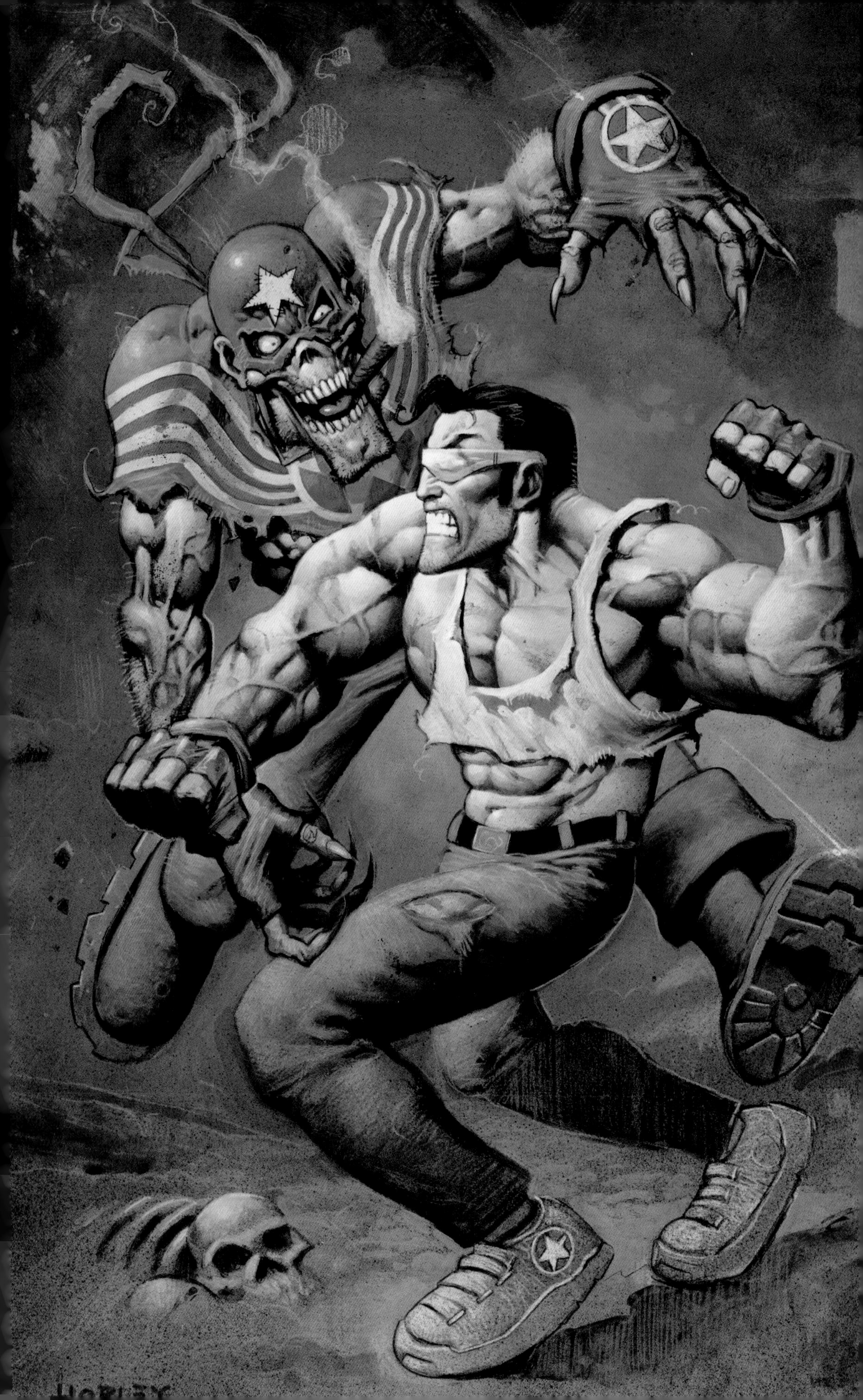

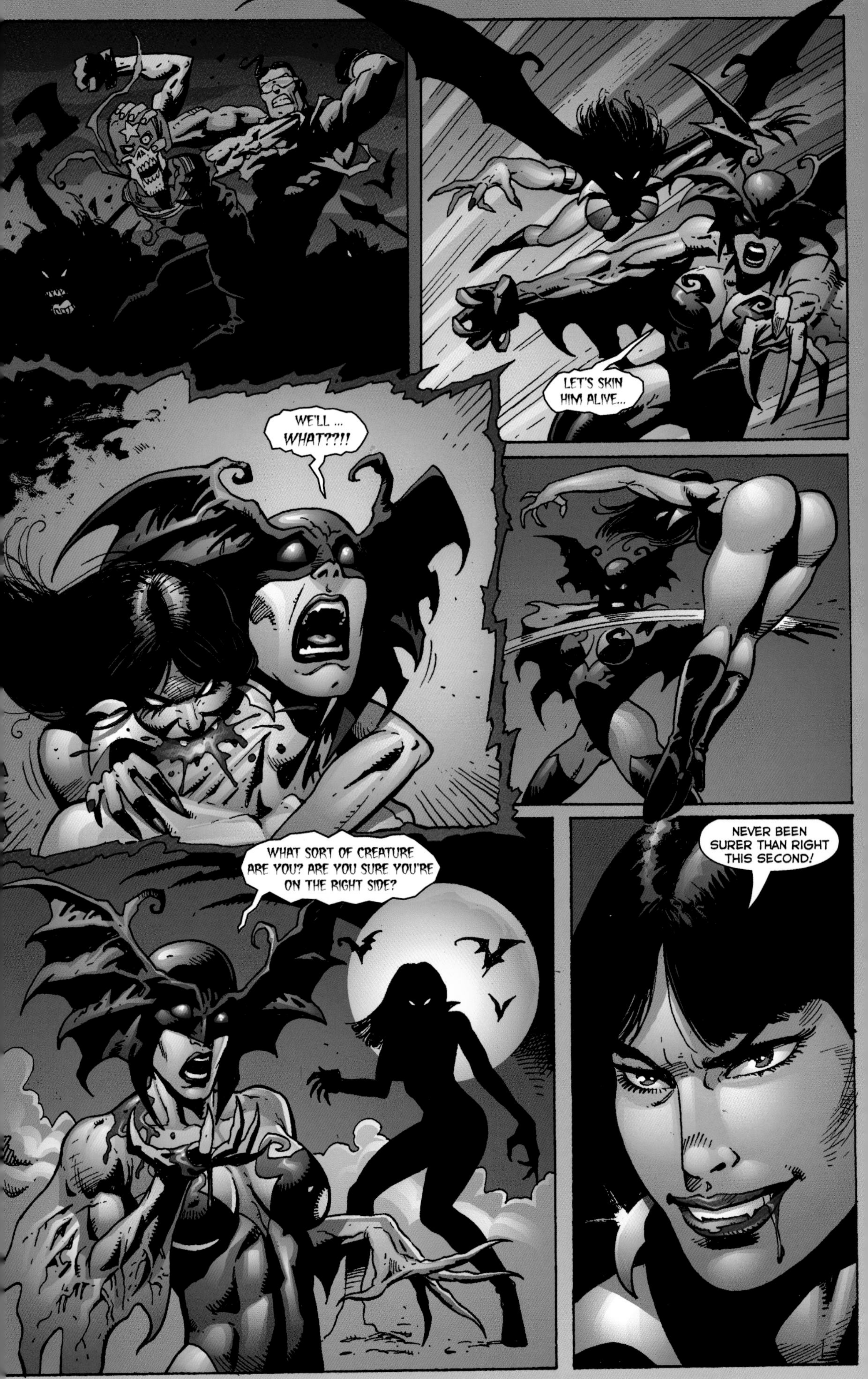
LET'S SKIN HIM ALIVE...
WE'LL ... WHAT??!!
WHAT SORT OF CREATURE ARE YOU? ARE YOU SURE YOU'RE ON THE RIGHT SIDE?
NEVER BEEN SURER THAN RIGHT THIS SECOND!

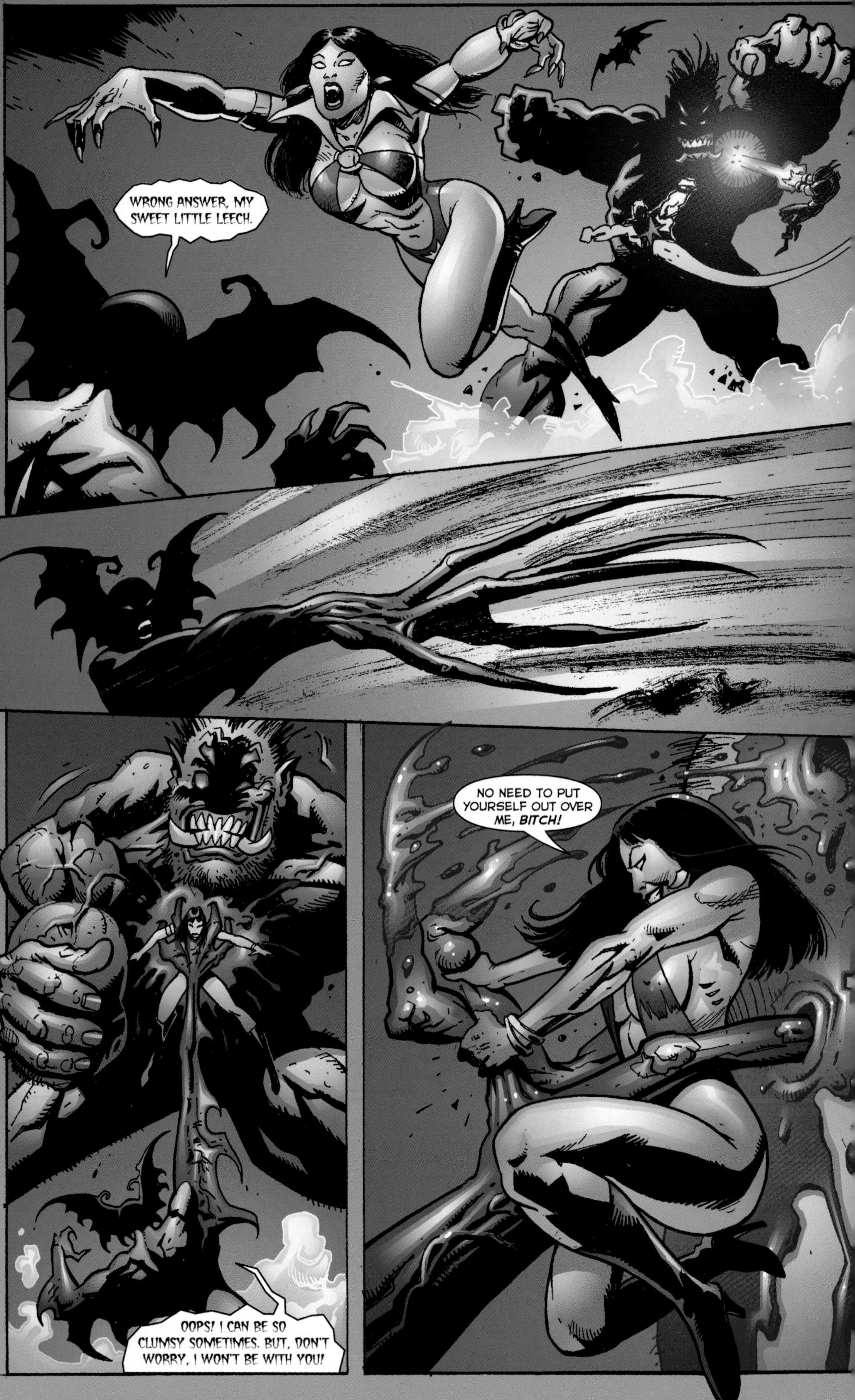
WRONG ANSWER, MY SWEET LITTLE LEECH.
NO NEED TO PUT YOURSELF OUT OVER ME, BITCH!
OOPS! I CAN BE SO CLUMSY SOMETIMES. BUT, DON'T WORRY, I WON'T BE WITH YOU!

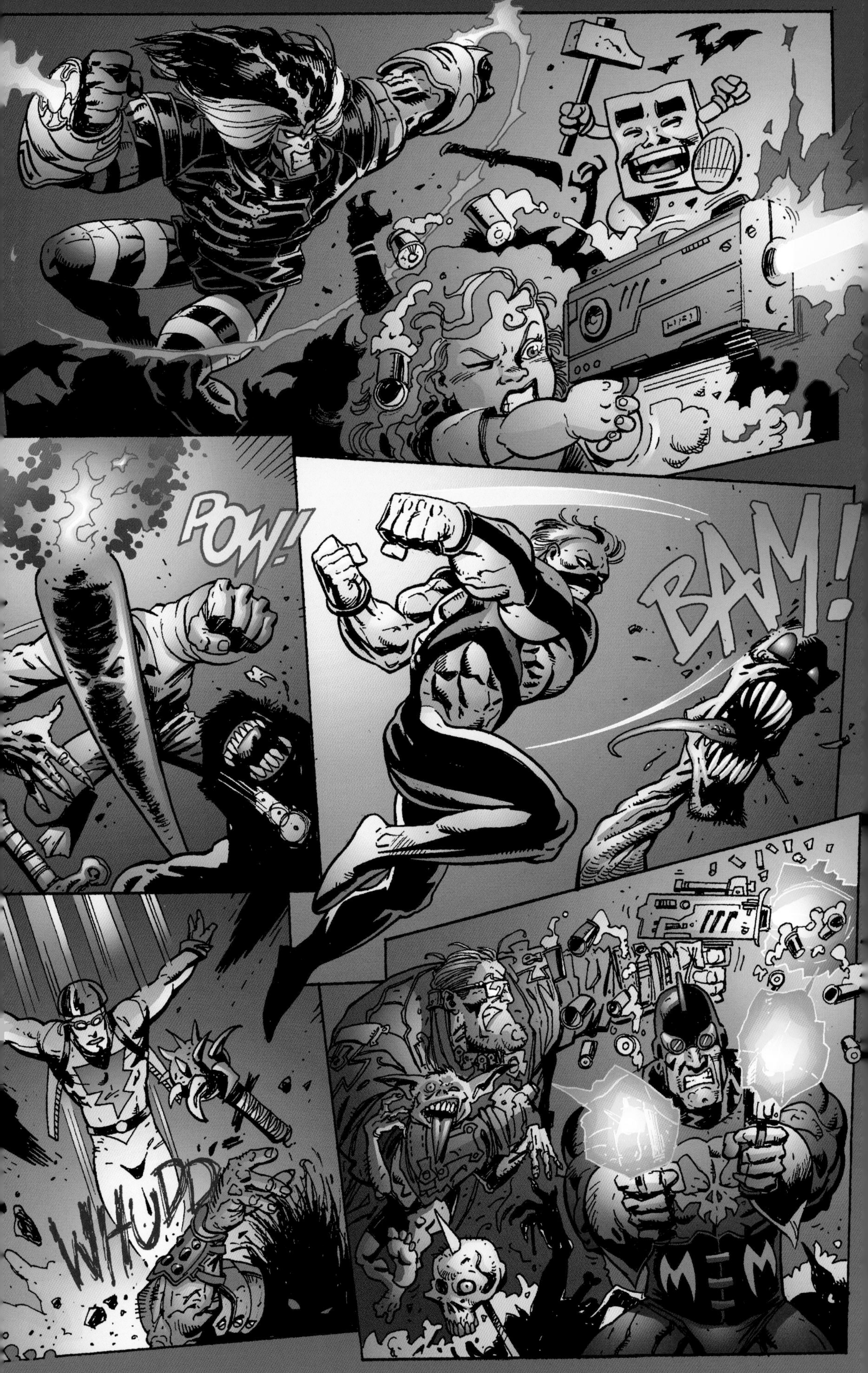
POW!!
BAM!
WHUDD

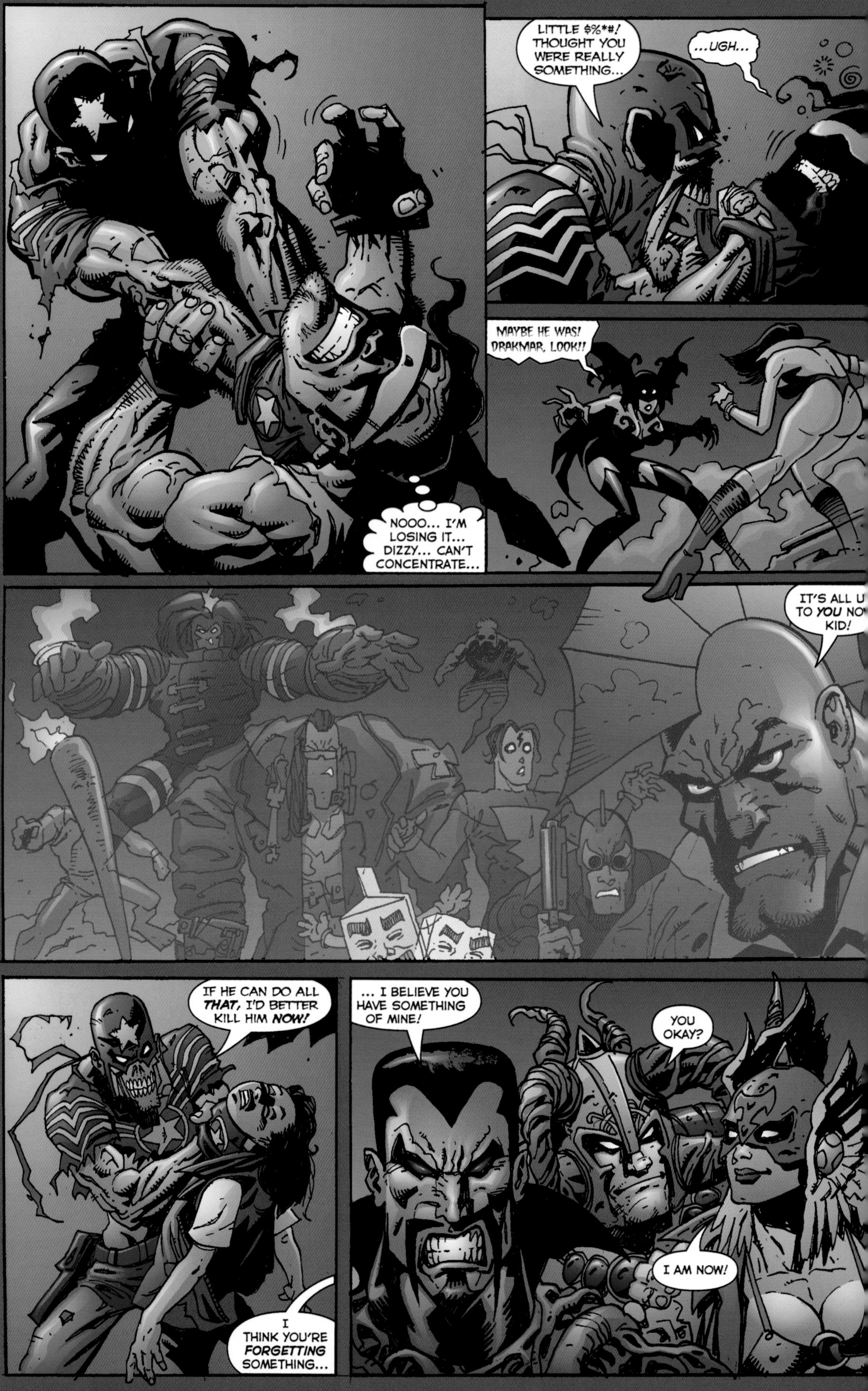
LITTLE $%*#! THOUGHT YOU WERE REALLY SOMETHING...
...UGH...
NOOO... I'M LOSING IT... DIZZY... CAN'T CONCENTRATE...
MAYBE HE WAS! DRAKMAR, LOOK!!
IT'S ALL U TO YOU NO KID!
IF HE CAN DO ALL THAT, I'D BETTER KILL HIM NOW!
I THINK YOU'RE FORGETTING SOMETHING...
... I BELIEVE YOU HAVE SOMETHING OF MINE!
YOU OKAY?
I AM NOW!

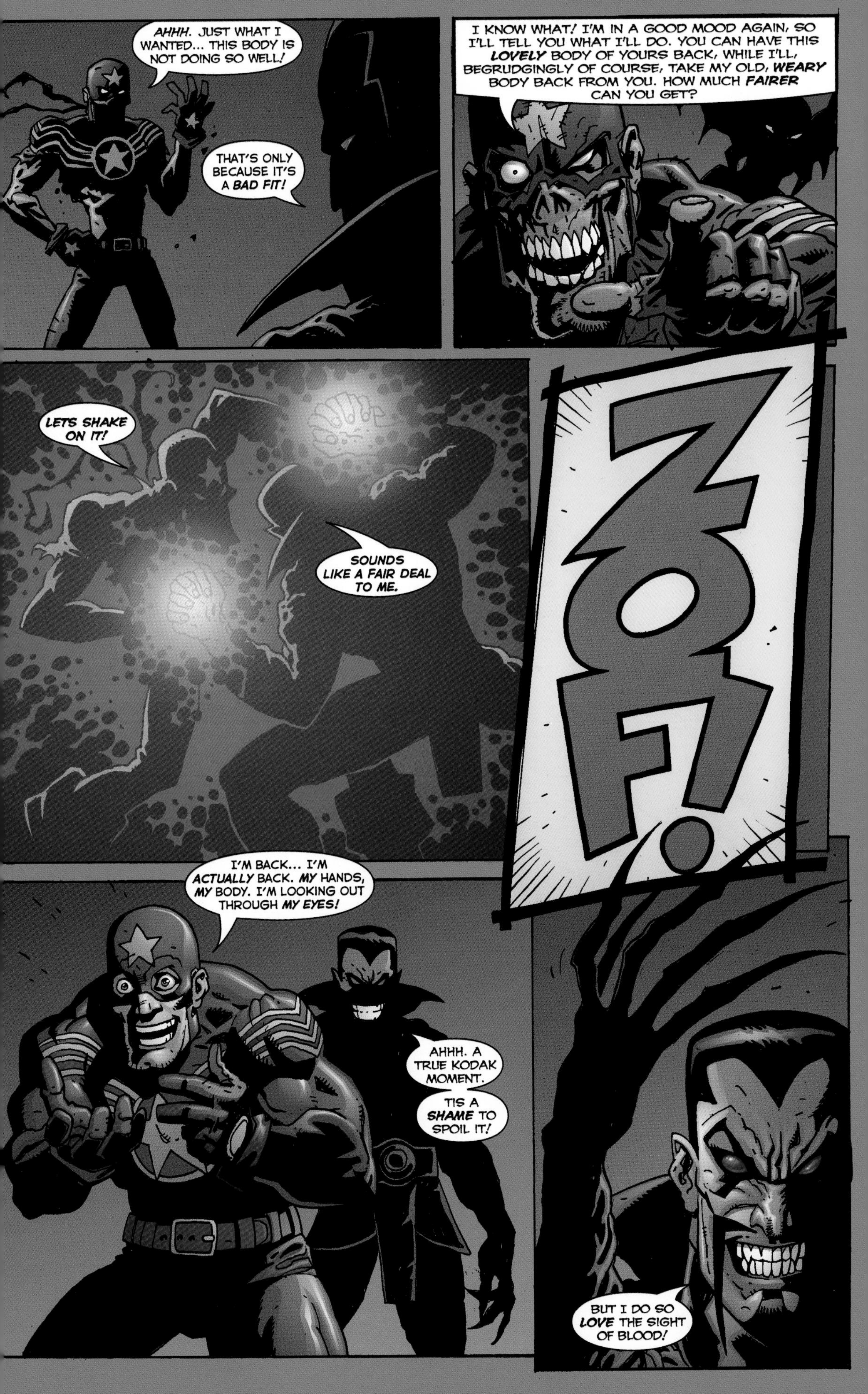

AHHH. JUST WHAT I WANTED... THIS BODY IS NOT DOING SO WELL!
THAT'S ONLY BECAUSE IT'S A BAD FIT!
I KNOW WHAT! I'M IN A GOOD MOOD AGAIN, SO I'LL TELL YOU WHAT I'LL DO. YOU CAN HAVE THIS LOVELY BODY OF YOURS BACK, WHILE I'LL, BEGRUDGINGLY OF COURSE, TAKE MY OLD, WEARY BODY BACK FROM YOU. HOW MUCH FAIRER CAN YOU GET?
LETS SHAKE ON IT!
SOUNDS LIKE A FAIR DEAL TO ME.
ZOF!
I'M BACK... I'M ACTUALLY BACK. MY HANDS, MY BODY. I'M LOOKING OUT THROUGH MY EYES!
AHHH. A TRUE KODAK MOMENT.
TIS A SHAME TO SPOIL IT!
BUT I DO SO LOVE THE SIGHT OF BLOOD!

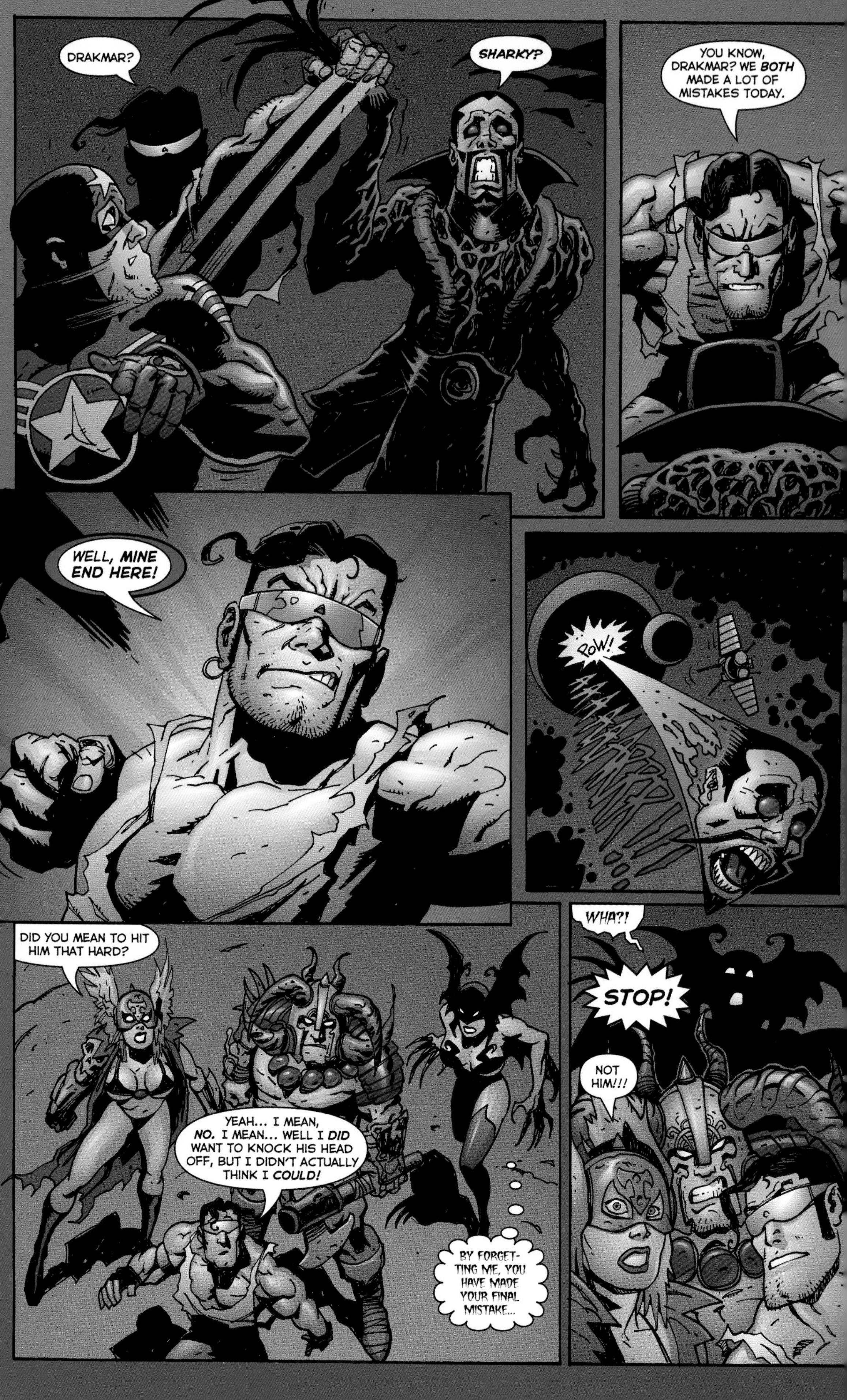

DRAKMAR?
SHARKY?
YOU KNOW, DRAKMAR? WE BOTH MADE A LOT OF MISTAKES TODAY.
WELL, MINE END HERE!
POW!
DID YOU MEAN TO HIT HIM THAT HARD?
YEAH... I MEAN, NO. I MEAN... WELL I DID WANT TO KNOCK HIS HEAD OFF, BUT I DIDN'T ACTUALLY THINK I COULD!
BY FORGET-TING ME, YOU HAVE MADE YOUR FINAL MISTAKE...
WHA?!
STOP!
NOT HIM!!!

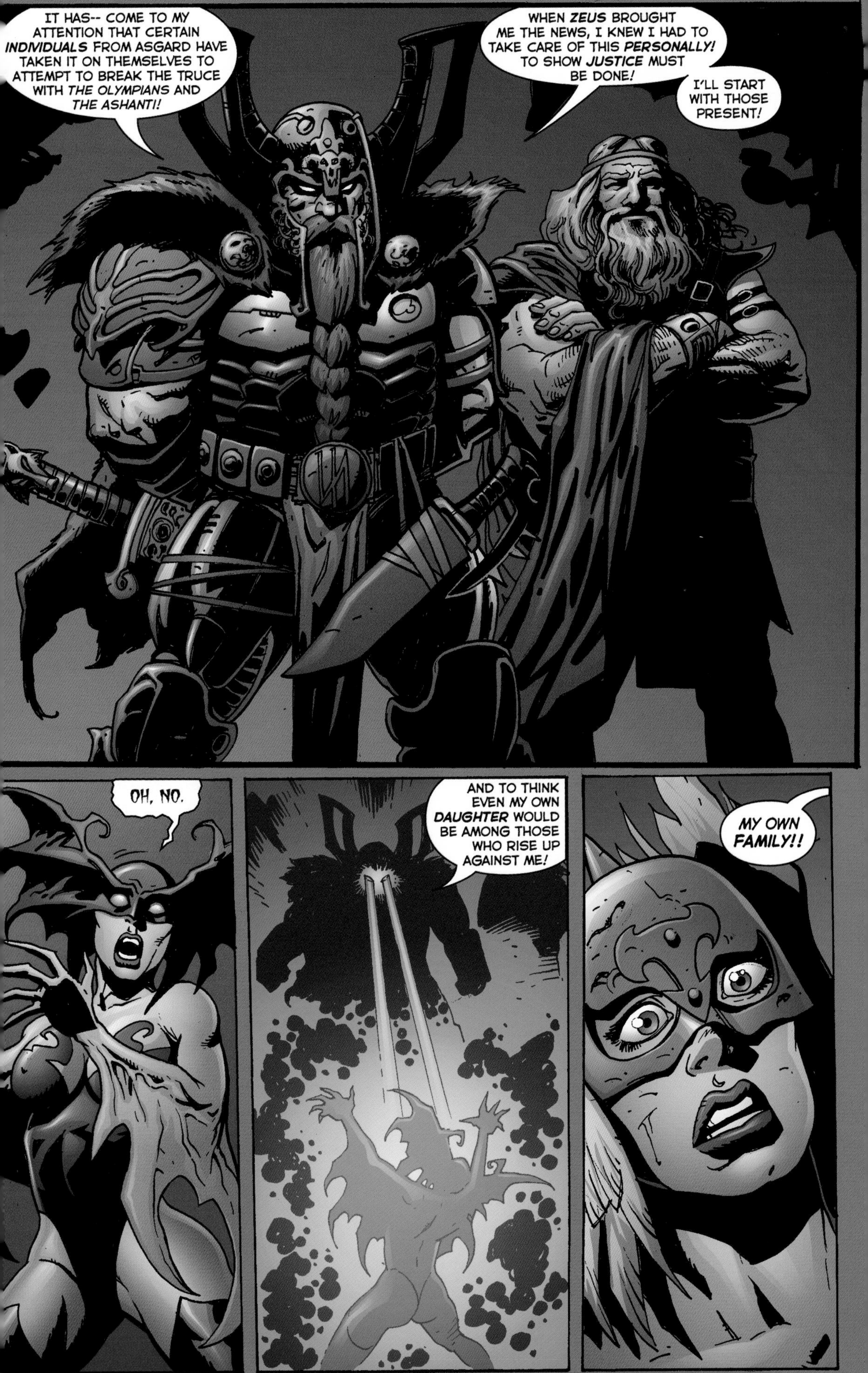
IT HAS-- COME TO MY ATTENTION THAT CERTAIN INDIVIDUALS FROM ASGARD HAVE TAKEN IT ON THEMSELVES TO ATTEMPT TO BREAK THE TRUCE WITH THE OLYMPIANS AND THE ASHANTI!
WHEN ZEUS BROUGHT ME THE NEWS, I KNEW I HAD TO TAKE CARE OF THIS PERSONALLY! TO SHOW JUSTICE MUST BE DONE!
I'LL START WITH THOSE PRESENT!
OH, NO.
AND TO THINK EVEN MY OWN DAUGHTER WOULD BE AMONG THOSE WHO RISE UP AGAINST ME!
MY OWN FAMILY!!

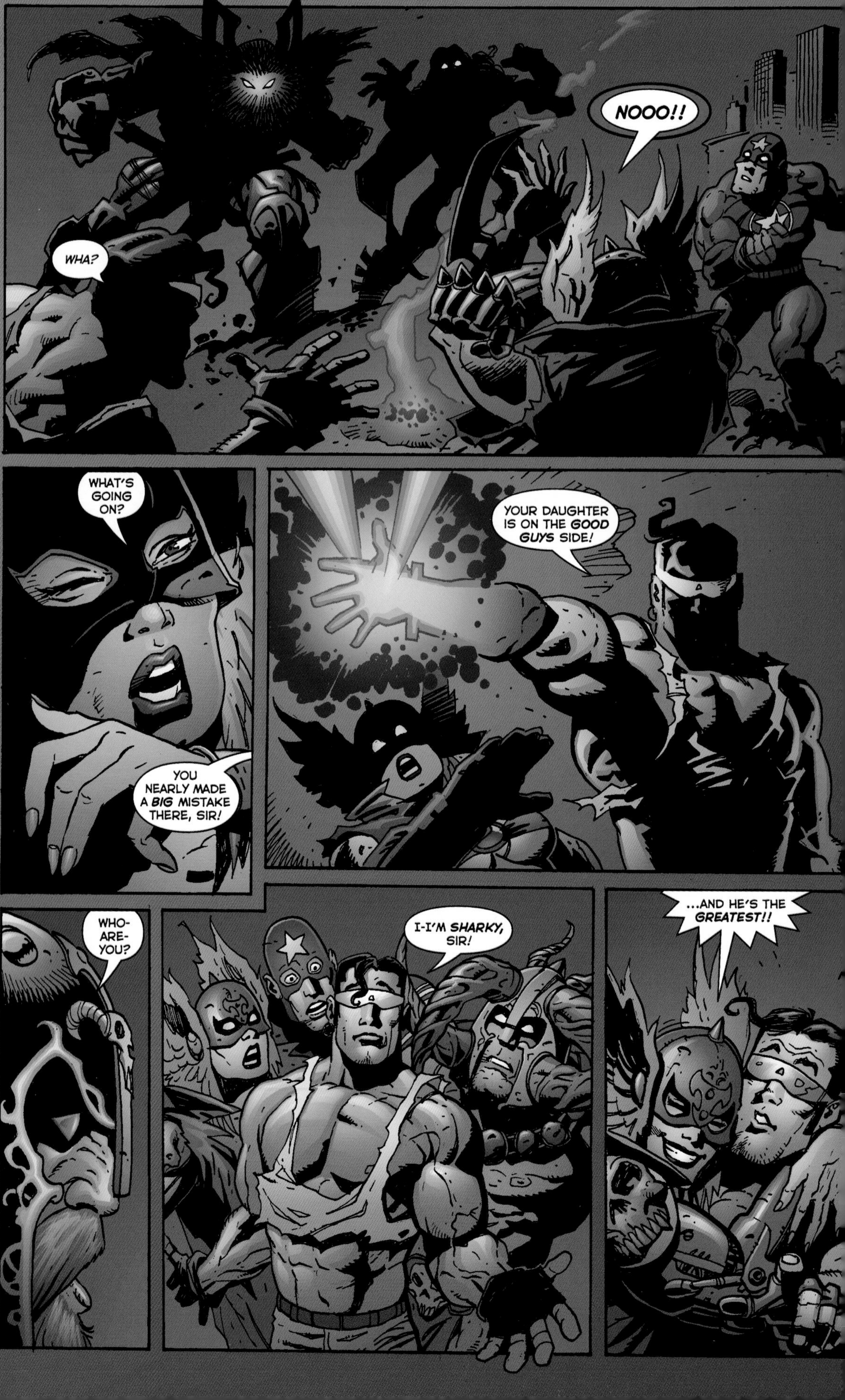
WHA?
NOOO!!
WHAT'S GOING ON?
YOU NEARLY MADE A BIG MISTAKE THERE, SIR!
YOUR DAUGHTER IS ON THE GOOD GUYS SIDE!
WHO-ARE-YOU?
I-I'M SHARKY, SIR!
...AND HE'S THE GREATEST!!

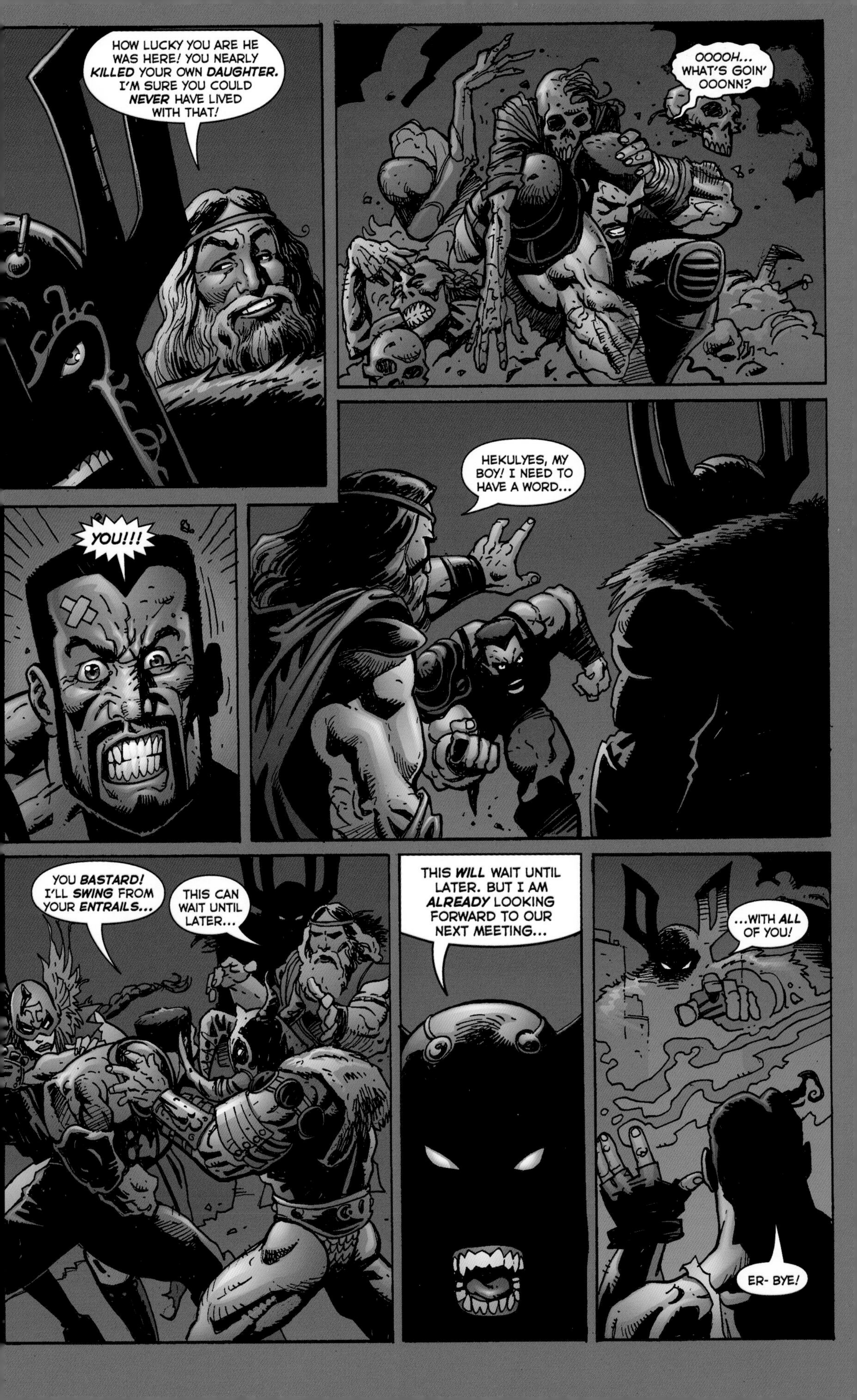
HOW LUCKY YOU ARE HE WAS HERE! YOU NEARLY KILLED YOUR OWN DAUGHTER. I'M SURE YOU COULD NEVER HAVE LIVED WITH THAT!
OOOOH... WHAT'S GOIN' OOONN?
YOU!!!
HEKULYES, MY BOY! I NEED TO HAVE A WORD...
YOU BASTARD! I'LL SWING FROM YOUR ENTRAILS...
THIS CAN WAIT UNTIL LATER...
THIS WILL WAIT UNTIL LATER. BUT I AM ALREADY LOOKING FORWARD TO OUR NEXT MEETING...
...WITH ALL OF YOU!
ER- BYE!

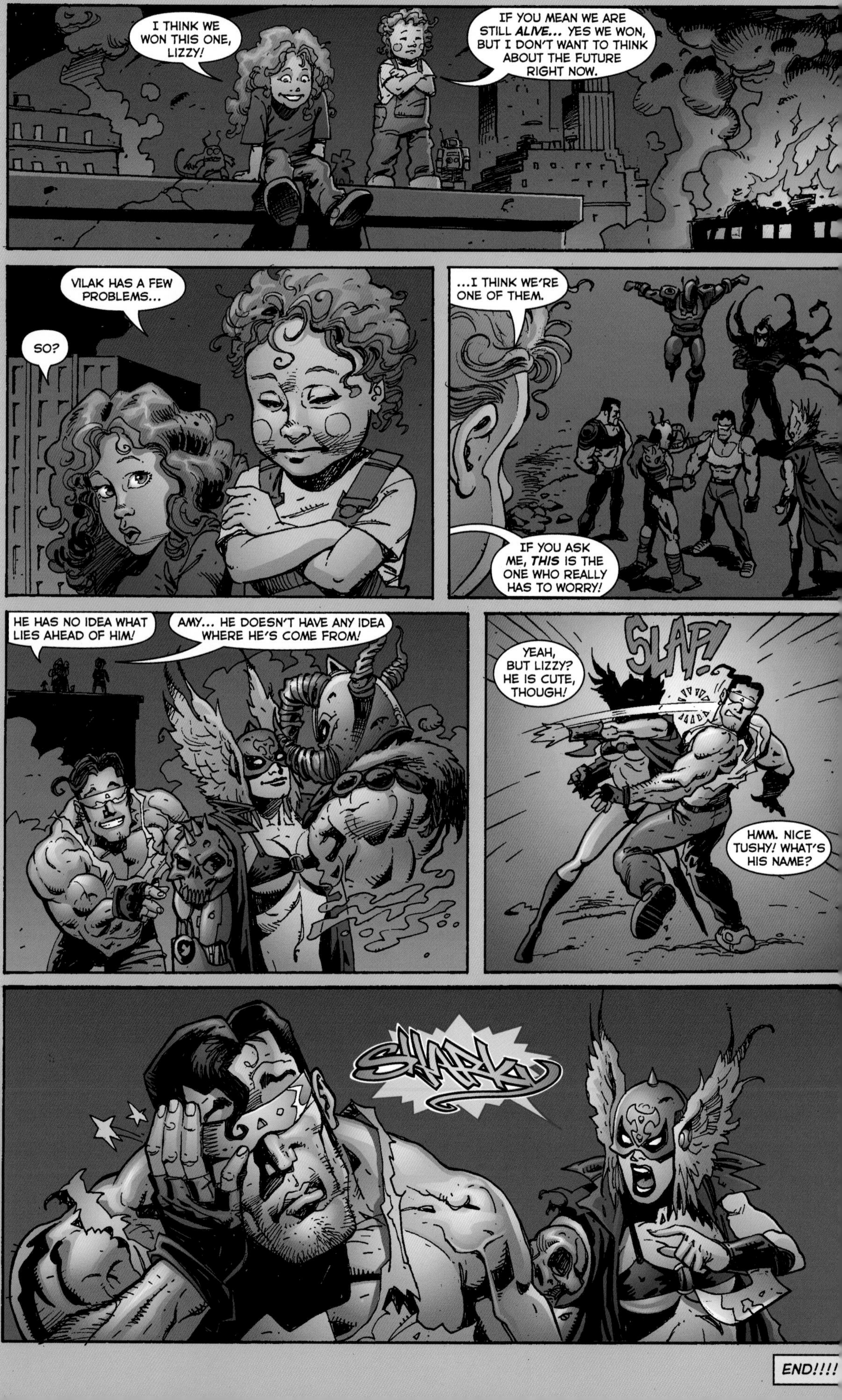
I THINK WE WON THIS ONE, LIZZY!
IF YOU MEAN WE ARE STILL *ALIVE...* YES WE WON, BUT I DON'T WANT TO THINK ABOUT THE FUTURE RIGHT NOW.
VILAK HAS A FEW PROBLEMS...
SO?
...I THINK WE'RE ONE OF THEM.
IF YOU ASK ME, *THIS* IS THE ONE WHO REALLY HAS TO WORRY!
HE HAS NO IDEA WHAT LIES AHEAD OF HIM!
AMY... HE DOESN'T HAVE ANY IDEA WHERE HE'S COME FROM!
SLAP!
YEAH, BUT LIZZY? HE IS CUTE, THOUGH!
HMM. NICE TUSHY! WHAT'S HIS NAME?
END!!!!

THE SECRET ORIGIN OF... SHARKY!

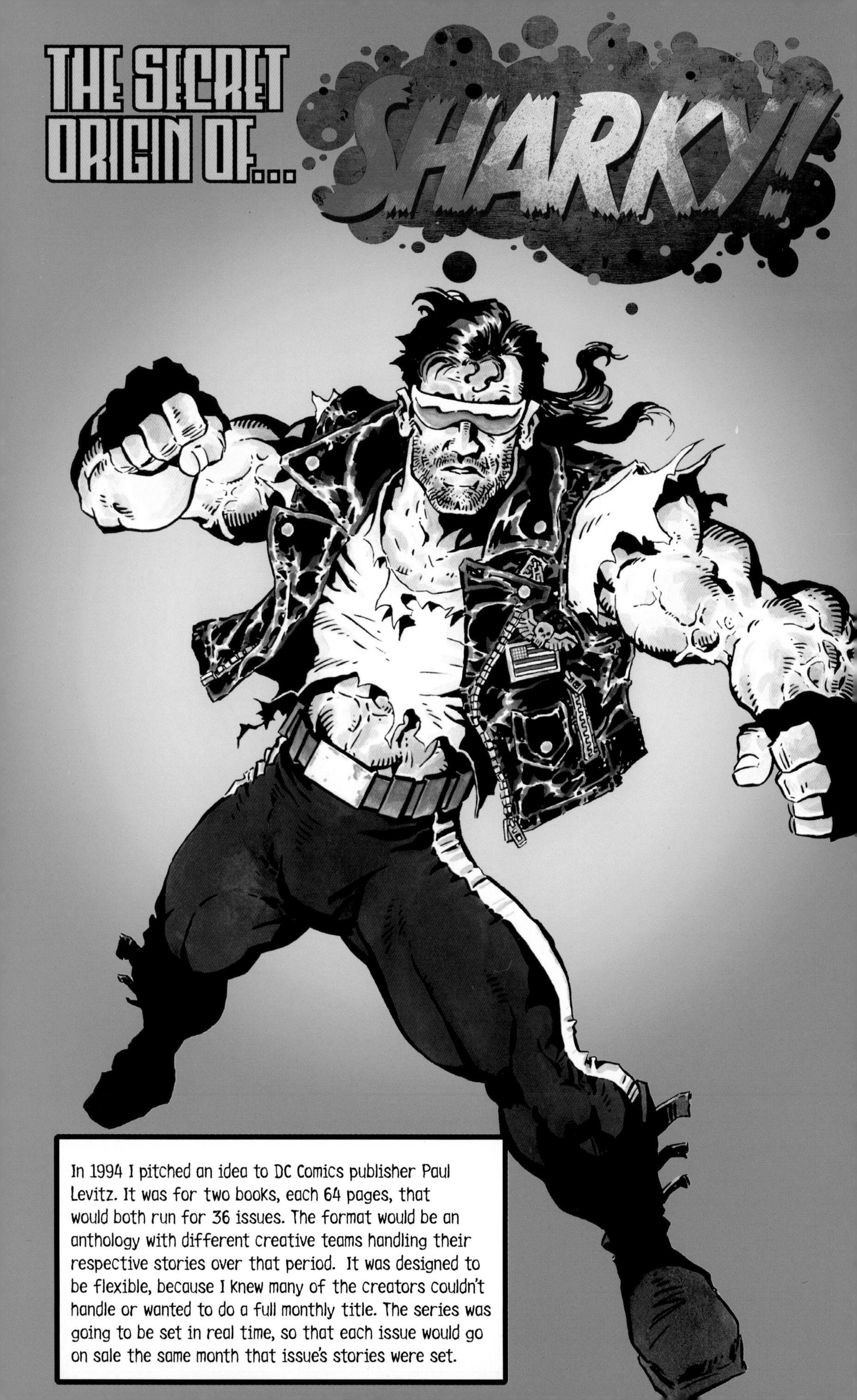

In 1994 I pitched an idea to DC Comics publisher Paul Levitz. It was for two books, each 64 pages, that would both run for 36 issues. The format would be an anthology with different creative teams handling their respective stories over that period. It was designed to be flexible, because I knew many of the creators couldn't handle or wanted to do a full monthly title. The series was going to be set in real time, so that each issue would go on sale the same month that issue's stories were set.

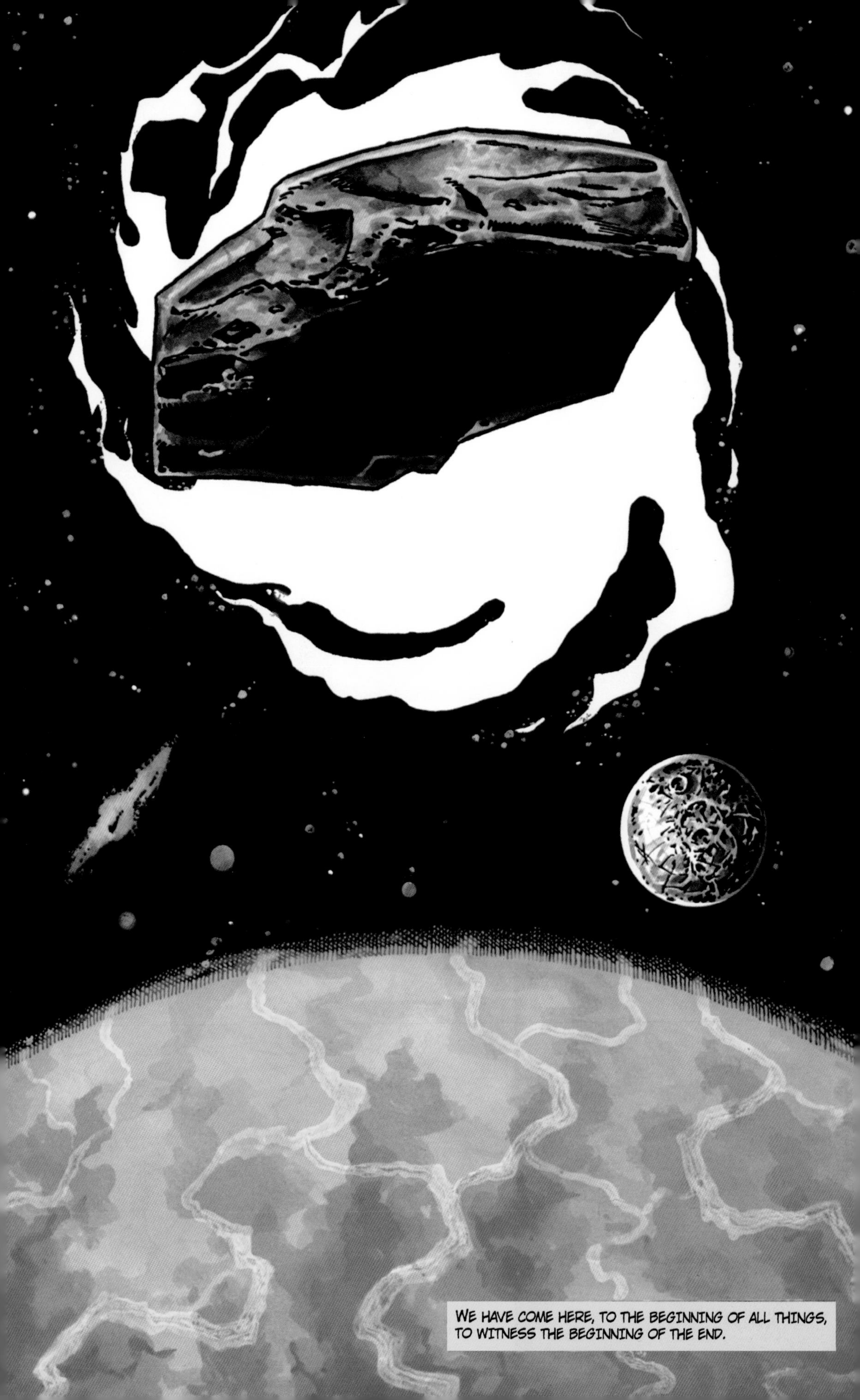
WE HAVE COME HERE, TO THE BEGINNING OF ALL THINGS, TO WITNESS THE BEGINNING OF THE END.

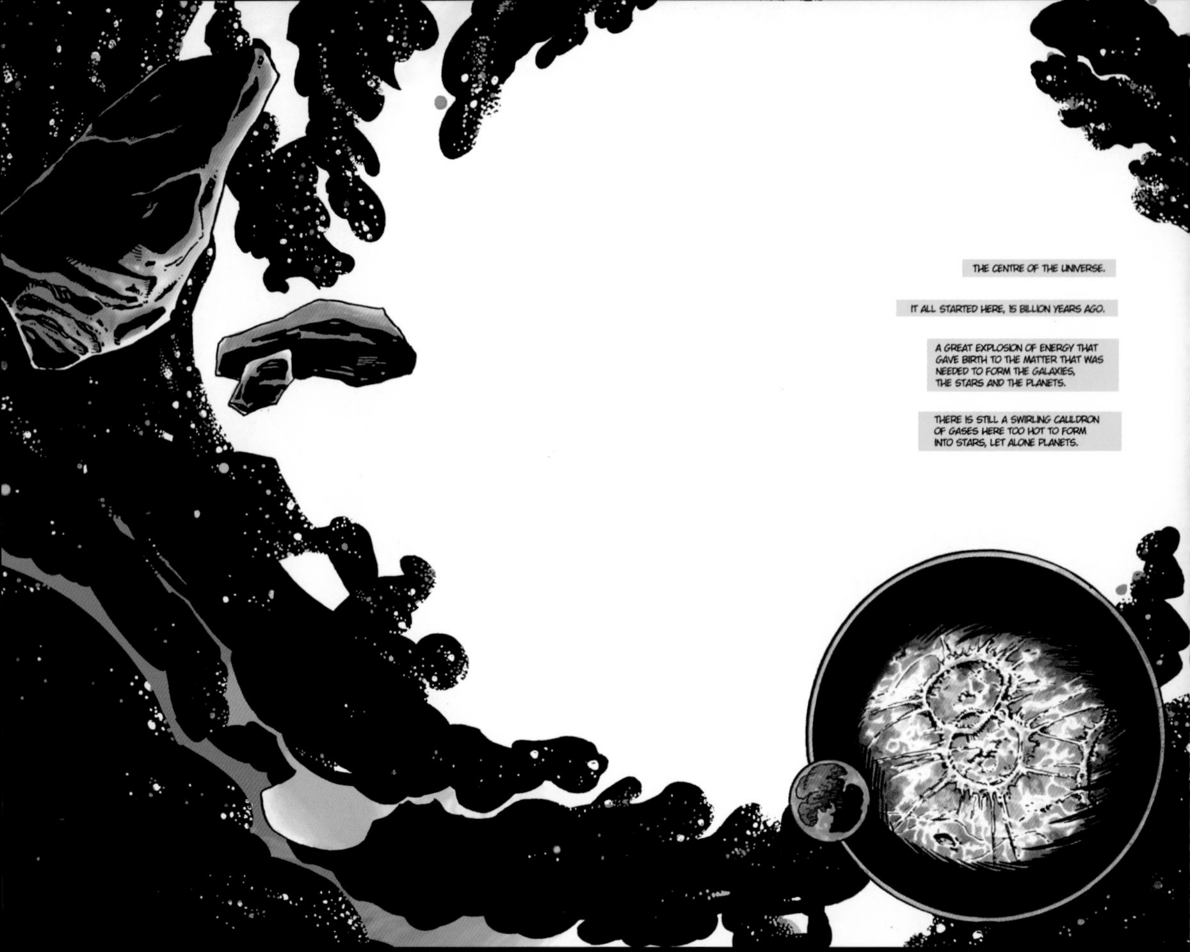
THE CENTRE OF THE UNIVERSE.
IT ALL STARTED HERE, 15 BILLION YEARS AGO.
A GREAT EXPLOSION OF ENERGY THAT GAVE BIRTH TO THE MATTER THAT WAS NEEDED TO FORM THE GALAXIES, THE STARS AND THE PLANETS.
THERE IS STILL A SWIRLING CAULDRON OF GASES HERE TOO HOT TO FORM INTO STARS, LET ALONE PLANETS.

The big story was timed for three years, starting in 1997 and ending in 2000. It would be a new universe – but in the last issue, everyone dies. Not just the heroes, or Earth, but the entire universe dies.

An event no hero could stop.

What you see here are the pages I drew (and a couple from young whipper snapper Simon Bisley) as the opening of the pitch document. The series came within a gnat's testicle of happening...

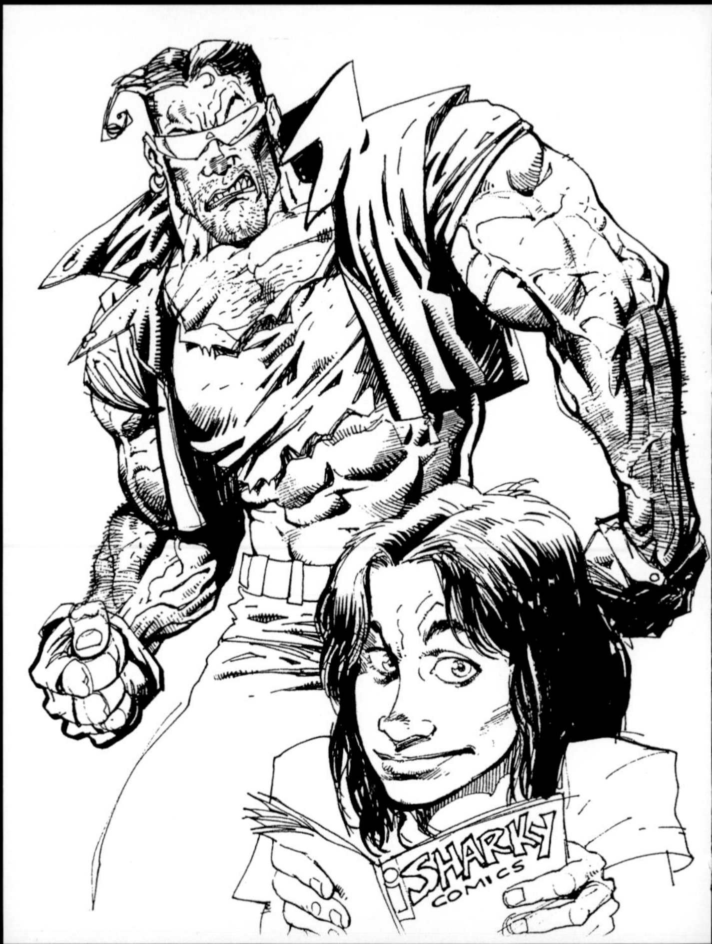
SHARKY
COMICS

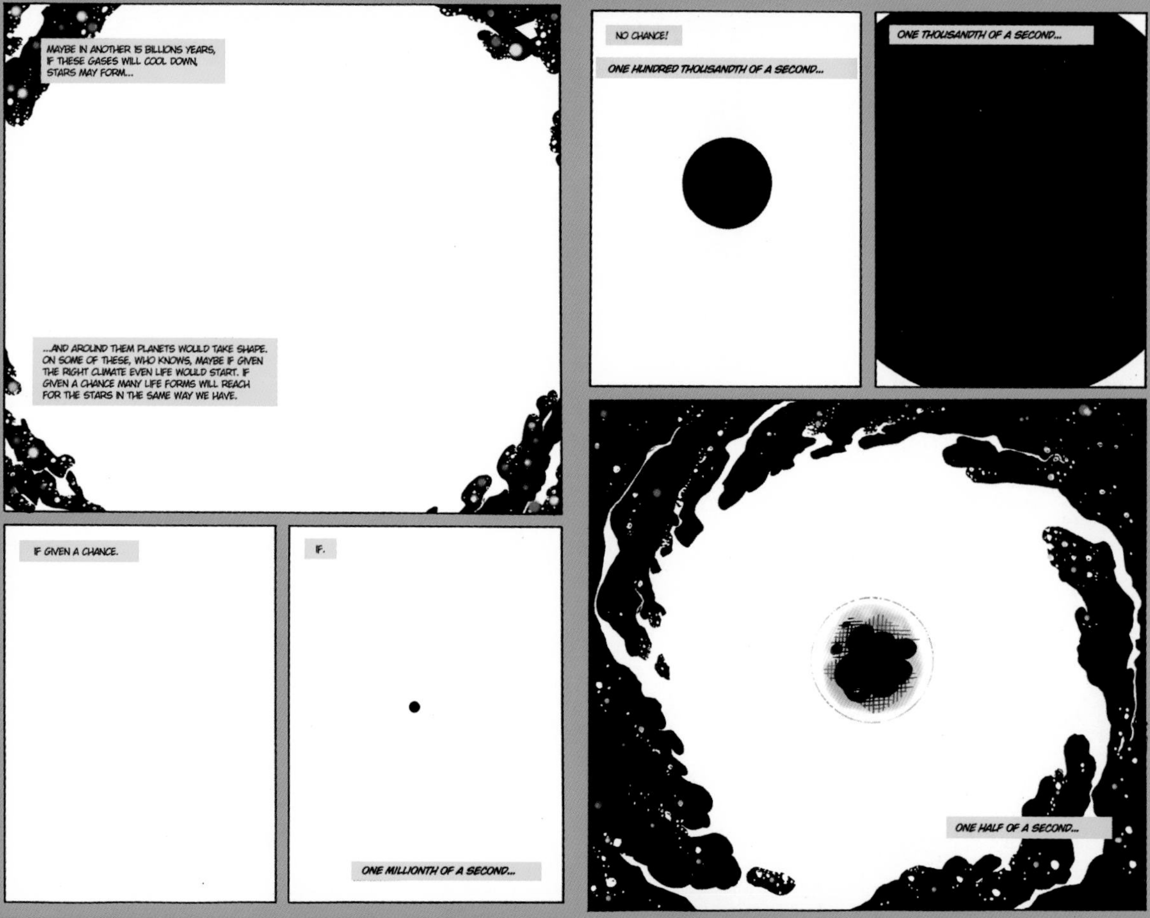
MAYBE IN ANOTHER 15 BILLIONS YEARS, IF THESE GASES WILL COOL DOWN, STARS MAY FORM...
...AND AROUND THEM PLANETS WOULD TAKE SHAPE. ON SOME OF THESE, WHO KNOWS, MAYBE IF GIVEN THE RIGHT CLIMATE EVEN LIFE WOULD START. IF GIVEN A CHANCE MANY LIFE FORMS WILL REACH FOR THE STARS IN THE SAME WAY WE HAVE.
IF GIVEN A CHANCE.
IF.
ONE MILLIONTH OF A SECOND...
NO CHANCE!
ONE HUNDRED THOUSANDTH OF A SECOND...
ONE THOUSANDTH OF A SECOND...
ONE HALF OF A SECOND...

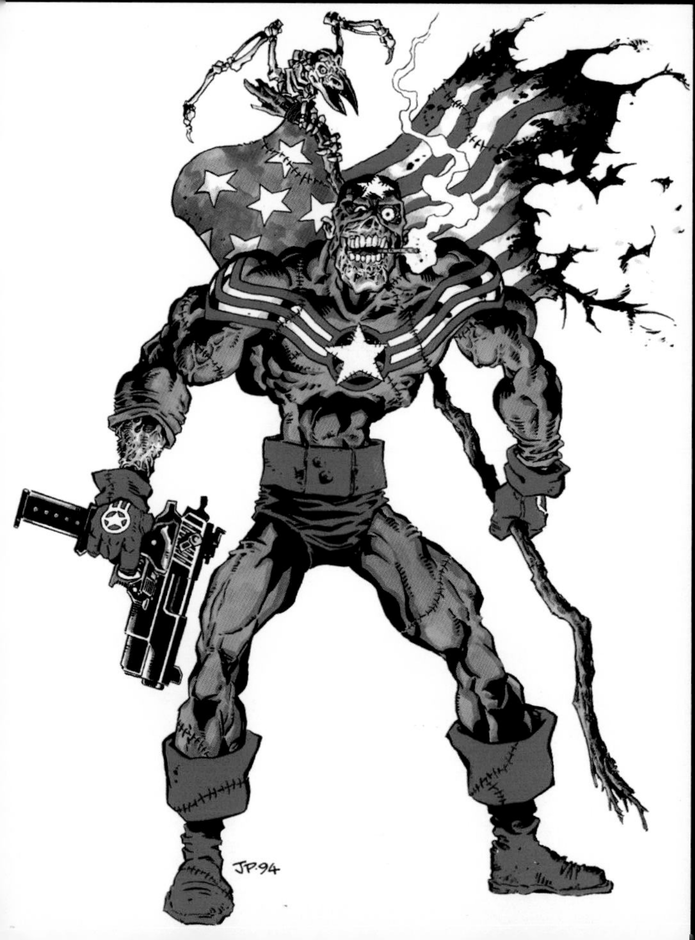
JP.94

Not one to waste anything, I started playing with some of the characters I'd created and decided to do something with them myself. Something that wasn't as high concept as the end of the universe but did deal with one of the planned themes, how a new breed of hero, or anti-hero, was replacing the heroes we grew up on. I was someone who loved the attitude that creators like John Wagner, Alan Grant, Pat Mills, Alan Moore and Kevin O'Neill had brought to the table with *2000AD*, along with the classic comics of yesterday from the pens of Jack Kirby, Curt Swan, Steve Ditko, John Buscema and Wally Wood that were scripted by Roy Thomas and Stan Lee.

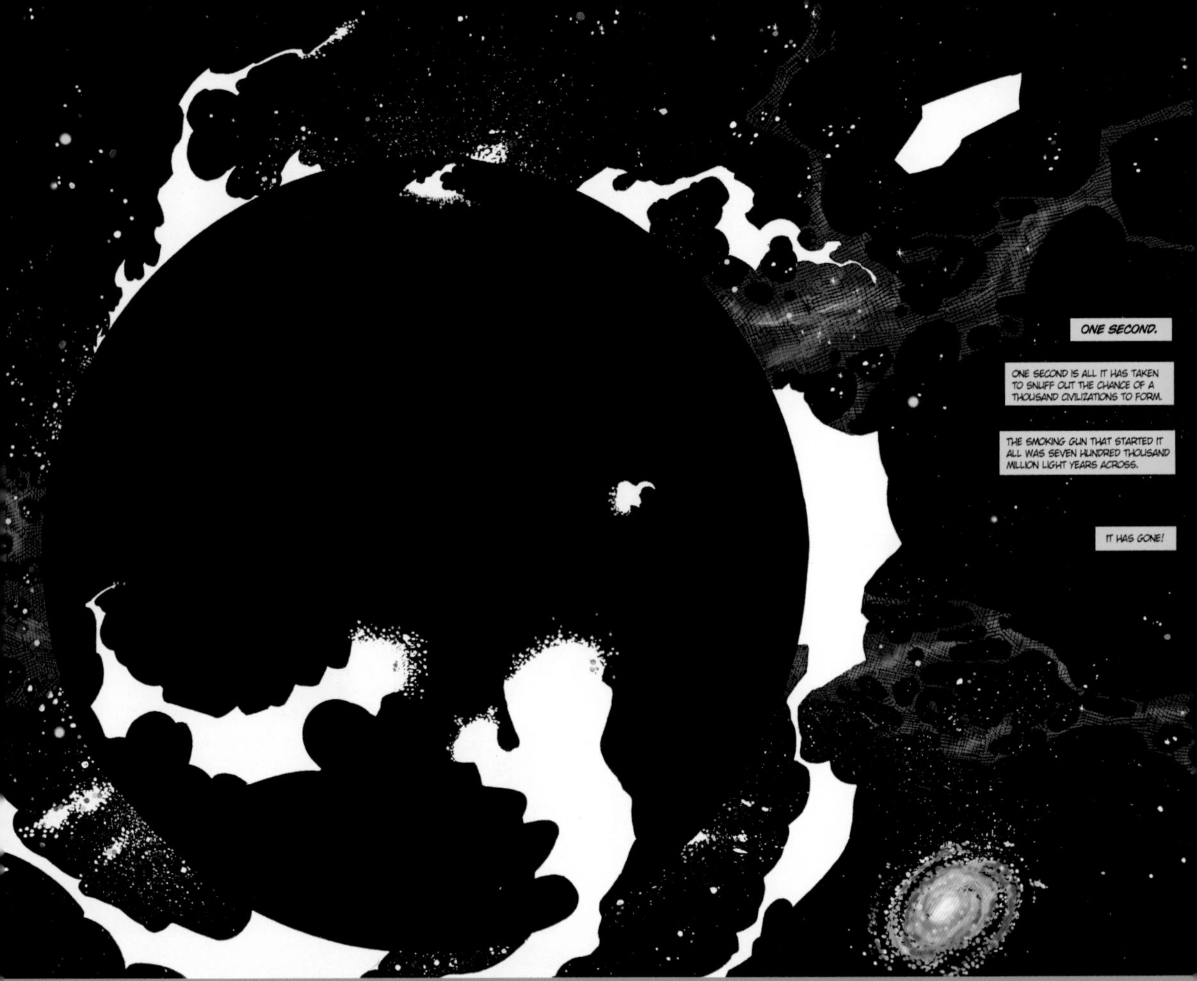
ONE SECOND.
ONE SECOND IS ALL IT HAS TAKEN TO SNUFF OUT THE CHANCE OF A THOUSAND CIVILIZATIONS TO FORM.
THE SMOKING GUN THAT STARTED IT ALL WAS SEVEN HUNDRED THOUSAND MILLION LIGHT YEARS ACROSS.
IT HAS GONE!

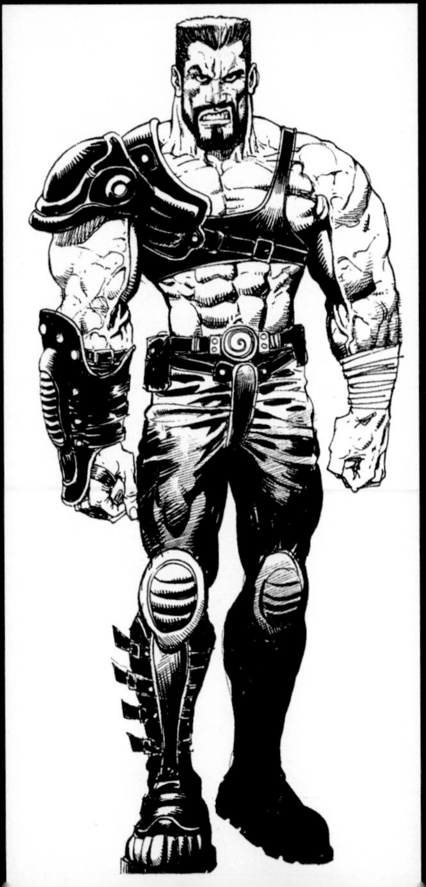

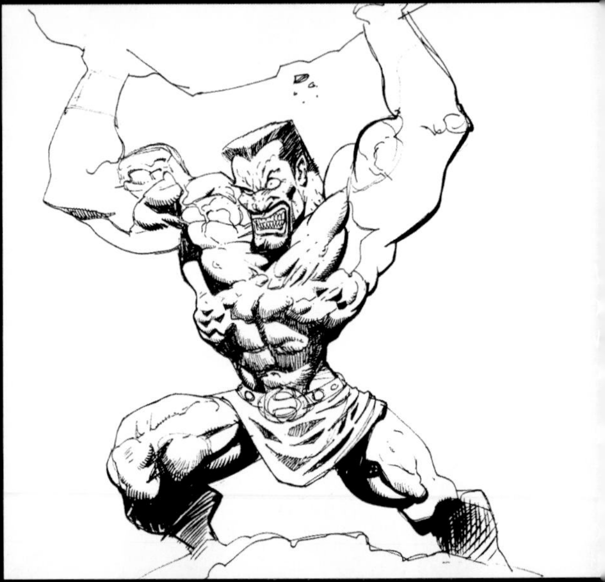

I'd pitched the project to DC shortly after the collapse of Tundra publishing, and as I was just starting to work with Bob Guccione and George Caragone at Penthouse Comi[illegible] There was an artist who had traveled all the way from Italy to visit the Tundra offices. He arrived shortly after we had been told the company was shutting down. His name wa[illegible] Alex Horley and we started working together shortly after.

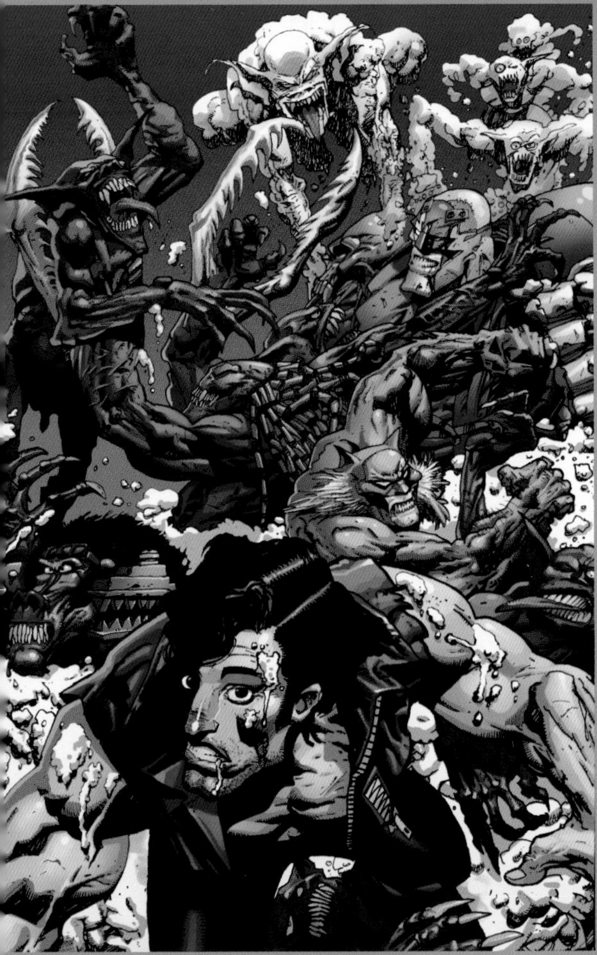

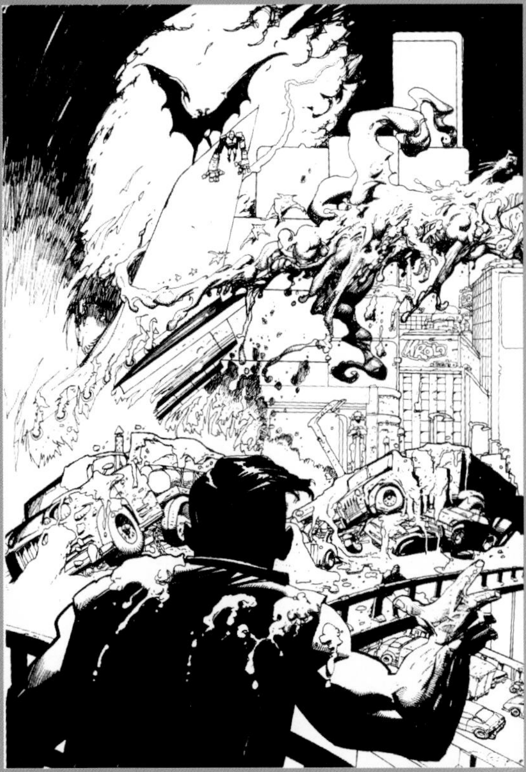

Our warm-up was the sequel to *ibby in the Lost World* in Penthouse omix called *Latischa in the Lost World.* 'e had a blast and established a way of ollaborating we would bring to *Sharky.*

Both Alex and myself were huge irby fans. We were also fans of antasy and science fiction, so our lan was to build something that we ould have a lot of fun with. Where terally 'anything goes'.

Before starting the scripting, I sked Alex for a list of what he wanted o draw. It was a long list, but every hird word was 'monsters' or 'zombies'. was only too happy to cover those oints. We beat *Marvel Zombies* and *'alking Dead* to the punch by several ears!

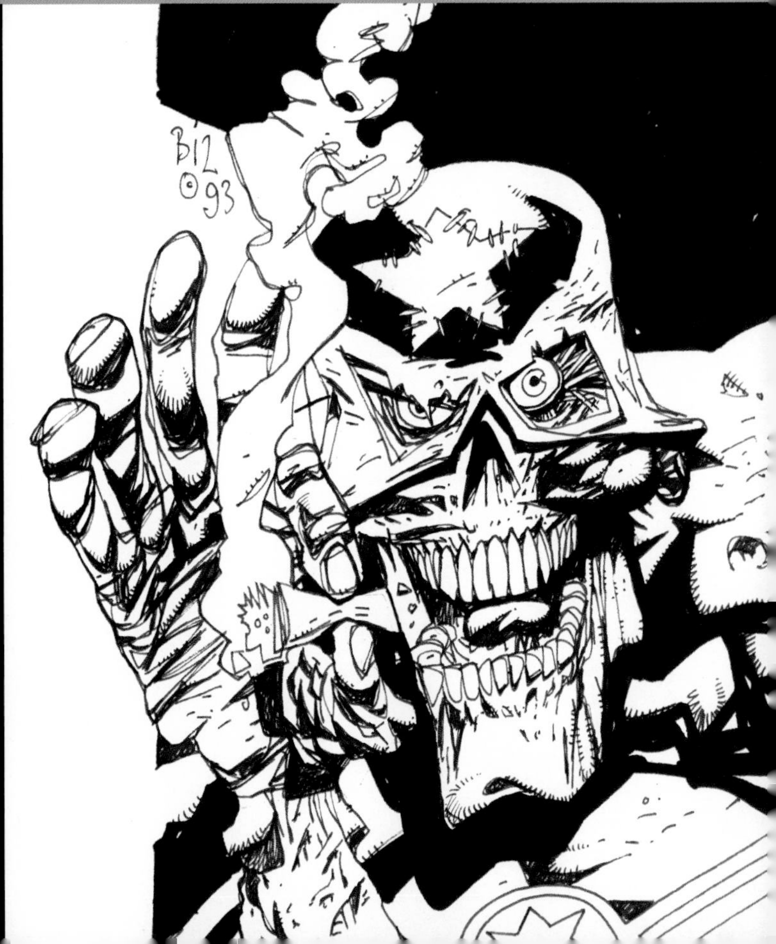
BIZ
©93

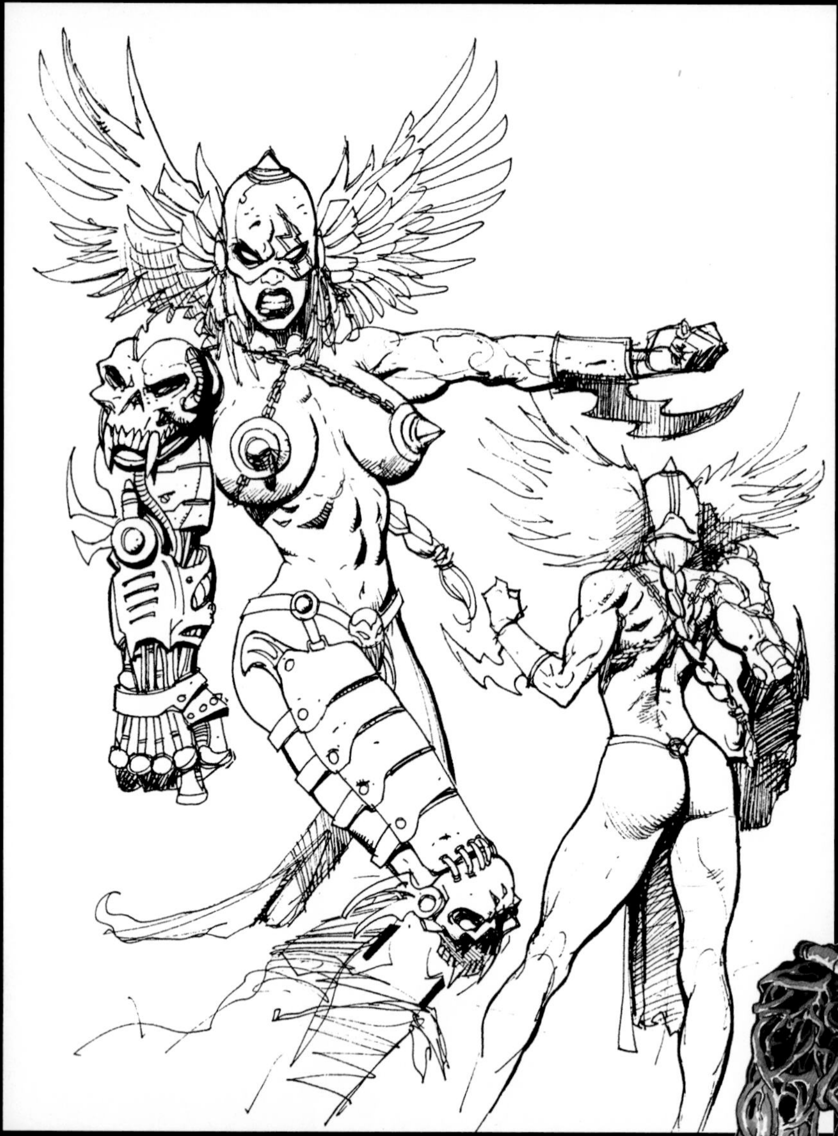

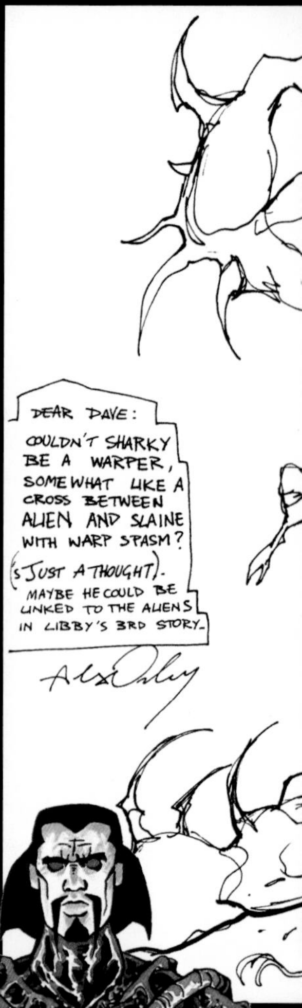

DEAR DAVE:
COULDN'T SHARKY BE A WARPER, SOMEWHAT LIKE A CROSS BETWEEN ALIEN AND SLAINE WITH WARP SPASM?
(JUST A THOUGHT).
MAYBE HE COULD BE LINKED TO THE ALIENS IN LIBBY'S 3RD STORY.

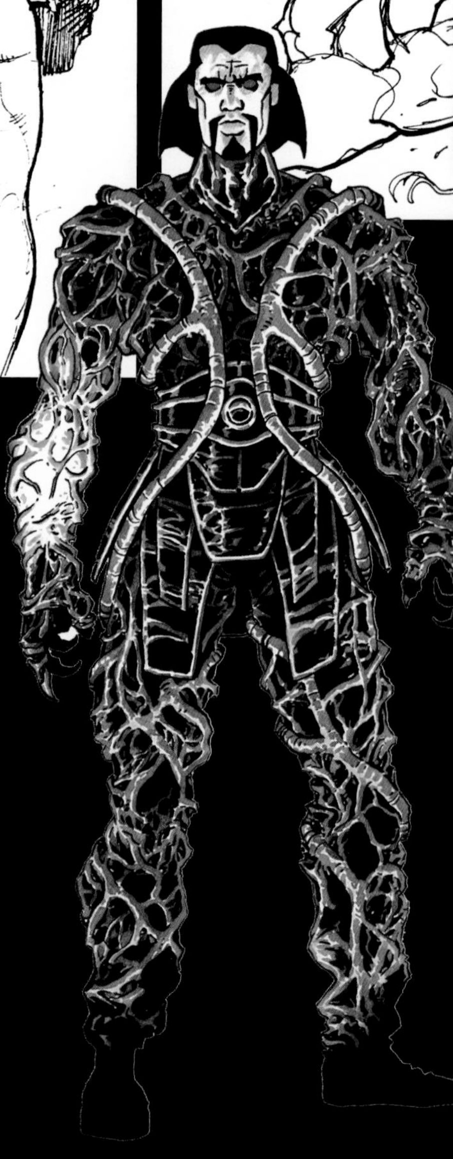

I'd always planned on *Sharky* being the offspring of both Greek and Norse gods, so there was a reason to bring the various pantheons into play. I also wanted to play off the fact that most myths, legends and religions were sexist, written and controlled by men. What if Thor was female? What if Freya hid her from Odin and tricked him into giving this girl the power of the elements, and control of the hammer Mjölnir?

Thus was born Thor, Goddess of Thunder. Because of the power inherent in her and the hammer, Vilak (Odin) has been trying to arrange her death for years – but has so far succeeded only in making things worse. When she had her arm bitten off by a dying monster, it also took the hammer

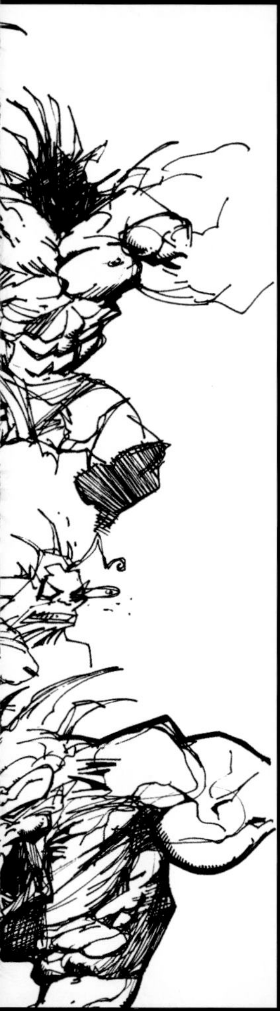

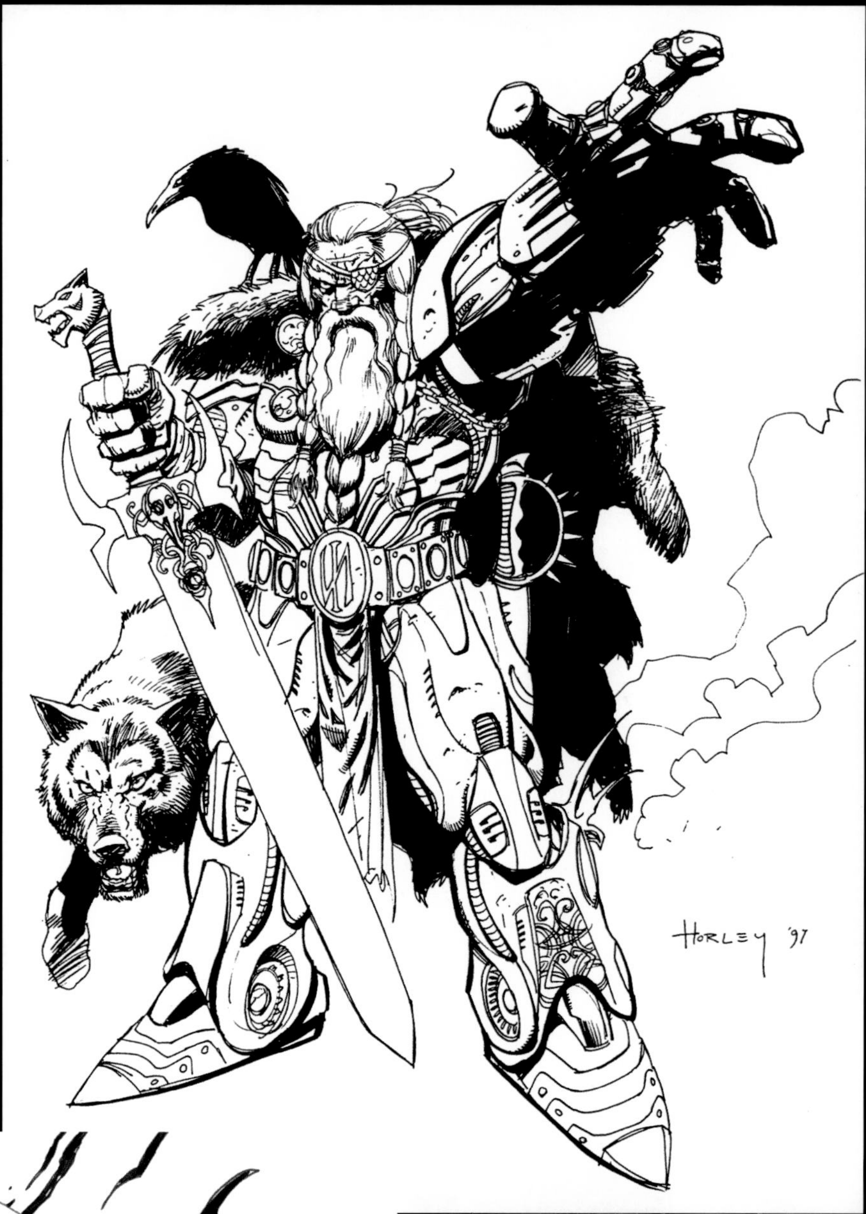
HORLEY '97

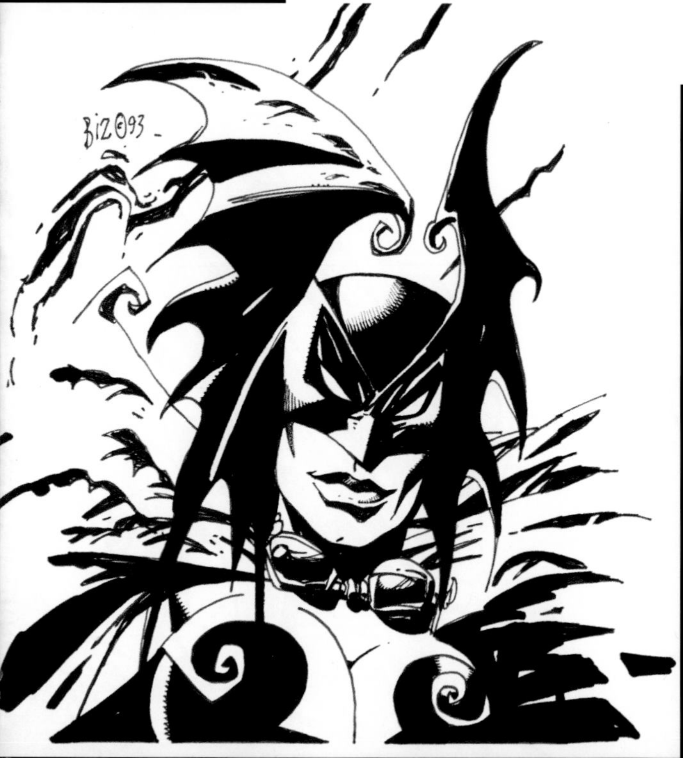
BIZ©93

in its death throes. Now only Thor knows where it is and she's finding it amusing to frustrate her father.

'Odin' in *Sharky* is a term used on Asgard like we use 'King' or 'President'. Vilak is the current ruler of Asgard and therefore is referred to as "Odin". Like many Odins and Zeus', he is fond of coming to Earth and taking advantage of the women here. Freya is well aware of this and was one of those who made sure Sharky's existence was kept secret, knowing one day he might prove an ally against Vilak.

I love playing with perceptions of what a character may be because of what he or she looks like. I did that with Thor and I also did it with GunnMetal. I didn't get to cover GunnMetal's background in the series so what I will reveal here is the answer to the question I was asked at several signings. "Is GunnMetal a man or an android?" To which I would reply, "wait and see." In reality, he is neither. He is an alien from a planet where people are literally pure energy, barely contained in human form. The energy erupts in contact with oxygen, even though they don't need that to survive. GunnMetal's armor is nothing more than a containment suit. The energy from his feet that he uses to fly or as blasters from his hands is purely the expulsion of that energy through vents after he has opened them to let oxygen in. GunnMetal is trapped on Earth along with Thor, both of whom were members of the group The Senturians along with Blazing Glory, Rokk'Ed, Zephyr, Blaster Bunny and Black Death.

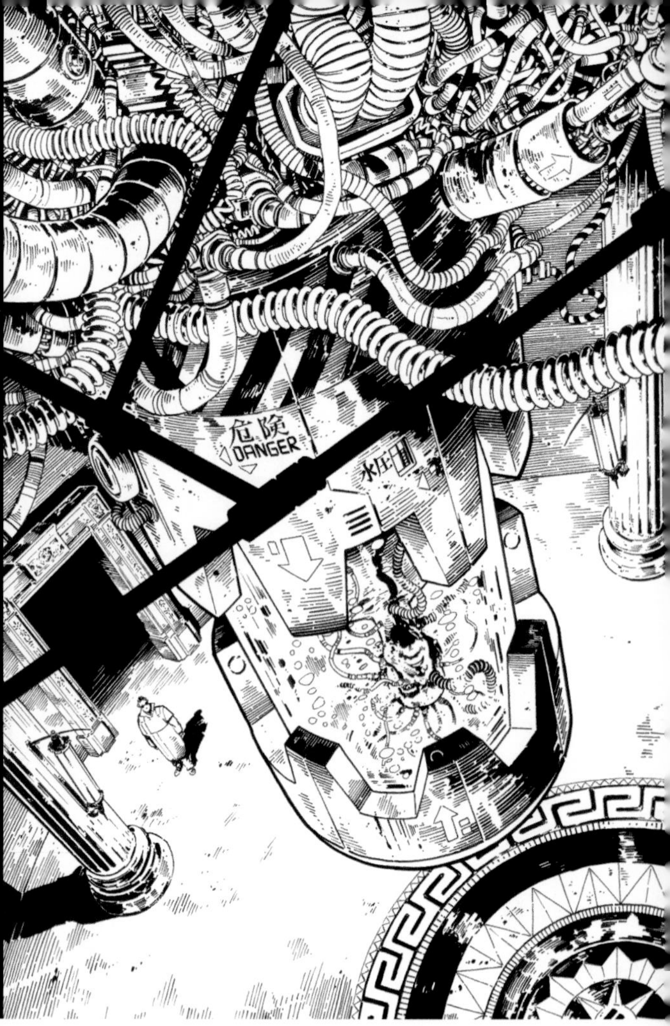
危険
DANGER

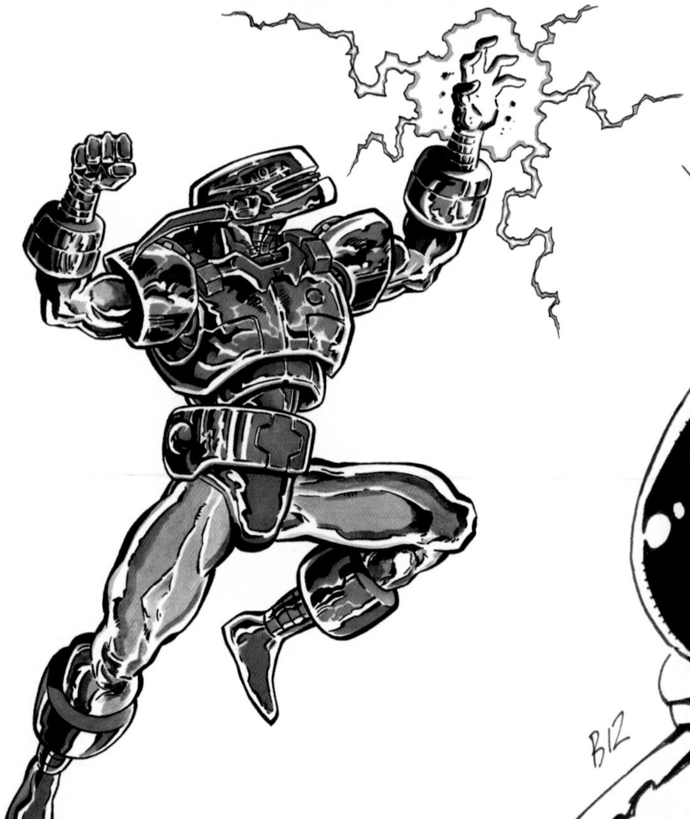

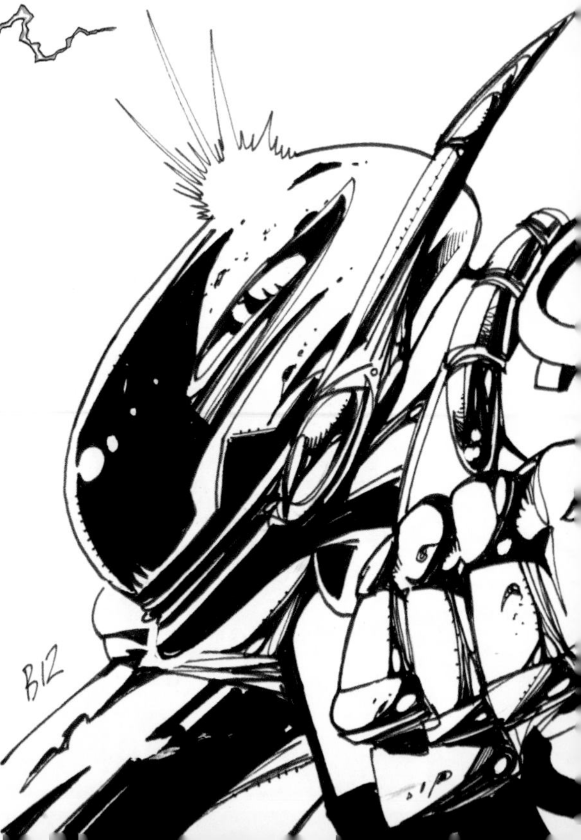
BIZ

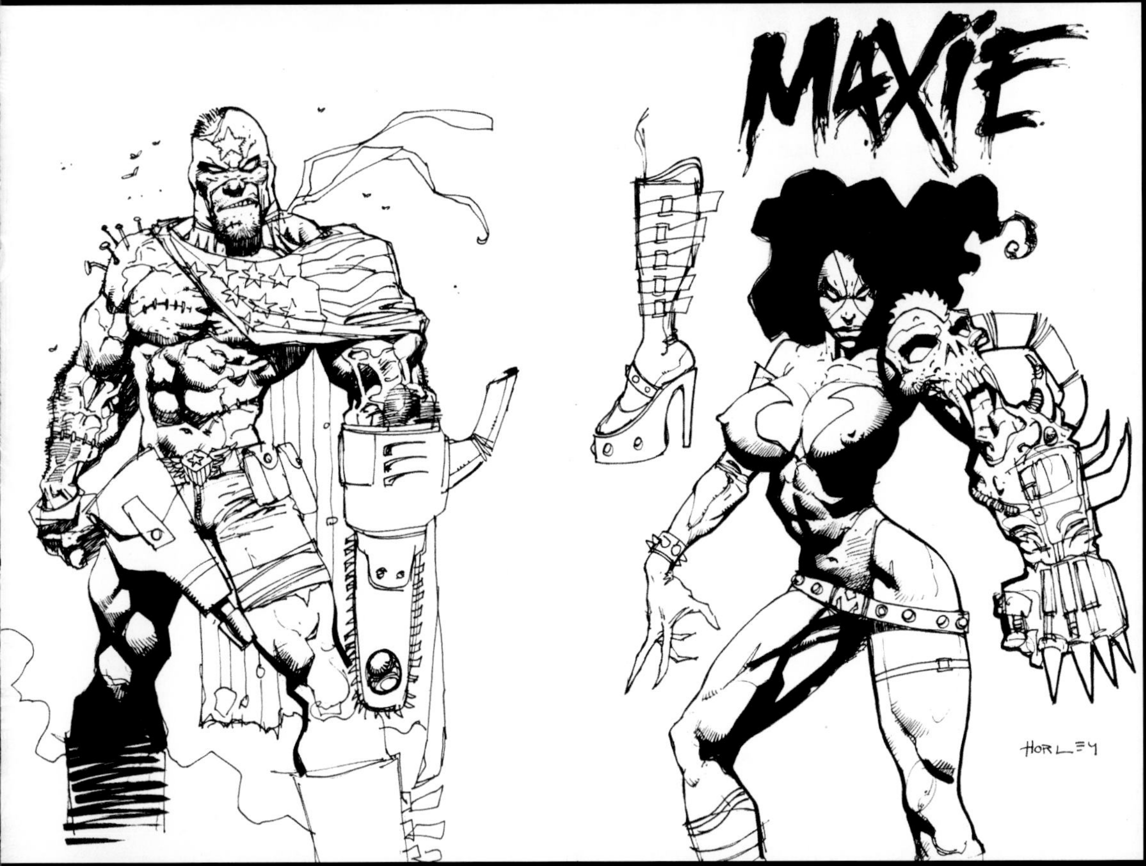
MAXIE
HORLEY

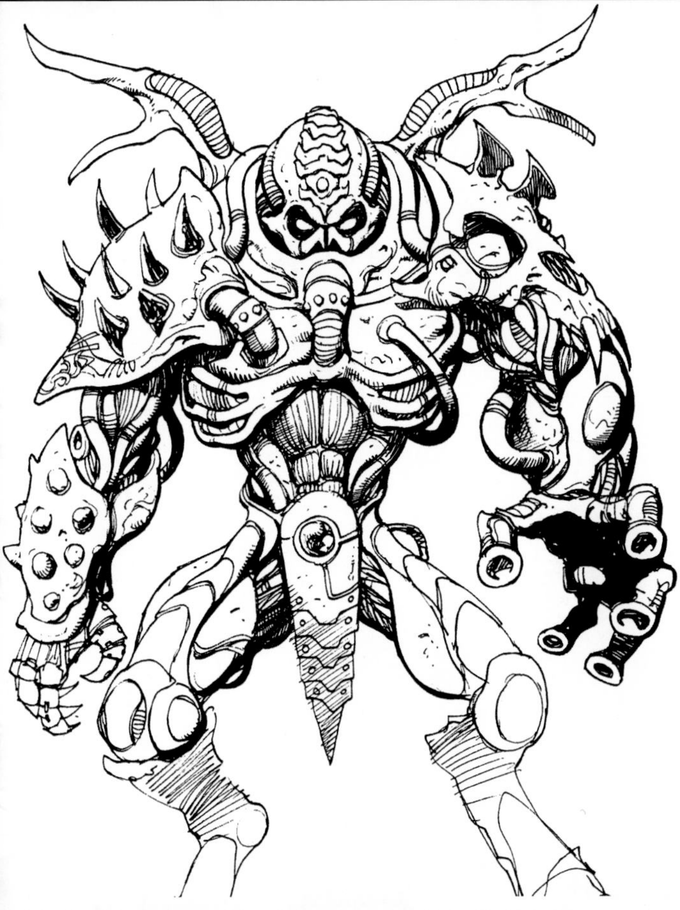

The series quickly became a love letter to Jack Kirby and many of the Marvel-style stories in the 60's and 70's. From the original DC proposal, I kept the concept of a world transitioning between the hero worship of yesteryear to the more negative anti-heroes of Lobo, Punisher and Wolverine.

In Volume 2, you'll be able to see how my attempts went, as far as trying to merge current storytelling with the older Silver Age style.

Hope you enjoyed the book!
Let me know at:

http://deevelliott.deviantart.com/

https://www.facebook.com/AtomekaPress

Creator Bios

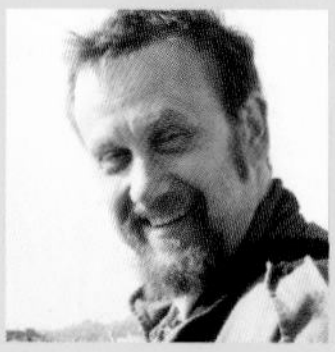

DAVE Elliott has more than 25 years of experience working in every aspect of the comic book industry from writer and artist to editor and publisher. Dave created *Sharky* and *Maximum Force* and has worked on titles as diverse as *A1, Deadline, Viz Comic, Heavy Metal magazine, Penthouse Comix, 2000 AD, Justice League of America, Transformers, GI Joe* and *Doctor Who.* He recently worked with the band Fall Out Boy, and with NASCAR/MMI to create and brand new intellectual properties which he cites as examples of new media integration for a more immersive entertainment experience.

In 2006, Dave co-founded Radical Studios. As both the co-publisher and Editor-In-Chief, Dave was integral to the development and launch of Radical's premiere comic book titles, several of which have now begun development as film properties including *Hercules* (Starring Dwayne Johnson, directed by Brett Ratner and to be released by MGM), *Freedom Formula* (New Regency), *Schrapnel, Caliber, Hotwire, Last Days of American Crime* and *Oblivion* (starring Tom Cruise, directed by Joe Kosinski and released by Universal).

Currently, Dave is relaunching his company ATOMEKA, started with his partner Garry Leach, as an imprint of Titan Comics. Atomeka's titles include *A1*, *WEIRDING WILLOWS* and *MONSTER MASSACRE*, followed by *ODYSSEY*. Dave is easilly accessible on both Facebook and DeviantART.
https://www.facebook.com/AtomekaPress
http://deevelliott.deviantart.com/

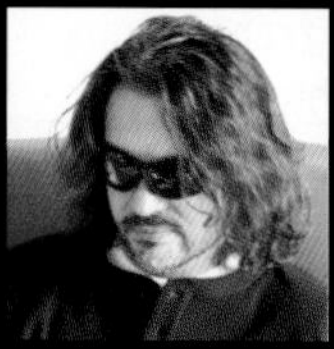

ALEX Horley (real name Alessandro Orlandelli) has worked for a wide variety of U.S. publishers in the last 20 years, including DC comics, for which he did two *Lobo* mini series and several covers, the *Sharky* mini series written by Dave Elliott for Image and several covers and a calendar for *Heavy Metal Magazine.* In recent times, he has mainly focused on producing paintings for CCG games like *Magic: The Gathering*, *Versus* and especially *World of Warcraft*, for Blizzard Entertainment. He's also been commissioned for production design and various illustrations by director/rockstar Rob Zombie. Currently, Alex is trying to find the time to work on various personal projects, between one deadline and another. His latest works can be seen on deviantART and at his web gallery.
http://alexhorley.deviantart.com/
www.alexhorleyart.com.

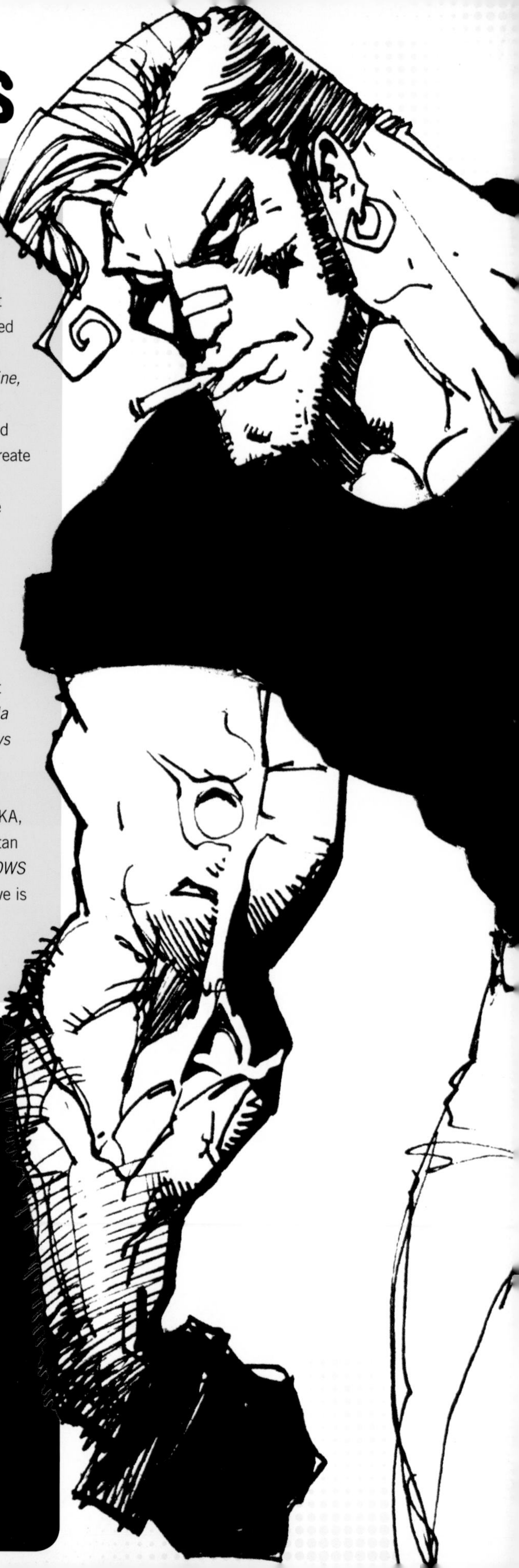

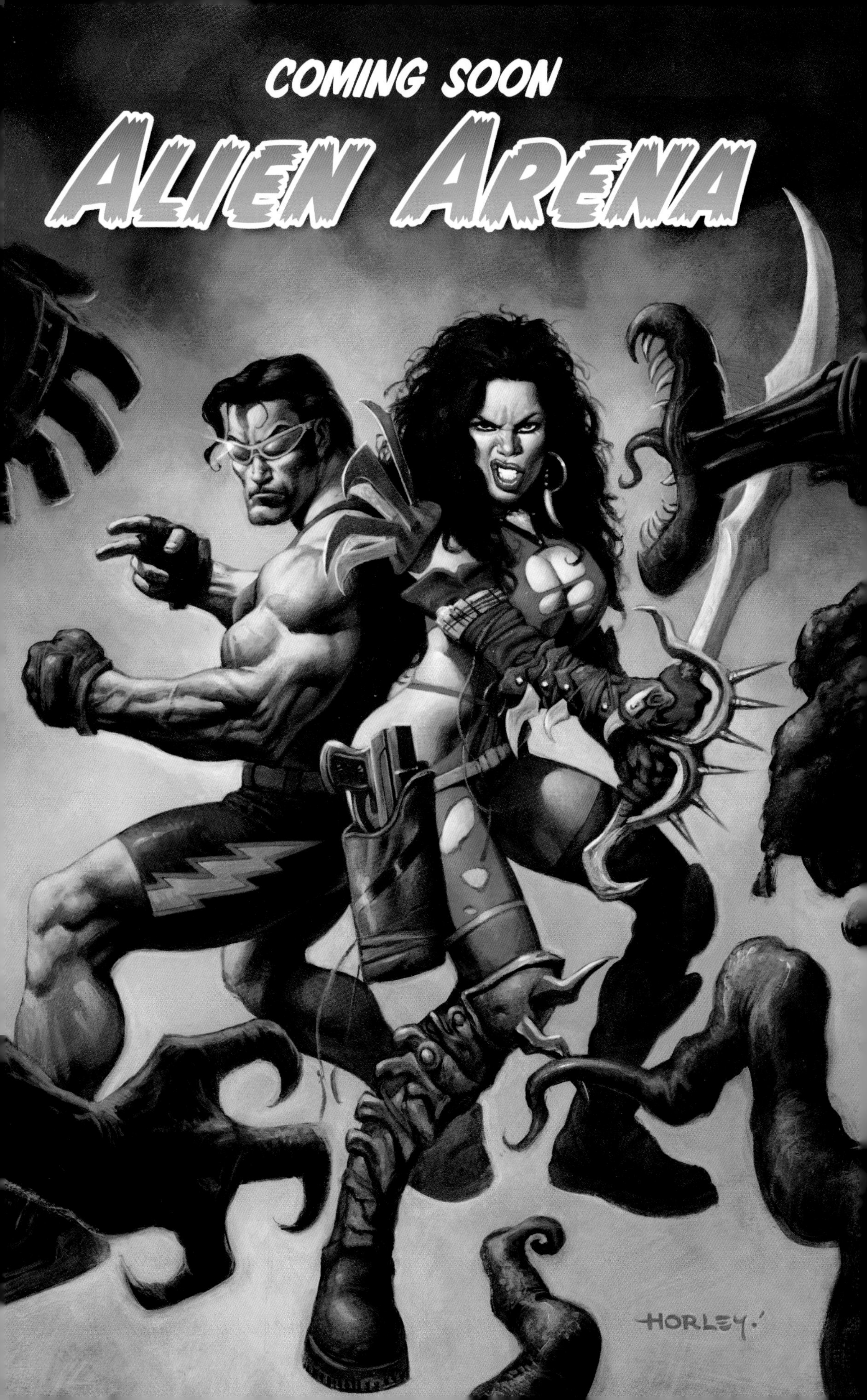
COMING SOON
ALIEN ARENA
HORLEY